Dr Tammie Matson is an Australian zoologist and author based in Sydney who specialises in human-wildlife conflict. Tammie has worked for over a decade to conserve African wildlife, including wild dogs, black rhinos and hippos, with a special focus on Namibia's threatened black-faced impala, the subject of her PhD and first non-fiction book, *Dry Water – Diving head-first into Africa*. Since 2005 she has worked with local people to reduce human-elephant conflict in southern Africa and north-east India. Tammie is working with Animal Media Australia on a documentary about human-elephant conflict. She is also an environmental consultant and speaks on conservation issues affecting threatened species around the world. She is addicted to Africa, the ocean, Caramello koalas and pies with mushy peas. You can find Tammie on the web at www.tammiematson.com

TAMMIE MATSON

ELEPHANT DANCE

Pan Macmillan Australia

First published in Macmillan in 2009 by Pan Macmillan Australia Pty Limited
This Pan edition published 2010 by Pan Macmillan Australia Pty Limited
1 Market Street, Sydney

National Library of Australia
Cataloguing-in-Publication data:

Matson, Tammie K. 1977–.
Elephant dance: a story of love and war in the kingdom of the elephants / Tammie Matson.

978 0330 42577 3 (pbk.)

Matson, Tammie K. 1977–
Zoologists – Australia – Biography.
Wildlife conservationists – Australia – Biography.
Elephants – conservation.
Wildlife conservation.

591.092

Internal illustrations courtesy of Nafisa Naomi
www.nafisanaomi.com

Typeset in Granjon by Post-Pre-press Group
Printed in Australia by McPherson's Printing Group

For Andy

A story is 'like the wind. It comes from a far-off quarter and we feel it.'

Kabbo, a great San storyteller whose name means 'dream'; as told to Wilhelm Beck, German linguist.

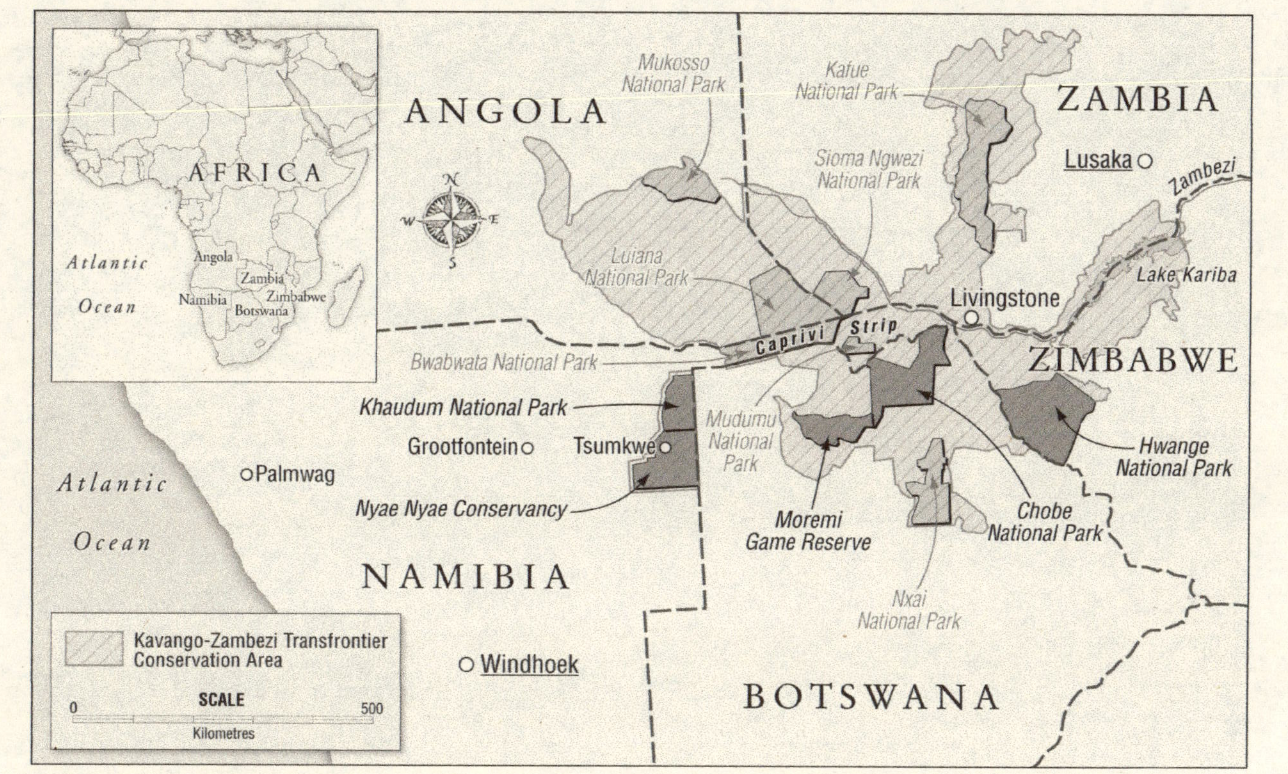

AFRICA
Atlantic Ocean
Angola
Zambia
Namibia
Zimbabwe
Botswana
ANGOLA
ZAMBIA
Lusaka
Zambezi
Mukosso National Park
Kafue National Park
Sioma Ngwezi National Park
Luiana National Park
Lake Kariba
Livingstone
Caprivi Strip
Bwabwata National Park
ZIMBABWE
Khaudum National Park
Grootfontein
Tsumkwe
Mudumu National Park
Hwange National Park
Palmwag
Atlantic Ocean
Nyae Nyae Conservancy
Moremi Game Reserve
Chobe National Park
NAMIBIA
Nxai National Park
Kavango-Zambezi Transfrontier Conservation Area
SCALE
0
500
Kilometres
Windhoek
BOTSWANA
N
S
E
W

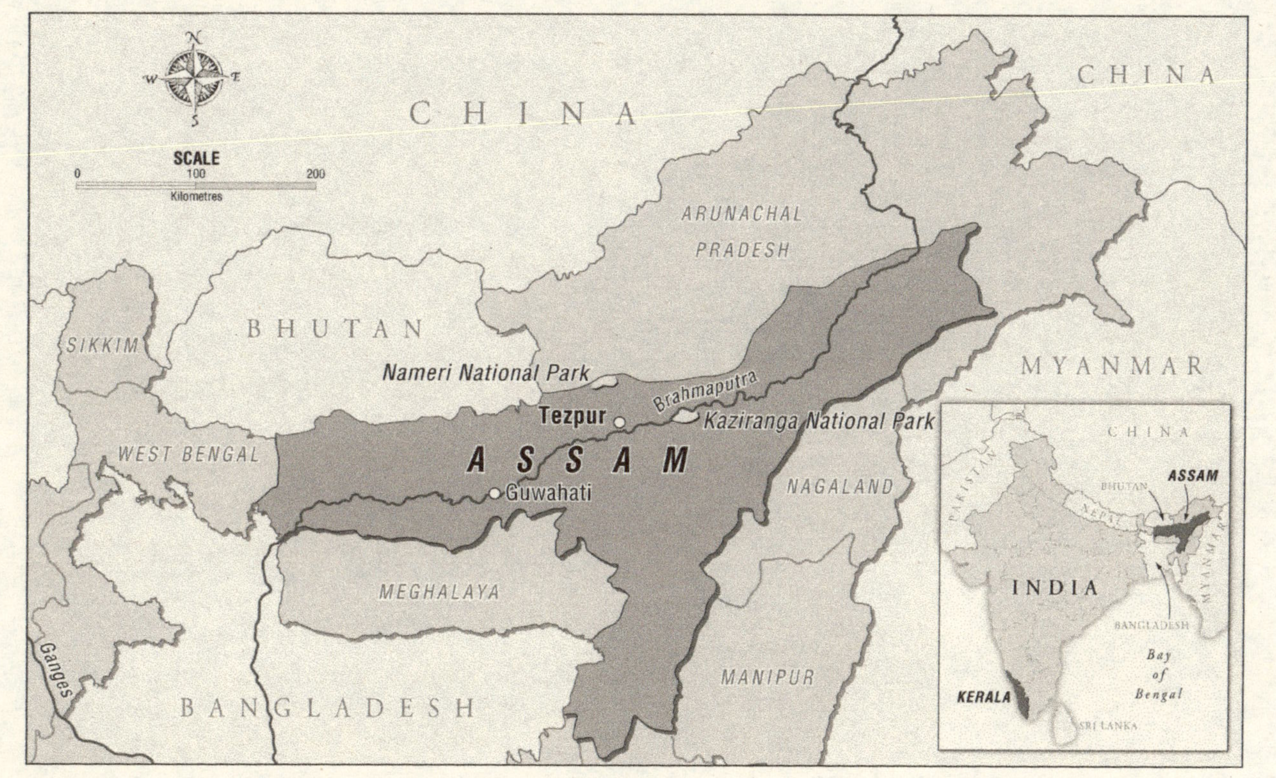
N
W
E
S
SCALE
0
100
200
Kilometres
CHINA
CHINA
ARUNACHAL PRADESH
BHUTAN
SIKKIM
MYANMAR
Nameri National Park
Brahmaputra
Tezpur
Kaziranga National Park
WEST BENGAL
ASSAM
Guwahati
NAGALAND
MEGHALAYA
MANIPUR
Ganges
BANGLADESH
CHINA
PAKISTAN
BHUTAN
ASSAM
NEPAL
MYANMAR
INDIA
BANGLADESH
Bay of Bengal
KERALA
SRI LANKA

PROLOGUE

The night was so quiet I could hear my own breath. Desert silence. So deep and pervasive it was like being inside a tomb. In a yogi-like meditation, I inhaled the spirit of this place, breathing softly. The high-pitched bark of a black-backed jackal punctuated the desert night, a reminder that even here, in the middle of nowhere, I was not alone.

Inside my tiny one-man tent I lay on a swag under a heavy duvet and waited for the heat of my own body to defrost my aching fingers and toes. On nights like this I wondered whether the single life of a roaming zoologist was really all it cracked up to be. Feeling strong and independent was one thing, but the benefit of the warmth of another body was not to be dismissed on freezing desert nights.

Earlier in the day, my translator, Munekamba, and I had set up camp at the Palmwag rhino base in Damaraland. It was cheaper than camping at the lodge nearby and, with no tourists around, it was a lot quieter. On this moonless night in Namibia's rugged north-west, we were the only ones in the camp. In the cold moonless night, a spray of diamantés glittered across a black silk sky.

Earlier, Damaraland had blushed crimson where the rays of the late afternoon sun touched its hard shell. For a moment it was easy to imagine that the ancient volcanos which once created this basalt desert were still active, oozing tongues of molten lava. Seductive fingerlings of light stroked the glowing crimson rocks. The earth pulsed with golden light. Then, too quickly, the sun departed, as it always did in Africa, and the mood changed. Dark shadows began to creep over maroon mountains of sharp shale and rock.

In the fading light Munekamba and I put up my tent on the rocky ground a few metres from the base of a large mopane tree. I liked the idea of sleeping under the branches of the old sentinel. There are very few large trees in Namibia's deserts, due to the paucity of water. The only ones that can grow to such a size are those nourished by underground springs or rivers, like the gigantic Ana trees lining the banks of the Hoanib River, which form a shady migration path for desert-dwelling elephants. Camping next to that old mopane I felt a strange sense of security, as if it were a kindred spirit watching over me in the darkness. It made me feel a little less alone.

I parked my double-cab Hilux about twenty metres away and we hoisted up the rooftop tent for Munekamba to sleep in.

'My house!' he declared, 'I am liking this very much.'

Munekamba and I had met for the first time the previous day in Namibia's capital, Windhoek. After driving for eight hours to get to Palmwag, this was our first night in a three-week expedition to find reintroduction sites for black-faced impalas in Namibia's remote Kunene region. Exhausted after the long drive, I'd cooked us some *boervors* (spicy Afrikaans sausage) on the campfire and then we'd both crawled into our respective tents shortly after eight. It felt good to be back on bush time. I planned to wake before dawn.

But the night had other plans for me. I woke with a start not long after I'd gone to sleep. I could hear crunching. It wasn't Munekamba munching on Maltesers. Not unless the Maltesers were *gigantic*. I'd heard this sound before and I knew it well. Elephant footsteps. Volcanic rocks cracked like shattered glass under proboscidean pads as slow steps plodded towards where I lay on the ground in my tent.

I didn't move a muscle. I could feel my heart beating fast and loud in my ears as a surge of adrenaline shot through my chest and into my stomach. Inside my windowless tent it was pitch-black, so I couldn't make out any shadows to guess how close the elephant was. Male elephants usually travel alone or accompanied by one or two other bulls, while females tend to move in larger groups called breeding herds, so I guessed this solitary elephant was a bull.

Just then, the elephant's stomach rumbled so loudly and so close to my tent that my heart temporarily stopped beating. It sounded like a tractor right next to my swag and I knew from the direction of the sound that he was right beside me, standing over the top of me, assessing me, just as I was assessing him.

He must have known I was there. As long as I stayed still and didn't panic, I was pretty sure I would be safe. I wondered for a moment whether Munekamba was awake, and if he was, whether he knew to keep his cool. It was not a good day to get trampled by an elephant frightened by a random Himba leaping to my rescue from a rooftop tent.

My ears were finetuned to every sound the elephant was making, and I listened intently to his heavy breathing. Volumes of air sucked in and out of lungs the size of large seals. Then, with great aplomb, he shot off a magnificent round of farts. At such close range, beneath the barrel, it was like being hit by machine-gun fire of composting vegetables.

It would have been humorous if it hadn't been so terrifying. One wrong step by this elephant and I was pizza. One Aussie meat-lovers with thin crust coming right up!

I listened to him rubbing his wrinkly buttocks against the old mopane tree, a sound like rough sandpaper against wood. His belly continued to grumble. Then I heard the crunching of rocks again. It was another elephant, coming from the same direction as the first.

I knew that as long as nothing disturbed the bull he would just get on with his business, which in this case seemed to be a vigorous butt scratch on the mopane tree. But now, with a second elephant coming along, I hoped that they were friends and were not going to pick a fight with each other. The second bull walked faster and with less care than the first one had, again plodding right beside my tent, apparently also intent on a good butt scratch. I held my breath as he walked by, rumbled a greeting to the first bull and then together they farted and rumbled an elephant ensemble to their huge hearts' content.

With the fresh tang of compost in the air and my heart beating frantically, I lay there for hours on high alert. I dared not move while two of the world's largest land mammals loitered beside my tent, jostling with each other and taking turns to scratch against the tree.

All I can say is that I felt very, very small on the ground. Rational thought was telling me I would be fine. As a zoologist I knew that an animal would rarely attack unprovoked. But logic was also telling me that there was nothing between me and ten tonnes of elephant bull except a flimsy piece of polyester. I fought the desperate urge to jump out of the tent and make a run for the nearest building with four walls, which was only a few hundred metres away. I knew I was being ridiculous, that by that very action I would frighten the bulls and probably provoke an attack; still, every cell in my body, every self-preserving instinct, was telling me to get out of that situation as quickly as I could.

Trying not to panic, I spoke to the stars and made a pact: *If you let me survive tonight I will give up Africa. I'll give it all up. Just don't let them stand on me.*

At about midnight I heard the bulls mosey off at last. I breathed a sigh of relief, but I barely slept for the rest of the night, expecting them to come back or for other elephants to arrive in their place. No longer my sentinel, the mopane tree had become my curse, an attractant for every elephant in the region with an itchy butt.

I'd been charged by elephants plenty of times in a vehicle, but I had never been this close to wild elephants and this was the first time I'd been unable to do anything to get away. Trapped in the tent, I was completely at the bulls' mercy. After more than a decade of working in the African bush, I realised I wasn't as tough as I'd thought I was. That really wasn't any fun. And sheer terror is not to be scoffed at – especially when it's happening to you.

In the morning, bleary-eyed after a sleepless night, I emerged from my tiny cavern of fear to see Munekamba creeping down out of the rooftop tent.

'Did you see this elephant?' Munekamba said, looking as tired as I felt. 'It was right beside your tent! I am thinking it is standing on you!'

I laughed. 'Man, I thought so as well.'

'I am watching it from up here. Aya! I have never seen this thing!'

'You mean you haven't been that close to one before?'

'No, this is the first one I am seeing with my own eyes.'

Although Munekamba had grown up in a Himba village in north-west Namibia, he had never seen an elephant until that night. Elephants had been heavily poached in that region until the 1990s, when Namibia gained independence and the war ended. Now, with appropriate community-based conservation programs in place, elephant populations were building up again.

I walked up to the mopane tree and placed my palm on the relatively smooth area where the elephants had been rubbing against the bark. Munekamba pointed out the elephant footprint a metre beside my tent. If the elephant had been any closer, he'd have been touching the canvas.

In the light of day, I knew I had never really been in any danger. The elephants had been relaxed and respectful, if a little too close for comfort. But I could still taste the fear I'd felt that night. It was real.

I'd been studying human-elephant conflict for the past year, but until now I hadn't really known how it felt. All around Africa and in many parts of Asia, this was how many thousands of people felt every night of their lives. That's how it feels to live with elephants.

Sorry, stars, I remembered. *About that pact . . . You see, I wasn't really serious. You knew that, right? I'm not done with Africa yet. And I'm definitely not done with elephants.*

PART ONE

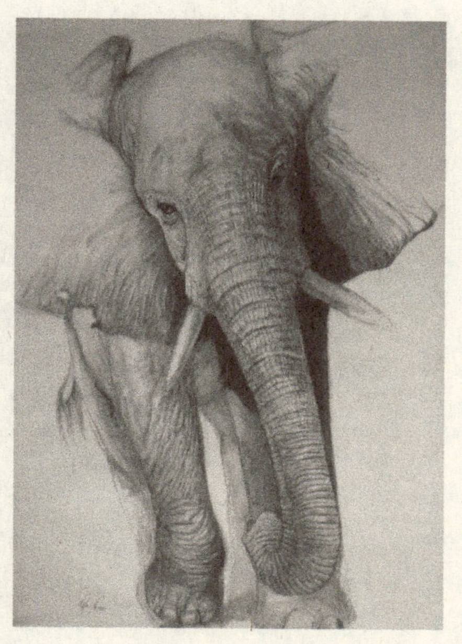

ONE

September 2007

There was a helicopter at eye level and it was staring at me with bulging, buggy eyes. Another six of its kind were whirring like overgrown cicadas around the peaks of the high-rise buildings of Sydney's city centre, circling for signs of suspicious activity. I wondered how they were going to spot a bomber from that high up, and even if they did, what they were going to do about it.

I was thirteen storeys up in one of those high-rise buildings, looking out at the scene that was the week of the Asia Pacific Economic Cooperation (APEC) meetings. President Bush had arrived in Sydney two days before and outside it was utter madness. Inside the World Wide Fund for Nature (WWF), one of the world's largest wildlife conservation organisations, things weren't that dissimilar. My role at the Panda (as we on the payroll of WWF Australia affectionately called our employer) was to lead the national Species Program, a largely government-funded team of state-based, community-focused conservation co-ordinators known collectively as the Threatened Species Network.

'Tammie, I've got you booked in for an interview with ABC Radio National at four o'clock, and with 2Day FM at four-thirty. You'll have your work cut out for you tomorrow. Your first interview starts at six-thirty and your last one's not till six. You've got about ten in between.'

Helen was the Threatened Species Network's communications officer and my right-hand woman on all things to do with the media. Her voice sounded miles away as I watched a black hawk swerve menacingly between two high-rises, dipping in for a closer look at something I couldn't see.

'Yep, sure. Lock them in,' I replied, trying not to look as distant as I felt.

Helen had worked hard to get so many interviews lined up. Putting conservation messages out to the public is a crucial part of what WWF does. Even so, I felt my stomach lurch at the prospect of all that public speaking. Knowing that it wasn't about me, that it was really about the animals, helped a little to assuage my nerves, but that didn't mean I wouldn't be clutching a paper clip or a pen or whatever the hell I could get my hands on to stop them shaking so much.

I'd worked for WWF at their Australian headquarters in Sydney for nine months and I still had regular moments of disbelief that I was actually there. The roller-coaster ride had begun almost a year earlier when the combination of being almost thirty, broke, single and homeless had led me to apply for the position of manager of the Threatened Species Network. To my astonishment, I got the job. Two weeks into it I was promoted – more through good luck than talent – and christened 'Program Leader – Species', a senior management role answering to the conservation director. I gathered from the way I was treated that it was a title that carried with it a fair bit of power and status. This was a new feeling for me. I kind of liked it.

For the last six years, as a young woman working in Namibia as a foreign researcher, I'd been at the very bottom of the conservation barrel. In terms of status, I hadn't been much higher than a *nyamtuta,* or dung beetle, the name I was given as a teenager in Zimbabwe for what a brazen safari hand once described as my habit of 'organising shit'. I'd fought my way up the African conservation ladder through a churning sea of sexist macho men trying to put me in my place, had my mettle tested by charging rhinos, hungry lions and deadly cobras, and lost my lippy in the desert dunes, never to be found again. Now, more by accident than intent, thirteen years after my first trip to Africa, I had emerged somewhere near top of the conservation castle wielding a budget of millions and quite a high level of influence. In a very Austin Powers way, I wanted to shout, *Yeah, baby, yeeeeah!* And then, a split second later, *Oh shit . . .*

The only problem with my newfound status was that I knew almost nothing about Australian species. I felt like a fraud. On paper, I was perfect for this job. After over a decade of working on African species, I knew my stuff when it came to impalas and elephants. I could tell you about the desert plants of the Kaokoveld and the water-saving behaviours of arid-adapted antelope in Namibia. I could talk at random about anthrax and its impact on the mammals of Etosha, about translocation of impalas and how to maximise its success, about how to reduce human-elephant conflict in places where elephant populations were growing rapidly.

But ask me about wombats and rat kangaroos and I wouldn't even have known where to start. My glossy qualifications and experience in Africa masked a bottomless black hole in the part of my brain where my knowledge of Australian species should have been. Unfortunately, Aussie critters were the subject of my new job. For an Australian with a PhD in zoology, I was an overqualified, unpatriotic ignoramus, a creature cretin among those I was expected to lead. The fact that I came from the same part of Australia as Steve Irwin did not help my reputation. I didn't know what a quoll was, let alone how to conserve one. This lack of Australian faunal knowledge was not something I was terribly proud of. There was no way I could have faked it. Sooner or later, people were going to find out I was a fraud.

I had said to my new boss, 'You know I don't know anything about Australian species, don't you? I mean, I'm flattered that you would even consider me for this opportunity, but really . . . are you *sure*?'

Nine months of long days, rapid-fire speed reading, copious domestic travel and strenuous social posturing later I was still trying to live up to my illustrious job title. It was exhausting. I glanced at my watch. It was after six and the choppers were still whirring their way around the city. I decided to call it a day.

In amongst the heaving throb of commuters that characterised Central train station in peak hour were police and other broad-shouldered beefy men who looked like elite security forces. The security measures in the city were beyond anything Sydney had ever seen. The Opera House had been shut down for the week of APEC and a five-kilometre-long, terrorist-proof fence erected around the area where the official discussions were being held. Australia's illustrious prime minister, John Howard, was doing his best to ensure that President Bush was treated like a global superstar. Unfortunately for Howard, the nation's then opposition leader, Kevin Rudd, had realised that the real celebrity at the APEC was not Bush, who was on borrowed time in his presidency and influence anyway, but the President of China. While Howard focused on schmoozing the brash Texan, Rudd modestly greeted the Chinese leader and had a friendly conversation with him in fluent Mandarin.

Politics aside, I frankly had bigger things to worry about than the APEC meetings. Animals were dying out there! Come on, people, let's get some perspective! Australia had – and still has – a mammal extinction crisis and tomorrow was National Threatened Species Day. Howard had it all wrong – he was trying to save the wrong Bush! America's Bush had become a real threat to the bush we were trying to save because he was literally dominating the media. Who the hell did he think he was? WWF relied on National Threatened Species Day to communicate messages about species threats to the Australian public. With APEC going on, we struggled to get a look-in with any major newspaper or radio station.

The communications team eventually resigned themselves to the fact that if we couldn't beat 'em, we'd have to join 'em. We constructed a press release about the most endangered and charismatic species in each of the APEC countries, focusing on popular animals people could identify with, like orangutans, tigers and pandas, and encouraging those countries to move trade in a more sustainable direction. Come 7 September, National Threatened Species Day, I was all over the media talking about species that I had never even seen in a zoo. I talked my way through dozens of radio interviews in several states throughout the course of the day and night. And I was talking to interviewers as though I knew precisely what I was talking about. Something that, even as I was saying the words, I was completely amazed by.

By the end of the day I was so exhausted from pretending to be an Australian threatened species expert that I needed a very stiff drink. Helen and I headed for the pub.

As we cut across a pedestrian crossing in Paddington, stopping the bumper-to-bumper traffic coming home from the city,

I was reminded that it wasn't very long ago that my life involved real zebra crossings and traffic jams caused by elephants. Now all I could smell was the pungent fumes of a bus that roared past, rather than the sweet smell of campfire smoke after sunset. Instead of dust from the hooves of antelope filling my nostrils, it was the foul emissions of cars. There had been a time when my days were filled with wild animals and even wilder people – not so different from a night at the pub in Sydney, some might say, but I knew which animals I'd rather have been dealing with.

It wasn't that I was unhappy. God knows, I'd been lonelier in Windhoek on a Sunday than I ever had in Sydney. In this throbbing Australian city, I didn't have time to be lonely. I'd never been so busy in my life.

'Watch out, Tammie!'

Helen grabbed my arm just as I was about to cross a small lane where a car was pulling in at forty kilometres per hour. I'd been charged by lions and elephants, rhinos and buffaloes, and now, nearly murdered by a maniacal Mazda.

'Thanks, man. You saved my life.'

In appreciation, I bought a bottle of red wine for us and let the alcohol take the edge off the day's adrenaline.

Soon, as one wine led to many more, I was telling poor Helen my life story and she was pretending to be interested.

'Do you ever wonder what you're doing here?' A dangerous start, I know. Put it down to the drink and the long day.

'All the time!' she exclaimed. 'Well, I know what I'm doing here really. I came to Sydney to work for the Panda. I probably wouldn't be here otherwise.'

To some extent, it was the same reason I was in the big city. Such is the pull of the WWF brand that conservationists long to work there, even if it means being miles and miles away from the animals we became conservationists for. But there had been more to my return to Australia in January than that. After so long in Africa, I certainly wasn't ready to give up the adventures but I was looking for a little stability. I was tired of being at the whim of the Ministry of Home Affairs of Namibia who regularly rejected foreigners' work visas, if they ever addressed them at all. At some point in my life I wanted a house, a hound and a husband (not necessarily in that order). My life in Namibia wasn't getting me any closer to those goals. Above all, I had been flat broke and the idea of a regular income had sounded like heaven in a pay packet.

'Let's face it,' Helen went on, 'I'm not here for the men.'

A dashing but decidedly gay man in a smart suit sashayed past us and blew a kiss at a man at the bar, just to prove the point. We both giggled shamelessly.

I scanned the pub. There were a lot of very good-looking men there. It was something about Paddington. It seemed to attract handsome, well-dressed young men with designer stubble and brand-name shirts.

'The truth is,' I asserted, eyeing off the talent in the room, 'you'd have to say there are men here. It's not the quantity. It's an issue of availability.'

'Stop the press,' cried Helen. 'I've got the answer! They need to introduce a quality assurance standard for men in Australia. Like a panda stamp. A man-da stamp! They get a stamp if they're single, available, love animals and the outdoors, ideally have money . . .'

'. . . a house, no stalking ex-girlfriends, *not* on drugs, mental and emotional stability . . .'

'. . . and not in the army!' Helen's ex-husband had been a military man.

'That's not asking too much, is it?'

We both burst out laughing.

'Let's face it, Helen. These criteria are ridiculous. It just doesn't work like that. My last boyfriend didn't meet any of my criteria. With me, falling in love usually has more to do with a bad case of khaki fever than anything else.'

'Khaki what?'

'Khaki fever. You know, that fatal combination of boots, a collared khaki shirt and facial hair.'

'You are definitely in the wrong place then!' Helen exclaimed.

And didn't I know it. My first brush with khaki fever had been at the humble age of fifteen on my first trip to Africa. I had joined my father on a safari at a ranch called Humani in Zimbabwe. Dad's professional hunter was about twenty-four, which at the time seemed ancient, but in an irresistibly attractive way. I loved the way he read the signs of the bush, recognising the tracks of a leopard that were invisible to my eye but obvious to his in the small shift in river sand its paw left on the bank, the way he could detect the faint smell of elephant when a herd was a kilometre away, his intimate knowledge and appreciation of nature, the way he glided through the bush like an animal. After that, just a whiff of khaki and it was all over for me.

That first accidental trip to Africa, made possible by the fact that my mother had been too daunted to join my dad on his first safari, literally changed the course of my life. Fresh out of Catholic girls' school I returned to Humani in 1995, my gap year after high school, to work as a safari slave. Humani, a 150 000 acre safari property, part of the Save Valley Conservancy in Zimbabwe's lowveld, was a wildlife lover's mecca. Elephants and rhinos had been reintroduced and now formed healthy populations. Lions, leopards and cheetahs roamed the plains, dining on a cornucopia of antelopes, from the most common impalas to the rarer nyalas.

So much for the law degree I had deferred to take a year off. I didn't care if I never made a cent. From then on I had my heart set on being a wildlife conservationist in Africa.

'You must have really loved it there to stay so long,' Helen mused.

I nodded, suddenly feeling wistful.

How could I explain the extent to which Africa had changed my life? Africa was part of me now, tattooed forever onto my soul. I had to be careful not to sound like an obsessive, crazy weirdo when I talked about the place. It was part of the constant juggle I played out between my two lives, the one in Africa and the one that was, well, Out of Africa.

The truth was that Africa had taught me what I was made of. I was seventeen years old when I began teaching grade six English at a Zimbabwean school to pupils who were older than me by several years. I had to fight off the local witchdoctor, who was determined to put a curse on the headmaster because he was my friend. And, for a couple of weeks, I ran a hunting camp in the middle of nowhere in Zambia on the smell of an oily rag. In an average day I could be cursed by a witchdoctor, run over by a rhino or lost in the jungle, and I absolutely loved it. Africa was my initiation to life in the real world.

There it was. I'd done it again. I'd turned a perfectly normal conversation about men into one about Africa. It was as if the continent were a living, breathing sex god. Some days I just wished I could be normal. Oh well, it was too late to worry about that. I was in my stride now, talking about my favourite subject.

'I don't know,' I tried to explain, 'Africa just made me feel invincible.'

It hadn't been an easy journey. Apart from the fact that I'd taken all of the necessary high school subjects to be a lawyer, none of which were in any way useful in my training to be a scientist,

I had to face the subjects I had hated most at school in order to get an environmental degree – chemistry, physics and maths. My brain rejected these disciplines just as vehemently the second time round, but somehow I got through the first year of university and scrambled my way up to an Honours degree, majoring in Zoology, just as the twentieth century drew to a close.

In my final year of undergraduate studies, still obsessed with my goal to become a wildlife conservationist in Africa, I scavenged enough funding to do a study at Humani on impalas, Africa's most abundant antelope, eaten by everything from leopards to humans. Tumbling around the savannah for three months in a jeep with no roof, suspension or brakes, accompanied by a wonderful local tracker, stalking and observing the vigilance behaviour of impalas, I was in my element. After that I knew I could do wildlife conservation in Africa solo; the question was how to make it a permanent arrangement.

With one small research study under my belt, I reckoned the world was my oyster. Even before I left Zimbabwe, I was plotting how to get back there. I was cocky enough to think that the Australian government might give me a scholarship to do a PhD on the same species, using the rationale that impala were kind of, sort of, like, well, kangaroos. They ate grass, tasted great as steaks and jumped around a lot. Astonishingly, in the year 2000, Howard's mob bought it, granting me enough money to survive as a doctoral student for the next three years.

What a way to start the century! Everything was on track, to plan and on schedule. Naturally that was when Zimbabwe turned into hell. With impeccable timing, just as scholarship funds started trickling into my bank account, Robert Mugabe's war veterans began invading white-owned farms, including Humani. By June of 2000, when I was finally able to fly there, Zimbabwe was a mess. So-called war vets, some of whom weren't even born during the country's independence war, were crawling all over the Save Valley Conservancy, claiming land at their will and poaching the wildlife that had grown so abundant. Humani's game scouts collected hundreds upon hundreds of snares and local people were brutally intimidated and beaten. It was devastating to see a once thriving game reserve reduced to a bloody war zone. And, after a couple of personal scares with men wielding pangas, I realised with deep regret that my previously bright prospects for wildlife research in Zimbabwe were fizzling out.

I was devastated to leave Zimbabwe, but I wasn't about to give up on my PhD. I'd heard about an endangered subspecies of impala that lived in Namibia, mostly in Etosha National Park – the black-faced impala. Apparently almost nothing was known about this subspecies, a gift for a budding zoologist like me. At the very least Etosha sounded like it was worth a look, so I convinced a friend who was travelling in South Africa at the time to join me, and together we sped across the Trans-Kalahari Highway, dodging donkeys and cows, all the way from Pretoria in South Africa, through Botswana up to Etosha in Namibia.

Etosha was everything and nothing I had imagined. A place of extremes, it took my breath away in equal measure with its raw, stark beauty and its devastating, life-sucking heat. Towering dust devils swept across a saltpan the size of a small European country; goliath elephants covered in white dust strode across the landscape like regal kings puffed with talcum powder; sinister black-maned lions hid in the long grass and occasionally jumped on car windscreens just for fun. Unexpectedly, out of the disaster that had become Zimbabwe I found a new home in the desert and the perfect species for my doctoral research, an endangered, little-known antelope.

Over the next few years as I studied the behaviour of the

black-faced impala, this arid land taught me how to live at the edge of the earth and be truly happy. To survive in Etosha you had to become like a desert plant, resilient and strong. It was no place for weaklings. *Toughen up or die*, her achingly dry, desiccating winds screeched. *Show no fear*, the heat haze hummed. I cried. I pleaded. *Get up*, it replied. *Shake the dust out of your ears and get over yourself.* After a while, I found my voice. As the sun beat down, merciless in its fury, I began to shout back, fearless, *Is that the best you can do?* And that was just the weather. Similarly, when it came to surviving the sexism of my male colleagues in Etosha, the key was never to show weakness. When trying to fit in with the boys' club, it was simple: buy lots of beer and learn how to swear in Afrikaans.

A barman learned in over the top of Helen to wipe a recent spill of red wine off the table.

'It was her,' Helen said to him. 'She's a little bit drunk.'

He gave her a knowing smile.

But heaven forbid, I would never have imagined that I would end up working on elephants. Of all the species in Africa they were the last I wanted to study. It wasn't that I wasn't fascinated by them. I was. I loved nothing more than watching elephants bathing in a muddy waterhole with light-hearted, blissful joy, and then showering themselves with dust in the late afternoon sun. Unfortunately I knew that the world of elephant conservation wasn't nearly as carefree as the elephants themselves. The problem with working on any of the Big Five in Africa – elephant, rhino, lion, buffalo and leopard – is that they can attract big egos. Crossing into those territories can be fatal, even before you've unwittingly left a scent mark, because many researchers guard their domains like Rottweilers. Funding is scarce in the world of wildlife research and this invites a world of fierce competition, especially in the realm of large mammals. So, quite intentionally

I had always worked on impalas, because they didn't attract a lot of attention and I could just get on with the job without being particularly threatening to anyone.

But by a twist of fate, in 2004 I found myself among elephants, studying the underlying causes of the problems they were inflicting on a tribe of people who had suffered more than enough conflict in their lives already. For generations the Bushmen had been hunted, enslaved and persecuted by all other tribes, including my own, which classified them as vermin and hung them by the neck from trees. I was a displaced impala researcher with a missionary zeal who knew almost nothing about elephants. And yet, with no trace of bitterness or anger, the Bushmen welcomed me into their world as though I were family. They had a big problem – elephants – and although I knew almost nothing about human-elephant conflict, they were desperate enough to think I could help them fix it.

I stared hard into my merlot, seeing the ancient baobab trees of Bushmanland as clearly as if they had set down their roots through the table and were growing arthritically right out of my wine glass. I saw Chief Bobo's wrinkled old face breaking into a thousand furrows as he chuckled, his kind eyes narrowing into deep smile lines. I saw elephant bulls standing under an erect ilala palm tree, sucking and slurping loudly, imbibing water from an underground spring into their agile trunks and spraying it into their mouths. The images swirled in the ruby red liquid, and for a few moments I was right back there with them. I was home, in the land of the little people.

TWO

August 2004

'I'm looking for Dries . . . Dries Alberts.'

The drive from Namibia's capital city, Windhoek, to Bushmanland's capital village, Tsumkwe (pronounced 'Choom-kwe') took over eight hours at an average speed of one hundred and twenty kilometres an hour. The last three of those were on an infamous white gravel road, which alternated between dead straight and boring at best to bone-jarringly corrugated at worst. The Hilux careened and sometimes flew over sections of deep, thick sand with hidden potholes the size of small cars. It felt like the road to never-never. We were never-never going to get there.

What I didn't know yet was that it was a necessary journey of the metaphysical kind. The endless glary road led us out of relative civilisation and all its trappings into the land of the Bushmen, a place where nothing was what it seemed, where life danced to a different rhythm. It was literally like being transported from one world to another by three long hours of white gravel road.

'If you pass a chicken on the road, you've gone past Tsumkwe,' the warden, Dries Alberts, told me on a phone line that crackled and delayed for several seconds, as if this were an international call rather than a national one. 'It's so small that if you blink you'll miss it. But don't worry, another forty kilometres and you'll hit the Botswana border post, which takes you into the Okavango Delta. If you go through there without stopping they'll shoot you. So I'd advise you to look out for the chicken.'

Dries's voice had the deep timbre of an elephant's stomach rumble, vibrating with the strong, guttural accent of a Kalahari Afrikaner. He didn't sound like someone you'd want to mess with.

I'd lined this trip up to coincide with the visit of my dear friends, Sally and Jeremy Henderson. Sal and I had become great mates as soon as we had met, bonded by a mutual fascination with Africa, a passion for writing and a connection that sometimes went beyond words. A deeply spiritual person, Sal could pick up on whether something was wrong with me long before I typed her an email. Her intuition bordered on the psychic. Her husband, Jeremy, was simply a legend, a gentle giant you could always depend on to create laughter and calm, no matter how trying the situation. Like me, Sal and Jer had always wanted to see Bushmanland, a place that few tourists go to because of its remoteness. An anthropologist by trade, Sal had read about the Bushmen in her studies and met some when she and Jeremy worked at a safari camp in Botswana. My boyfriend, Tristan, had been to Bushmanland as a child, but hadn't been back since. Ever since he was a small child he'd been called 'Bushman', so it seemed somehow fitting that we all go there together.

I had an ulterior motive for going. It had been a year since I'd finished my work on the black-faced impalas in Etosha and I was thoroughly impala-ed out. I was looking for a new mission.

While I wrote up my PhD in Australia for nine months, Tristan had taken a job managing a game farm near Kamanjab in north-west Namibia. Soon after my return we had moved closer to Windhoek so that I could try to get work and he could start up his own business as a safari guide, professional hunter and mechanic. I was doing bits and pieces of environmental work and trying to get my PhD papers published in scientific journals, but what I really wanted to do was to run another conservation project.

Enter Bushmanland! In conservation circles, Bushmanland, now recognised as the Nyae Nyae Conservancy, was known as a place that was wild and magical but in great need of wildlife research and conservation support. Critically endangered African wild dogs and rare roan antelope, a growing elephant population, lions and leopards were just a few of its animal residents, but only limited research had been conducted on any of the species in the region. Listening to people talk about the place, I felt a familiar missionary zeal rising to the surface. It was conservation converts I was looking for, not religious ones. Nyae Nyae sounded like just the sort of place I could sink my teeth into, if I could find the right project.

There were no signs indicating that this was Tsumkwe. A skanky looking chicken darted onto the road. We had arrived.

There was only one main road in the sprawling capital village of Bushmanland. It wasn't much of a road, more of a wide dusty track jagging sharply off the main road to never-never. Traditional huts fringed the track, disappearing into dust clouds whenever a vehicle passed by. These small homes had been stuck together haphazardly with everything from grass, mud and rock to torn sheets of plastic and rusted corrugated iron. In stark contrast to these ramshackle exteriors, a shiny, near-new building painted in all the bright colours of the rainbow stood on the corner like Paris Hilton on a grey day in London. *Tsumkwe Craft*

Centre, it declared itself in silver letters. Beside it, somewhat dwarfed by its bawdy neighbour, stood a small office building surrounded by a high wire fence with a sign that said *Nyae Nyae Conservancy Office*.

On the other side of the road, opposite the craft centre, was a typical rural African shop with a couple of old fuel bowsers and signs advertising Castle Lager. Goats and people milled around, puffs of white dust billowing from scuffling hooves and feet. A skinny goat picked up a piece of plastic that looked like an empty Simba chips packet, chewed on it for a second or two, then, finding it wanting in nutritional value, promptly spat it out again. Obviously not a fan of salt and vinegar. The packet blew down the street in the wind before catching on a spiky bush, harpooned on thorns. Crushed Afri-cans of Coca-Cola and Mountain Dew, supersized for Africa, lay scattered in the dirt.

Lapping Tsumkwe's only official street, we passed a couple of churches, more scrawny goats, a large building with a sign that said *Community Hall*, another shop with advertisements for Coca-Cola and a health centre. Before we knew it, a few hundred metres down the road, we were at the end of the street.

'Well, then,' Jeremy commented in his gravelly Australian accent, 'I think we've just seen Tsumkwe.'

It had taken us all of two minutes. That's not to say the experience was dull. Things were happening in Tsumkwe. Tiny barefoot people scuttled along the street, filtered in and out of the shops and sat around in conversation under trees. The Bushmen. With their small statures, lighter skin and Asiatic features, they were unmistakable.

The women radiated colour. Wearing T-shirts with American brand names and long skirts, I recognised instantly the foreign-aid clothes designed for much larger westerners. Their necks, ankles and wrists were encircled by brightly coloured, handmade chains of beads. Some wore vibrant scarves on their heads. Others had babies strapped to their backs with blankets, secured with ties under their breasts. A gaggle of women held up dozens of necklaces as we passed, calling out in their clicking language for a sale.

Now I'd be lying if I said I hadn't always imagined what it would be like to meet a real live Bushman. I'd watched *The Gods Must Be Crazy* about a hundred times. I'd heard that the main actor in that film came from a village outside Tsumkwe. I had a somewhat idealised view of what I would find in the land of the little people. I hadn't quite expected to see nymph-like, primitive beings running around in loincloths and carrying bows and arrows, but it's fair to say I'd brought a whole swag of preconceptions with me. I certainly hadn't been expecting to see so many random Coke bottles lying around (such things naturally being messages from the gods).

The road ended at a T-junction. Remembering the instructions that Dries had given me over the phone, we turned left into a dirt track that wandered off the main drag. It was about a hundred metres long and its main feature was the office of the Ministry of Environment and Tourism (MET), where Dries had told me I would find him. Three dark green Landcruisers and a beaten-up German Unimog truck with two flat tyres were parked out the front. Half-a-dozen men from a range of African tribes – very few of them Bushmen, judging by their size – stood around out front in ragged uniforms. They were smoking, chatting, nodding, grunting and doing what people in Africa do a heck of a lot better than we do in the western world – not very much at all. Waiting patiently (something I am hopeless at). Being (even worse). Going with the flow (nearly impossible). Avoiding heart attacks and strokes from overexertion (inevitable).

Being Deepak Chopra is easier in Africa. There's something about the heat that sucks the initiative out of you. Some days you can physically feel the energy being drained slowly but surely from your body. Like wisps of exiting life-smoke, you exhale it until there's no choice but to have a little rest under a tree and think about your life.

'I'm looking for Dries. Dries Alberts,' I said to one of the men.

He raised his arm limply and pointed into the office.

Inside, there was a reception area with no receptionist. All around me was a kaleidoscope of the region, a display of the good, the bad and the ugly of Bushmanland. The walls were covered in photographs of stressed or dead elephants wedged into cement waterholes, huge maned lions in long grass, MET staff carrying elephant tusks stained with vegetable juices, antelopes with weird back-to-front or missing horns, recently translocated Cape buffalos inside a *boma* (enclosure), Raleigh International volunteers proudly standing in front of wooden hides, and a variety of people in official uniforms striking poses with dead and living animals. Line graphs of the results of annual waterhole game censuses took up a large chunk of one wall, showing how the populations of species like elephants, giraffes and roan antelope were faring in Nyae Nyae and the national park north of here, Khaudum. Judging by the graphs, most of the populations seemed to be on the rise.

Belatedly, a canine with short-dog syndrome growled, then came charging out of the office beside the reception area with its teeth bared.

'Pundi! Get in here!'

I recognised Dries's guttural accent immediately. I hoped he was talking to the dog and not me.

'Hello?' I called out.

Sometimes even to my own ears my voice sounded so foreign.

After more than a decade in Africa, I still stood out like a sore toe.

A more restrained, almost dignified, 'Come in.'

Tentatively I stepped into the dingy office where the voice was coming from. It smelled of dust and mutts – musty, you might say. Dust, because there was a layer of it about a millimetre thick on everything in the room. Mutts, because there were about six of them sitting under Dries's long wooden desk, baring their canines at me.

As Dries rose to shake my hand, the pack burst into a terrifying outburst of barking.

'Shut up!'

Dries's outburst subdued the dogs as if he'd just cracked a whip. One mangy mongrel whimpered plaintively. Dries sat down again, lifted it onto his lap and began stroking it gently behind the ear. He skirted my eyes.

'Sorry, Tammie . . . Take a seat.'

The wooden desk was covered in various piles of official-looking papers. In the middle of it all was an automatic rifle.

'Don't worry, it's not loaded,' Dries assured me, without meeting my eyes. 'Now, what can I do for you?'

'Nothing really. I just came to say hello,' I smiled.

'Nothing? Well, with respect, Tammie, you'd be the first foreign researcher coming here who wants nothing.'

'Well, no –'

'Frankly, I know what *I* can do for *you*. I'd like to know what you can do for us . . . for Bushmanland. You researchers come in here trying to change the world, take what you need, then fuck off. Sorry, Tammie, but it's true.'

I don't know how he did it but Dries said my name with a roll at the back of his throat, which was quite impressive given that there aren't any 'r's to roll in 'Tammie'.

I felt the all too familiar sinking feeling, the smack across the thin skin of my self-esteem – *remember your place, girl*. I'd been in this position so many times with men of the African bush who didn't know me. I remembered the first time I'd walked into the Etosha Ecological Institute five years earlier and been lectured about following the 'right channels' by the acting chief warden, as if I, at twenty-two and just beginning my PhD, was already responsible for all of the foreign researchers who'd broken the rules before me.

I'd toughened up since those days, but I was still too quick to feel the need to run away and cry in a corner when faced with a bellowing male in uniform. I knew that this was a test of my mettle. Even if I didn't feel terribly brave at that moment, I had to lay the ground rules or pay the price later. I took a deep breath.

'You're right, Dries. There have been too many researchers in Namibia who've come out, got their doctorate and buggered off back to their own country, taking their results with them. That's why I'm still here. I could have left Namibia a year ago, but I stayed. I'm not going anywhere.'

'That's all well and good, but you haven't answered my question. What are you going to do for us?'

'That's because I don't have an answer for you yet.'

Dries's face broke into a wide grin and he chuckled. When he laughed he didn't seem nearly as intimidating. I realised with a sudden intensity that he was very good-looking. His dark brown hair and matching eyes against a deep tan were quite striking. And, of course, the khaki collared shirt and shorts didn't hurt either.

He poured the small dog off his lap, stood up and grabbed the rifle off his desk in one swift movement. I took the hint and stood up too. He came around to my side of the desk, still clutching the rifle, and I realised that even in my boots (which gave me almost an inch of extra height) I only came up to his left nipple.

'Well, we'll see then. Meet me here tomorrow morning at nine.'

And with that, he charged out of the office, leapt into his Landcruiser along with the barrage of yelping dogs, and roared off in a cloud of dust.

We arranged to trail Dries on his daily travels around Nyae Nyae Conservancy for the next few days. It had been a freezing first night camping out in canvas tents at Klein Dobe, the government-owned camp twenty kilometres north of Tsumkwe, where most visiting researchers stayed when working in the area. After the long drive, we had *braaied* some sausage over the campfire and snuggled under duvets that were no match for the Kalahari night temperatures. The next morning, tired and not yet defrosted, we pulled up at Dries's house, two doors down from his office, in Tristan's old double-cab Hilux.

It seemed that Dries had adopted most of the local dogs in Tsumkwe, as an even bigger pack of hounds than had been in his office the day before raced out to bark at us. I hesitated in getting out of the car as they bared their teeth and growled, before one peed on the tyre. They were a mixture of half-breeds, big ones and small ones, skinny ones and fat ones, all of them typical of the dogs you find in remote parts of Africa, almost a breed of their own, adapted to living on the edge of survival. Later he told us that every so often a hyaena wandered into Tsumkwe and ate one.

'Dogs!' Dries called them over and loaded a couple into the front seat of his Landcruiser. 'Stacey! Let's go!'

In contrast to everything around her, Dries's girlfriend,

Stacey, was an apparition as she emerged from inside the old government house, a dwelling that looked like a veteran of war with its decayed exterior of water stains and peeling paint. She appeared from within a cloud of dust created by the barking pack of mangy mutts, looking as though she'd just stepped out of the salon. A gorgeous American with a halo of big blonde locks, she wore high wedge heels and just enough make up to look truly glamorous. So incongruous was she with her surroundings, so utterly, totally Hollywood, that everyone in our car went silent for a moment, just watching her.

In any other setting a well-groomed woman wouldn't be so extraordinary. But in Tsumkwe it was nothing short of miraculous. I had already learned that this was a place where there was no mains power, so a large generator powered the whole town. It broke down several times a week, making things like a simple blow-dry rather challenging. The closest thing to a restaurant or a nightclub or even a pub was the Tsumkwe Lodge, tourist accommodation on the outskirts of town. It only opened when they had guests. Tsumkwe wasn't the sort of place where you got dressed up to go out. There was nowhere to buy make-up or get a facial. The local stores sold the absolute basics. Soap, if you were lucky.

I looked down at my khaki shorts, dirty singlet and scuffed hiking boots. I caught a glimpse of my au naturel face in the rear-view mirror of the Hilux and grimaced. There was grit under my nails and I hadn't shaved my legs in a week. I knew Sal was thinking the same thing. I noticed her scuffling around in her handbag and wondered if she was looking for some lippy.

But there was no time for a rapid *Oprah*-style makeover now. Dries's Cruiser tore out of his driveway and hurtled down the gravel road, trailed by all of the dogs that hadn't scored a ride in the front with him and Stacey. The wheels of our Hilux spun on loose gravel as we hightailed after him. We had to drive fast to keep up.

As soon as we left Tsumkwe we were in sand. Nyae Nyae was four-by-four country all year round and not for the faint-hearted rally car driver. The deep, soft sandy roads required low ratio often to plow through them. And on sections of rocky calcrete, it was rough. Head banging on the roof, holding on for your life, axle-breaking rough. Toyotas may be unbreakable and perhaps the only cars that can truly withstand the conditions in Namibia, but you couldn't say a Hilux is the most comfortable car in the wilderness.

Not that I was complaining. I was in my element.

One thing about Namibia is that it's largely one big desert. Some of it is your typical rolling orange sand dune desert (the kind you see in tourist pamphlets of the Namib). Some of it is the red corrugated sand dunes of the Kalahari, which are peppered by arid-adapted bushes and colonies of meerkats. Then there is Damaraland, a place of volcanic, red rocky mountains, all jagged shale and sharp rock, from which toxic Euphorbia bushes grow like pale green cottonwool on an immense maroon landscape. At the Skeleton Coast, where the angry Atlantic Ocean meets an equally hostile desert, it is often freezing cold, but when the east winds come from the inland, their extreme dry heat sucks out every last droplet of moisture from your body. And of course there is Etosha, which isn't exactly desert but, being semi-arid, it is just about as hot, dry and dusty as one. There are a lot of different types of deserts and Namibia's got just about all of them. They are gob-smacking, incredible places.

Thing is, I'd done my time in the desert. Not that I had *issues*, but I'd had enough of the long hot dry seasons that made you want to die just so you could escape their torture. I'd had my share of eyeball sunstroke and glare headaches. I'd had it with itchy, flaking, dried skin and brittle, hard hair that resembled a vulture's nest. I used to stare at the mirage that is Etosha's 5000 square kilometre saltpan and long for the water that my mind could see on the pan to be real. Now I just wanted big trees and lots of them. I wanted rain. I wanted heaps of animals and plenty of luxuriant water.

As we drove through the Nyae Nyae Conservancy over the next few days I found what I'd been looking for. Ancient gnarled baobab trees towered like lighthouses above a sea of smaller trees and bushes. Their twisted, arthritic limbs hung over all of the lesser trees like giant guardians. I'm afraid I have to call them 'lesser' trees, because when you meet a baobab you realise that not all trees are created equal. Dries showed us one so large that allegedly it had once held prisoners inside it. Some baobabs in Bushmanland, he told us, have been dated at over a thousand years old. Tall ilala palms shot up like straight-backed soldiers next to barely bubbling underground springs. Some of the natural pans in the conservancy still held water – *real* water, not mirages – glittering in the sun like reflective glass.

Trees! Glorious trees! I wanted to run around hugging them, but I managed to restrain myself. After all, I had my reputation to uphold in the presence of the warden. The last thing I wanted Dries to think was that I was a crazy tree-hugging greenie.

But I couldn't stop myself. When I thought he wasn't looking, I reached out and gave a baobab a hug. How could I not? It was crying out for it. Sal couldn't help herself, either. I wondered how many hugs this tree had received in its hundreds of years on earth. Its trunk was as wide as a small house.

There is something about baobabs that makes it nearly impossible not to anthropomorphise them. I wanted to talk to them, and felt somehow that they could talk back if they chose to. The one we were hugging was an old, old lady with saggy baggy skin, possibly a thousand years old. Putting it in perspective, some of these trees had first sprouted from a humble seed at the end of the Dark Ages. A thousand years ago the Vikings were still conquering parts of Europe and the Chinese had only just discovered gunpowder. Clinging onto the smooth bark and squeezing this old, old grandma, I must have looked like a barnacle on a humpback whale. But it was worth it.

Dragging ourselves away from the tree, we turned around to see Dries looking at us and stubbing out his cigarette in the sand.

'Women,' he grunted, a flicker of amusement in his eyes.

The air was smoky. Fires lit by the Bushmen blazed across the bush, creating a constant grey haze. Like Indigenous Australians, the Bushmen have used fire to manage the country for thousands of years. It makes hunting for game easier and reveals roots and tubers that are hard to find in the thick bush. Crackling through the dry winter grass, orange flames rampaged across the bush, leaping like excited children from one piece of fuel to the next, cartwheeling across tracks, charring tree trunks black and toppling those that were dead or close to it. Swirling devils of smoke, dust and burning leaves swept across the landscape after the fires, leaving a scene as black as night behind them. Devastating as they seemed at the time, these fires made way for the new life that would follow. Just days after a burn, new green shoots were already breaking through the earth, even though it hadn't rained for at least six months.

Where the fires hadn't recently burned, the bush was so dense it was hard to see the animals. A steenbok sped across the road at breakneck speed, followed swiftly by its partner. Steenboks are one of the smallest of the antelope species in Africa and one of the most interesting. It's rare that you see them drink water because they get most of what they need from their food. How's that for an impressive metabolism? Unlike many of the other antelopes, which have males with large harems of females, steenboks form partnerships with a single mate *for life*. You've got to respect that.

In what I'd taken as an auspicious sign that we would see plenty of elephants, on the drive out to our campsite on our first afternoon in Bushmanland, we found two elephant bulls standing together under an ilala palm, sucking water from a temporary underground spring. The sky at dusk was pastel pink behind them, a scene of utter peace and harmony. They took their time drinking. There was no rush. Elephant bulls are, after all, the biggest and most powerful animals in the bush. It wasn't like a garrulous warthog was going to come along and say, 'Come on, guys, get a wriggle on!'

It was a good thing they let us watch them for a while, because they were the only elephants we saw during the whole trip. There were signs of elephants everywhere in huge piles of dung and branches strewn across the roads. Sometimes we could smell their intense vegetable aroma, but the bush was so thick that even animals the size of elephants vanished into it. They walked through flooded areas in the wet season and left footprints that dried to create deep, gaping cavities in the ground. The grass then grew chest high over the top of them, disguising the hazards. At one stage I watched Stacey follow Dries on foot across one of these grasslands and saw her delicate form promptly disappear into an elephant footprint. One second she was there, the next she was gone. A few seconds later she re-emerged, apparently unscathed, with hair and make-up intact. *Hurrah for the hair!*

Dries was a man of few words, but when he did speak it was often about what he considered the biggest issue in the region – human-elephant conflict. I found it hard to believe him, given that we had hardly seen any elephants.

'It's only August,' Dries explained. 'You don't get the big numbers of elephants coming in here until it gets really hot. October. Then they head in to the conservancy for the water. In Khaudum, just north of here, that's when you get hundreds of elephants at a waterhole at a time. That's when they cause the *kak*,' the shit, 'pulling up the water pumps and solar panels.'

I tried to imagine an elephant attacking the solid metal installations that fed the waterholes during the dry season when the natural pans dried up. It seemed counterintuitive to destroy the things that gave you water when there was so little in the environment. I just couldn't visualise an elephant thundering around, trumpeting at the top of its lungs while it caused thousands of dollars of damage. I hadn't seen this side of elephants. Sure, I knew elephants got angry. I'd felt the wrath of a cow having a bad-hair day and had to back up a long way when she charged. Mock charges aren't uncommon, but usually when I'd been charged it was by a matriarch protecting a herd with youngsters in it. So it was understandable. As far as I could see, this aggression wasn't. There had to be a good reason for it.

On our last night, Stacey and Dries joined us for a *braai* (barbeque) and drinks at our campsite. They reclined in BYO camping chairs by the fire, sipping on vodka and sodas. It was another freezing night and everyone stayed close to the campfire. Dries began sombrely to tell us about a woman who had been killed a couple of years ago by an elephant bull.

'She was out collecting bush foods. An old lady. There were two of them and four bulls. By the time she saw the elephants it was too late. They were too close. One woman ran away, but the other . . . she was mincemeat.'

I'd watched Dries's interaction with the Bushmen in the villages we visited over the past few days and I could see that the people respected him. He wasn't much older than me, also in his late twenties, but he was responsible for the largest communal conservancy in the country and one of its most extraordinary and wildest parks, Khaudum. I could tell that he loved the Bushmen as much as he loved wildlife by the way he interacted with them. He joked with the people in the villages, spoke a little of their clicking language and had less of the colonial attitude I'd seen in some other parts of Namibia.

But I also knew that there was a hard edge to him, a side that would put a bullet in an elephant's brain with barely a flinch if given the official instruction. I knew that killing elephants designated as 'problem animals' was a part of his job. He'd told me that he shot animals for the conservancy when they needed meat for a community function. I was under no illusions that this was a man of practicality, more comfortable with a gun in the bush than with a pen in his office. A man whose territory was the size of Switzerland. That's a lot of scent-marking for one guy.

And yet I liked him.

After dinner Dries invited some of the local villagers to join us. Four women came with an old man known as *Alf Oor*, Half Ear. The story went that Half Ear got very drunk one night and his wife was so pissed off with him that she bit off his ear. Half Ear's wife was amongst the small group of women now sitting by our campfire. In the flickering light of the flames, the old lady seemed wise and kind, not at all the kind of woman you'd expect to bite off someone's ear.

A friend of Dries began to play an acoustic guitar and sing traditional Afrikaans folk songs. The women were intrigued, listening as though they'd never heard music like it before. The two younger girls seemed utterly enraptured.

After a few Afrikaans songs, Dries invited them to sing their own. And that was when I felt the magic of Bushmanland.

It's almost impossible to describe the traditional music of

the Bushmen. It involves a lot of rapid clapping and singing in several rounds at the same time. Trying to join in or keep up is nearly impossible. It's just not like any other kind of music. The Bushmen use singing to go into trances that are used in healing. Initially it sounded out of key and without rhythm, but as it went on and I allowed myself to really listen to it, I realised that it had an amazing complexity. The women stared into the flames as they sang and clapped, concentrating on the sound, absorbed by it.

Watching the fire, their high-pitched voices swept me away. My chest throbbed with the rapid clapping of their hands. Staring into the flames, I felt the music lifting me up. I think it is the closest that I have come to the sense of timelessness people describe experiencing during meditation. In one way I could feel myself expanding into the universe, but in another, I was completely alive and accurately aware. I felt humbled and at peace, adrift and yet a part. For a moment, the Bushmen had enabled me to glance through a secret window to another world, a place where time and space were irrelevant. Though I could not explain why, I felt elated.

When they stopped, I looked over at Sal and I could see she felt it too. Her eyes were wet with tears.

The next day, our last in Bushmanland, Dries arranged for us to meet the Honourable Chief Bobo, the man who was appointed many years ago by the government as the representative of his people. Now there was a conservancy, which had a chairman called Kievet, a board and almost eight hundred members. The conservancy wielded considerable influence because most of the community's income was derived through Nyae Nyae's wildlife-based enterprises; in particular, the lease of their lucrative trophy hunting concession.

In 2002 the conservancy signed a five-year-deal with

trophy-hunting operator Kai-Uwe Denker. WWF brokered the deal. The attraction of the hunting concession in Nyae Nyae was its elephants, particularly its large tusker bulls, which foreign trophy hunters would pay big bucks to shoot. The quota was set for half a percent of the population and only males could be taken. Compared with the population growth rate of elephants in the region (Dries believed it was higher than the typical rate of increase in southern African elephants of five percent), the impact was minor. Like it or hate it, it was impossible to ignore the benefits. An elephant trophy hunt could be sold in the realm of US$50 000. For the people of Nyae Nyae, this meant income, jobs and meat. In 2005 the conservancy paid out US$43 to each of its 770 members. That may not sound like much, but it is when you consider that the average annual income of a person in Nyae Nyae is less than US$100.

In the way Dries and others spoke about them, I gathered that both Kievet and Chief Bobo were highly respected elders. Chief Bobo wasn't an easy man to track down because no one ever really knew where he was and he moved around a lot. He didn't have a mobile phone and there wasn't coverage outside Tsumkwe anyway. There was no email or reliable postal system. If you wanted to find Chief Bobo, you had to put the word out.

'Have you seen Chief Bobo?'

'Yeah, I saw him last week at so and so village, but I heard he was going to so and so.'

'I saw him at so and so. Now he's in Windhoek.'

'Windhoek? I saw him yesterday at so and so village. I heard he was going to Grootfontein.'

And then sometimes you could get lucky. You could be driving along in the middle of nowhere and suddenly see an old man in a cowboy hat riding alone on a donkey, and that would be him. The Honourable Chief Tsamkxao# Oma Bobo.

Dries had put the word out several days before and learned that the chief was due to arrive in Tsumkwe for a meeting with the conservancy board on this day, so we took the chance that we might be able to meet with him. There were no guarantees that he would turn up.

We were in luck. When we arrived at the conservancy office mid-morning, Chief Bobo was already there, talking to some men in the small conservancy meeting room. One of the staff could speak good English, rare in Bushmanland as everyone largely spoke Ju/'hoan, their native tongue. Some people spoke a little Afrikaans, but very few spoke English. He was kind enough to translate for us. We all shook hands and smiled greetings.

For some reason I'd expected Chief Bobo to be bigger than everyone else, equal in size to his status, but, if anything, it was the opposite. This was one of the things I loved about Bushmanland. Here I was not vertically challenged. At a hundred and sixty-five centimetres, I was a *tall* member of society. The chief was even shorter and slighter than I am. He had a calm, humble way about him that reminded me immediately of the Dalai Lama. Sitting on a plastic chair, flanked by several young men who worked for the conservancy, he was like an old elephant bull surrounded by protective *askaris* (younger bulls with better eyesight). He was elderly, slightly stooped and infinitely wrinkly under his trademark navy blue cowboy hat.

I thanked him for letting us have some of his time and said how happy we were to be in Bushmanland. The translator conveyed this and the chief smiled. His eyes crinkled, forming deep smile lines as he spoke with gravitas in his native tongue. His voice was not loud but all in the room were silent. I had no idea what he was saying, but I was entranced.

'He thanks you for coming here and he asks what he can do for you.'

I said that we had spent several days looking around Nyae Nyae with Dries and that the area was very beautiful, and I was interested to know more from him about the problems in the conservancy. I explained that I was a wildlife conservationist and that I was interested in working in the area.

As the translator conveyed this message, the chief nodded and grunted sporadically, thinking deeply about it.

Several of the young men around him burst into opinionated chatter; although they were not speaking over each other, it was clear they all had views on the problems in Nyae Nyae. The chief again nodded and listened attentively as they spoke animatedly but respectfully. It was fascinating to hear the language being spoken quickly, so rhythmic and lyrical, with clicks of five different types interspersed with the words. This went on for some time, and then the chief spoke, looking me straight in the eye. I waited for the translator to explain.

'Elephants. This is the biggest problem here. You can help us with the elephants. It used to be there were not so many elephants. Now there are many! They are breaking things, hurting people, taking our food. This problem, it is very big.' The translator paused, and asked shyly, 'But what can you do to help us?'

'I don't know,' I replied.

I didn't want to make any promises to this old man with his smiling eyes and gentle humility, not if I couldn't keep them. I'd never worked on elephants and knew barely anything about human-elephant conflict. I was just a humble impala researcher, fresh out of a doctorate.

But I knew that I would not see him for a long time, that even if I wanted to contact him again it would nearly be impossible. His wise, kind eyes were compelling me to give him an answer here and now. The chief had highlighted the very same problem that Dries had been telling me about for days.

Answering with my heart, not my head, I heard myself make a promise to him that I would come back. Somehow, I would try to help them do something about those pesky elephants. How hard could it be?

THREE

Nothing ever goes to plan in Africa. That is the only given.

I knew the second I promised to help Chief Bobo that things weren't going to be as easy as the words that spilled from my mouth like happy baby cichlids. But I really wasn't prepared for everything that came next.

Returning with Tristan to our home, a number of things were just not right. Firstly, we were broke. There was nothing new about that. Wildlife conservation is not a lucrative profession. I had never been under any illusions about this. I felt privileged that I got to do my dream job. In the bush where the living was cheap, money had never been an issue and how much I had in my pockets had never mattered. But now, having moved from the bush to the outskirts of Namibia's largest city, we were barely covering the rent.

And then there was the wee small issue of my visa. Naturally no one would give me a full-time job without one. A year ago we'd employed a Namibian visa agent to take care of the process of applying for my visa with the Ministry of Home Affairs and had paid her an appropriate sum to do so on my behalf. We were told by her that even though my previous visa had expired, as long as I had applied for a new one I could stay in the country. After six months with still no sign of a visa, I started to feel less and less comfortable. More months passed and still she told us not to worry, it was in process. Then, after about a year, our agent disappeared into thin air, along with all of my original visa applications and supporting documents. Her office was empty and no one in the building knew where she was. It appeared that she had done a runner, taking my money and papers with her.

With no original papers providing evidence of my application and insufficient photocopies (I'd naively trusted this woman, so hadn't copied everything), the Ministry of Home Affairs was quite at liberty to throw me out of the country or, worse, into jail. I could only hope that the notoriously inefficient ministry had a record of my numerous applications on file.

Through a friend I obtained the contact number of a man quite high up in home affairs who I hoped would understand my predicament. I spoke to him on the phone and he agreed to meet me. I was desperate and sounded it. I knew he was making an exception for me. If I went through the standard route it could take me weeks to get a meeting.

I marched up to the gates of the Ministry of Home Affairs literally shaking in my boots, clutching a flimsy folder of all the documentation I had to offer, along with a passport with a long expired visa in it. Two surly security guards with automatic rifles let me past to talk to an official behind bars. He grumpily buzzed me in.

'Good morning,' a burly man greeted me, his large stomach

pouring over his belt as he let me into his office. He wore a suit and several flashy gold rings. I noticed a thick gold chain around a neck that folded neatly into several walrus rolls of blubber.

I tried to smile, but I think I looked like a sheep smiling into the face of a hungry wolf. Lips splayed back with a little too much gum.

He came around behind me and shut the door. Odd, I thought, given that everyone else seemed to have their doors wide open. I really hoped he wasn't going to hit me up for cash. Bribery is illegal in Namibia and they take it pretty seriously, unlike other places I've worked in Africa where it is more natural than breathing. I sure didn't want to go to jail for an expired visa *and* bribery.

'Ah, beautiful lady,' he purred immediately, 'are you married?'

Oh geez. Letting the comment slide, I said, 'Thank you, but I am here to talk to you about my visa.'

I explained my predicament, how I'd been waiting for my visa to come through for a year and now my agent had disappeared, so could he please tell me what had happened to my file and if it was still in process? It was a weak case and I knew it. I wasn't sure that he was even listening to me. He was staring at my chest like it was a large, juicy lamb chop. I lifted my folder of documents up to cover it.

'So you see, if you can just tell me what's happening with my visa I would be so grateful.'

He sidled outside and left me alone and sweating for about ten minutes. When he returned, he was carrying a thick manila folder. The Tammie File.

'Ahhhh . . . yes. I can see your visa is in the system. You have nothing to worry about. It is . . . how shall we say . . . *in process*.' He said the words slowly, lingering over them, letting the vowels drip off his tongue in a way that I think he thought was sexy.

I tried unsuccessfully to suppress the anger surging in my chest. Of course it was *in process*. It had been *in process* for a bloody year! The question was whether it was ever going to come out of the black hole of home affairs so that I could stay in Namibia legally. I took a deep breath.

'Can you tell me how long it will take, sir?'

'Ah . . . it must go to the minister. I cannot rush the minister, you understand. You must wait. Do not worry.'

He stood and came around to my side of the desk. I quickly rose to my feet, sensing danger. Sweat had left dark patches under the arms of his white shirt. Baubles of it shined on his neck.

'So beautiful . . . Tell me, do you have a husband?' He reached over and touched my arm with a clammy paw, then tried to slide it over towards my chest.

'Thank you for your time!' I exclaimed, then flung open the door and made a dash for the exit faster than a gazelle scenting lion.

If this was what it took to get a visa, it wasn't worth it.

I had to get out of the country fast or risk getting a lethal 'red stamp' in my passport. And I didn't need that, as not only would it ban me from Namibia, it would probably influence my chances of getting in to work in other African countries too. I hadn't intentionally done anything illegal, but it was unlikely that any government official would look at it that way.

I put both Tristan's and my return flights to Australia on my credit card. I had no idea how I was going to pay it off, but there was no alternative. What's was little more debt on top of a mountain of it?

Besides, that was the least of my worries. It was becoming increasingly apparent that not only were there cracks in my relationship with the Namibian immigration authorities, there were also cracks in my relationship with Tristan. Back home in safe, familiar surroundings, amongst family and friends who knew me perhaps even better than I knew myself, some of the things that had been wrong in our relationship were suddenly thrown into stark relief.

I remember sitting on the green grass of my parents' front lawn on their Darling Downs farm realising without a shred of doubt that it was over. It sounds sudden, and I suppose in a sense it was. But in another way, this had been coming for a while. In Africa I had chosen to ignore the things that had been wrong in the relationship because I couldn't cope with yet another problem on top of the pile of financial and visa worries I already had. Sal and Jeremy had voiced their concerns to me while we were in Bushmanland together, but I couldn't deal with it then. It was only now, removed from all of the other anxieties, that I could see just how much the relationship had been wearing me down. Finally, one night on my parents' farm, with Tristan asleep beside me, I made the decision. And then, for the first time in a long time, I cried myself to sleep.

I was angry about what felt like wasted years of my life and annoyed with myself for not seeing it sooner. In the end, some of the things that had drawn me to Tristan in the first place – the introspection, broodiness and intensity – had been the things that had driven us apart. Sometimes the things that you think are good for you in the beginning of a relationship – the very things that attract you – aren't what you need at all.

It was already over before the words were said, but it would still take all the strength I had to walk away. The love that we shared still burned, but I had disappeared into the fire and become a part of him, indistinguishable from the relationship, slowly becoming less and less myself, until after three years, I was almost completely gone. No longer strong and independent, I felt like a shadow of the girl who had first launched herself into

Africa as a teenager. It wasn't Tristan's fault; I had let this happen to myself. But in the haze of the sad goodbyes it didn't stop me feeling angry with him.

After Tristan flew back to Namibia without me, my younger brother, Davo, slept on a mattress on the floor of my bedroom for a week or so. He didn't say anything about me being a big sook or a crybaby while I was getting used to sleeping alone again. He even pretended that he preferred to sleep in that room anyway because it was airconditioned and a respite from the hot Queensland summer nights. I knew he was lying and I loved him for it. I was in debt, without a Namibian visa, a job or a home to call my own, and now I was alone. I knew I'd made the right decision to end the relationship, because I felt as though a weight had been lifted off my shoulders, but it didn't make the reality of the lonely nights any easier to deal with.

Mum cooked pea and ham soup, Droughtmaster beef roasts and caramel tarts imbued with all sorts of magical motherly healing ingredients. I put on the kilos, but I was putting on more than that. I was finding myself again. The old me was growing back at an astounding rate (unfortunately, most of it seemed to be on my thighs). I swore I would never again allow myself to be swallowed whole by a relationship. Next time, my independence and self-respect would not be left to walk the plank when the love boat sailed into harbour.

It's funny how often, when a whole lot of doors are closing, the sound of them slamming in your face awakens you to new doors you didn't see before. Just when my financial and emotional situation had hit rock bottom, something amazing happened. After the seven hundred and seventy-second rejection, a publisher took me on. The novel I'd been writing for the last year had got her interested in my writing style, but it was my own story she was interested in. I jumped at the opportunity to get published, not really believing my own luck, and I launched into writing as though I'd been doing it all my life.

Let me tell you that poring over many years' worth of diaries is one of the best and worst ways to get over a break-up. I retraced my life, my thoughts and feelings from the ages of fifteen to twenty-six. The good, the bad and the ugly of the last three years were in there. The reasons I'd fallen in love with Tristan, the things he'd done to piss me off, the times I had done the wrong thing, the gradual erosion of our dreams together. There's no escaping the truth when it's staring you right in the face in your own handwriting.

For someone who communicates well on paper, I realised I was a terrible communicator in relationships. I harboured the awful tendency, like many people raised Catholic, to be a martyr when it came to my own feelings, letting them build up until they exploded at an inappropriate moment. Most of the time, though, I didn't explode at all. I was an expert at control. I let things gnaw at my insides for a long time, fermenting into an evil stew of negative feelings. They'd find a way to pour out one way or another, usually translating into illness, often tonsillitis in my case (throat = communication – it kind of makes sense when you think about it).

Reading back through the pages of my life, the paper now smudged with tears, chocolate and yesterday's Vegemite cream crackers, all my own faults, failings and foibles were plain to see. *Now you're going to face every last shred of your past, Matson*, my diaries ensured, *and don't think you can ignore any of it*.

By the time I returned to Namibia four months and fourteen barrels of pea and ham soup later, I was nearly a new woman. I was three kilograms heavier and a soul-load lighter.

Did I say that I had my dream job when I was working as a wildlife researcher in Etosha? Let me take that back. That was before I started getting *paid* to do conservation work. Paid conservation work is definitely better than the unpaid kind.

My old friend Dave van Smeerdijk, the Aussie managing director of Wilderness Safaris Namibia, had secured me a work visa to help run the company's environmental program. He and his wife, Jen Lalley, an American geographer who had studied the lichens of the Skeleton Coast for her doctorate, set me up in the flat beside their house in Ludwigsdorf, a mountainous, trendy suburb in the flash part of Windhoek. I shared my flat most of the time with their two dalmations, two gigantic African cats and the very large personality of Zepa, who was a very small pug. Troops of baboons frequented the barren mountains around the house, occasionally coming down to drink from people's swimming pools and bare their teeth at local poodles.

My main job at Wilderness Safaris was to work with a Namibian woman, Basilia Shivute, to help run the environmental program, but I was also there to write proposals to the government to help Wilderness Safaris secure some of the best tourist concessions in Namibia, like the Skeleton Coast, for example, for which Wilderness Safaris had exclusive tourism rights.

It was awful. I had to drive a Land Rover all over Namibia to some of the most remote and extraordinary wilderness areas in the country, staying in luxury camps while advising on their environmental management, and forcing myself to suffer through crisp white wines on the savannah at the end of long hot days in the desert. I really can't fathom now how I managed it. I can only say that I tolerated with grim forbearance the royal red sunsets over the desert, the thousand-thread sheets inside canvas safari tents the size of houses, and the restaurant-quality meals in the camps. I mean, give me a break! I couldn't believe Dave was paying me to do this.

On the whole, life was good. This felt very different from the Windhoek I'd left behind the year before. There were pros and cons in that. After three years in a relationship, it was at first hard to disassociate the man from the country. I'd been with Tristan for more than half my time in Namibia. My journey in this desert land had largely been intertwined with his. I threw myself into my work in order to try not to think about it. But it was weird to be there alone and made worse by the fact that Namibia is a small place where everyone knows what colour underwear you wear.

One of my ex's mates at Wilderness Safaris literally ignored me now, making quite a large effort to give me a foul look whenever I said hello to him. Another, someone I thought had been a mutual friend, no longer returned my emails and phone calls.

'Is he in the bush?' I asked a male friend. 'It seems weird he's not answering my calls.'

'Don't ever tell anyone I told you this, Tammie,' my friend said, 'but Tristan's working for him now. You don't mess with the boys' club. As far as he's concerned now, you're a bitch.'

'But I introduced them! And he never even heard my side of the story!'

After the exorcism of a break-up, no one mentions that you still have to deal with the bloody aftermath. With genuine sadness I left some friends behind, but in the space that opened up, new ones flew in. Literally. Most of them were pilots. A bunch of them adopted me into their fray during evenings of zebra steaks and Windhoek lagers at Joe's Beerhouse.

'Never trust a pilot,' my new friend Ingrid warned me one night, during a typical evening of shameless flirtation at Joe's. She should know. She was one.

Most of the pilots at Sefofane were charming and notoriously shagaholic (there's a reason they call it the cockpit). They were great fun to hang out with, but definitely not the kind of guys you married. Perfect.

Despite the fun, though, Sundays in Windhoek were pretty depressing because everything was closed and most people stayed home with their families. I coped by working most weekends, which I didn't mind too much because it was a pretty cool job and it kept my mind off feeling lonely. I had more than enough work to do. When I wasn't working for Wilderness, I was writing the national management plan for black-faced impala and co-writing the Palmwag black rhino management plan with Jen for Save the Rhino Trust.

A month or so after I'd got back I received an official letter from the Ministry of Environment and Tourism. It was my research permit to study human-elephant conflict in Bushmanland. I was shocked. This was the last thing I had expected. It had been about six months since I had applied for it and so much had happened since then. I had been back to Australia, broken up with my boyfriend, written a book and started travelling all over Namibia with Wilderness Safaris. I'd all but forgotten my promise to Chief Bobo. In truth, I had only just got my life back on track and I wasn't sure I wanted to change it. I blushed as I recalled a conversation I had been having with one of the bush pilots at Joe's a few nights earlier. He had certainly captured my interest. With his French accent, aquamarine eyes and wavy dark hair, he looked like a pirate of the high seas. He had a way of looking at you that made you feel like you were the centre of his universe.

The first time he flew me to a camp for work I was in the front seat and he kept finding reasons to reach between my legs for some toggle or other, brushing my inner thigh quite purposefully. These were the oldest tricks in the book, but it had been so long since I'd flirted with anyone properly that I found myself enjoying the game.

Ignoring the din of locals, tourists and safari operators, he leaned in close to me and said, 'Tammie, I have been wondering . . . what is a person like you doing here? You should be in India or Nepal.'

'You can find like-minded people anywhere,' I said, trying not to be captured by those eyes. 'It's sometimes a bit harder in Namibia, but they're here.'

'This is true . . . I have been wondering why we met. I think you are very . . . fascinating.'

My heart skipped a beat. We stared into each other's eyes for a moment, before I pulled mine away. This was *fun*.

'Let me just say this,' he went on, 'I cannot say more. I am glad to know you.'

He picked up his *jagermeister* (German shots that are much like drinking straight petrol) and, against my better judgement, I found myself picking up mine too.

He paused, gazed deeply into my eyes and announced, 'To love and freedom!'

The following night, he phoned to ask me to come and pick up something for work from his apartment. We drank a beer and he played gentle music on his guitar while a couple of the pilots served up takeaway pizza. I watched his fingers as they plucked at the strings of the acoustic guitar. He had the hands of an artist, graceful in every movement.

'Tammie, come with me. I want to show you something.'

He led me upstairs to his bedroom and indicated I should sit on his bed. I scanned his bedroom. White curtains framed a large open window. It was spartan but romantic. Then he turned off the lights.

Don't worry, I'm not stupid. The direction this was heading was quite evident to me. But I had it all under control. At least, outwardly I did. Truthfully, I just wanted him to kiss me.

He knelt in front of me and leaned in close, then reached in next to my leg, his arm brushing my thigh as he felt around behind the bedside table. A switch flicked on. Suddenly the room filled with rays of light. He'd created a lampshade from a cardboard square with the symbol Om cut out of it. The square was covered with mosquito netting and now the Om glowed as light poured out of it.

'Do you like it?'

'It's beautiful,' I said, feeling breathless. *Are you going to kiss me or aren't you?*

Every so often in life you feel an incredible energy with someone, the kind of attraction that is basic, primitive and needy, like it came right out of the jungle. I think it's also known as two people being celibate for too long. Nonetheless, whenever I sat beside this pilot I felt an amazing heat emanating from him. I could *feel* it pulling him towards me like a magnetic force. The attraction was mutual, as the late-night text messages on my cell phone testified, but there was a problem. A big one. He was in a long-distance relationship.

Sitting on his bed, close enough to smell his subtle aftershave, it was taking everything I had not to jump him right then and there – and that tells you something about how strong the attraction was because I am really not that kind of girl. At least, I didn't think I was. Yet, at that moment, I could feel my lips tingling with the desire to be kissed. I might have made the first move if – thank God, I think – his phone hadn't rung then. It had to be a sign. Acting against every physical desire in my body, I went downstairs and rejoined the others.

God damn his dark locks and reef-blue eyes. Curse his deep gazes and purposeful caresses. This was one of life's little lessons in control. The thing was, though, even if we would only ever be ships passing in the night, I was enjoying being able to flirt myself silly, and disappearing into the bush to study elephants didn't seem very sensible from a social point of view.

From a purely practical perspective, I had no idea how I was going to fit a research project in with the work I was doing for Wilderness Safaris, and I wasn't sure I wanted to do this project solo. Bushmanland was a large step up from Etosha in terms of the levels of remoteness and ruggedness. I felt a barrage of self-doubts charge in. How was I going to do this on my own?

'Just put the funding applications in, Tam,' Jen said. 'If it's meant to happen, it will. If you get the money, you'll make a plan to get it done.'

I knew that Jen, always the voice of reason, was right. Anyway, I didn't fancy my chances of scoring much funding for the project with my nonexistent track record of working on elephants.

But I was wrong. The money for the elephant project came pouring in from the Namibia Nature Foundation, the Wilderness Trust in South Africa and the Rufford Maurice Laing Foundation in England, more than I needed to do the job. It seemed written in the stars that I would be able to keep my promise to the old chief. The wheels of fate had been set in motion the day I'd set foot in the land of the little people. There was no going back now.

FOUR

Jen, in all her wisdom, couldn't have imagined on that day she encouraged me to apply for the funds that she'd be the first to be roped in to join me on my initial field trip to Bushmanland that very August.

At six in the morning we packed the double-cab Hilux with two large safari tents, two swags and two boxes of bedding, camping gear and groceries. The Hilux groaned under the weight of it all on the eight-hour drive to Nyae Nyae. The CD player in the car didn't work so Jen brought along tiny speakers and her battery-run portable CD player.

'Turn up the tunes, baby!' I cried.

'I can't. They're on full blast!' Jen burst out laughing.

We could barely hear the music over the roar of the engine, but we bopped along to an imagined beat anyway.

When Jen was doing her fieldwork at the Skeleton Coast I'd spent a week with her driving across the desert counting lichens. I had never seen someone so excited about little chunks of pseudo-plant matter.

'They're not actually plants, Tam. It's fascinating, really. They're symbioses of algae and fungi living together. One can't live without the other.'

'Sounds romantic.'

Now, just a week after finishing her thesis and flying back to Namibia from Oxford, my favourite lichenologist had found the time to keep me company on my first reconnaissance mission to Bushmanland. It was a scoping trip to touch base with Dries and the conservancy, to get a feel for the area and see some of the human-elephant conflict sites. Until I had a sense of the logistics of getting around Bushmanland, the time it took to find conflict sites and record the relevant information, I couldn't really process whether the rough methodology in my head would actually work to assess human-elephant conflict on the ground.

My plan between now and the end of the year was to spend the two weeks of each month that I wasn't working for Wilderness Safaris up in Bushmanland collecting data. It was going to be a tight schedule, with very little time off at weekends or for socialising. I would need to visit all of the sites where human-elephant conflict had occurred and been recorded by the government over the last five years, and survey as many community members as possible, village by village, seeking their views on the problem.

Dries recommended I camp at Klein Dobe, where Half Ear's family lived. With the ample funding that had flowed in, I bought all the necessary camping gear and two big canvas tents at a discount from CYMOT. Satcom Namibia learned me a satellite phone in case of emergencies. Stacey recommended a good local translator called Leon, who also just happened to be the son of Chief Bobo.

If I managed to get enough data from the field in the next

five months, my plan was to analyse and write it up the following year for publication in a scientific journal, while providing regular reports to the conservancy and project sponsors. I planned to come back to Bushmanland and deliver the results personally to Chief Bobo, Kievet and the conservancy board. After all, they were the ones who would make the most use of the results. It looked like even with all that expenditure I would have money left over, so I decided that I would find some way to put that towards education among the village schools.

I couldn't have had anyone better with me to share ideas on my initial scoping expedition. Jen was an excellent scientist, but she was also bushwise after working for many years as an overland safari guide for Wilderness Safaris in Botswana.

It was almost dark by the time we arrived in Bushmanland and we headed straight out to Klein Dobe. The small community of Bushmen who lived there came out to greet us as we arrived. They lived in a small hut just a few hundred metres from the camp and they were responsible for its upkeep. I recognised Half Ear in the group and some of the women who'd sung and clapped on that magical night the year before. Half Ear stepped forward first to shake our hands, followed by all the others, including several small children, about twelve people in all. There was a lot of smiling and some tentative Afrikaans spoken on both sides. Even with very little common language between us, the warmth of this small family of Bushmen made us feel very welcome.

Klein Dobe was an environmental education centre that the conservancy used for meetings and gatherings. It was owned by the Ministry of Environment and Tourism and used when their staff were working in Nyae Nyae. Four small huts with roofs of corrugated iron and walls of thick wooden poles that smelled of creosote flanked the small education centre in the middle. To one side was a long ablutions block, also made of logs, with four separate cubicles, each with a shower on a cement floor. Two stand-alone flush toilets stood on either side beside it. Their wooden doors were held shut precariously with small loops of string slung around a rusty nail. There was no toilet paper and no water in them. It didn't look like they'd been used in a while. A green water tank perched on a high platform sat behind the showers, and beneath it a rusty donkey boiler for heating the water. The whole camp was sheltered by tall purple pod terminalia trees, characterised by their false thorns and bright maroon pods, now leafless and naked during the winter.

A roof over our heads, hot water, a comfy swag – what more did we need? Well, there was one more thing. The year before when we'd camped here in the dead of winter we'd almost frozen to death in our rooftop tent. This time, I'd come prepared. When Jen saw what I had for us both, she did a small jig of joy.

'Hot-water bottles! Tam, you are the best!'

When it comes down to it, it's the little things that matter.

I felt excited to be back. The camp had a nice feel about it. The only other person there, on and off, was African wild-dog researcher Robin Lyons. His tent was set up at one end of the camp, at the opposite end to the village, but he wasn't there now. It felt almost like we had the place to ourselves.

As the red orb of the sun sunk through a smoky sky, Jen and I threw our swags inside one of the rooms. We would put the tents up in the morning. It would be a big job and there wasn't enough light to do it now. They were large tents, easily fitting two single beds inside, and one had a veranda the size of another tent to keep the sun out when suicide season arrived. It was hard to imagine that this place would ever get hot as we barbecued chicken kebabs and toasted our freezing hands over the campfire, sipping on chilled bottles of piña colada from the car fridge.

My camping style had definitely improved over the years. No

more roughing it in a swag on the back of the ute and running barefoot to find a protective tarp to throw over me in the middle of the night when it started to rain. No more living on tinned beans and three-day-old bread in the bush for me. One thing I had learned is that if you're going to camp for a long period of time, you'll enjoy it a lot more if you're comfortable. These days, with camping fridges, comfortable tents and swags, and better quality long-life products, there's just no need to be a martyr.

A little later we heard the family singing and clapping by their campfire, that incredible sound of traditional Bushmen music. My heart felt happy to hear it again. I remembered that night, over a year ago now, when I had felt the singing and clapping of Bushmen lift me up to the edge of another kind of consciousness. With the recollection, a sense of warmth flooded through my chest. It was hard to pinpoint exactly what it was about Bushmanland that was so magical. I wondered if it was the friendliness and gentle humility of the Bushmen that made me feel so at home here. Perhaps it was related to being in a place of big trees, water and elephants that gave me a heightened energy. The Bushmen themselves were certainly connected to nature in a way that my own tribe has long ago forgotten and it seemed to give them a kind of wisdom. Whatever that source of magic was, there was no questioning its existence. I fell asleep to the rhythm of Bushmen music, filled with joy and gratitude to be back.

We both slept like logs that night. I woke at dawn to the sound of someone chopping wood. Wood doves and guinea fowls filled the sunrise with their calls, sounds so familiar to me that whenever I heard them I immediately felt that I was home. I lit the gas cooker to boil the kettle and make us a cup of tea to have with some *Ouma* rusks.

Before it was boiled, the Bushmen arrived.

'*Moro*,' I greeted them, smiling. '*Hoe gaan dit*? How are you?'

My Afrikaans was appalling, but I'd been in Namibia long enough to get a basic message across.

I showed Half Ear and some of the young men the two large tents in the back of the Hilux and, not knowing how to say 'tent' in Ju/'hoan, I said, '*My huis*.' My house.

They nodded enthusiastically. One of the men immediately started pulling the tents out of the car and pointed to a patch of sand close by.

Without any of us saying more than a couple of words we all understood, the four men set to work putting up the tents. They hoisted the thirty-kilogram bags out of the car and laid the tents out on the sand. A few of the women brought over handfuls of long dried grass, which they used to sweep the area of pods and thorny twigs. I made sure the tents were facing out towards the bush and under just the right amount of tree cover to ensure they'd get shade in the afternoon heat. There was no instruction manual with the tents, so we just had to take a guess at which pole went where and how. Everyone – and I do mean the entire resident community – launched into the tent mission as though it were an Olympic event.

The children were unbelievably cute, small nymphs with big brown eyes. The small ones' bellies bulged with what I could only guess was malnutrition. A little boy sat in a wheelbarrow watching Jen as though she were the most interesting creature he'd ever seen. Jen smiled and gave him a tent pole. He immediately leapt out of the wheelbarrow, holding onto the pole with his chest puffed out as if he had the most important task in the world.

'We did it!' Jen announced when the two tents were up.

'Almost . . . I've just got to work out how this bloody veranda goes up,' I cursed. 'I'm hopeless at things like this.'

All of us stood around for at least an hour trying to work out how the veranda came together over the top of the tent. I grew more and more frustrated, but the Bushmen simply looked amused by the whole experience. An old man called Petrus squatted to one side under a tree, a peaceful smile never leaving his face as he puffed on a cigarette made from strong local tobacco rolled up in a shred of old newspaper. Finally, my small research camp all came together, if a little more crooked than in the picture. Jen and I would never have managed without everyone's help. It had been a gigantic team effort.

I gave the men some money to thank them and their families for the help, not knowing exactly how much to give. They seemed very happy with the gift, so I guessed I'd been generous.

Petrus showed us a bow and arrow he had made from light commiphora wood and animal hide, then held it out towards us. Inside the wooden case were half a dozen handmade metal arrows, each with sharp triangular heads. Now if I got mugged in my flat in Windhoek, I would have a pernicious pug *and* a traditional bow and arrow for self-defence. No self-respecting burglar would dare mess with me.

For the next few days, Jen and I used a very basic map to find our way around the conservancy, discovering villages with great names like Xamsa and !Auru (both said with clicks at the start but, just to confuse you, different sounding clicks) and talking to people in the villages in haphazard Afrikaans and sign language. Most of our time was spent looking at some of the sites that Dries's official records said had experienced human-elephant conflict. We'd drive for a half-hour or so, sometimes passing barefoot people on the road walking to Tsumkwe, and then a clearing would appear with a gathering of grass-roofed huts. Children would often run out to greet us, shouting 'Sweetie! Sweetie!' in high-pitched voices. There were very few signs in the conservancy and the map we had was hopeless, so we spent quite a lot of time completely lost.

A typical conversation went something like this.

'Do you think we should go left here?'

'Well, if we are where I thought we were, there's no fork in the road on this map. So I guess left is as good as right.'

'Okay, I'll go left.'

'That last village we passed, was it called Xamsa or !Auru?'

'I have no idea. I thought it was Tjokwe.'

'Where the *hell* are we?'

'Somewhere in Bushmanland, mate, somewhere in Bushmanland!'

We saw recently erected circular enclosures made of cement and rocks protecting water pumps and solar panels at a couple of the villages. Dries described them as 'bomb proof'. At least twenty metres across and three metres high, no elephant could get past them. They were expensive, but Dries was confident they would work. We saw a circular enclosure that was only a metre or so high and made of large, loosely arranged sharp rocks. Inside was a well and a generator to pump water. I imagined a bull elephant easily shoving rocks away from the walls as though the rocks were soft marshmallows, but the people at that village assured us that elephants didn't like stepping on the sharp stones. We saw water tanks on high platforms surrounded by deep trenches and wondered if that would be sufficient to stop an elephant pushing over the tank to get water. We saw dried-up waterholes with elephant footprints indented solid into the dried mud.

We smelled elephants, saw fresh dung, trees recently debarked by elephants and, late one night, Jen swore she heard one near the camp, but there was not a real life proboscidean to be seen. Where were these great grey ghosts of Bushmanland? How on earth did a four-tonne animal manage to disappear like a silent wraith in the bush? How could an animal that big evade us so effectively? It was a complete mystery to me.

'Patience, Tammie,' Dries said, rolling the nonexistent 'r' in my name again. 'They will come. Soon you'll see more elephants than you want to.'

A few days into the field trip, we were driving through Tsumkwe when we spotted Half Ear's family loitering near the shop. One of the men, Xao (pronounced 'cow' but with a click at the start), flagged us down for a lift. The whole family piled in, all of the men taking prime position in the back seat, relegating the women and babies to the tray. Jen and I saw what was happening, took one look at each other and said, 'Nup.'

In my terrible Afrikaans I tried to explain that the men needed to go in the back of the Hilux and the women with babies and children in the back seat. They looked a little perplexed at my suggestion, but they seemed to understand what I was indicating and so willingly swapped places. The women looked like all their Christmases had come at once as they squished into the back seat. There were about four women, two kids and a tiny baby.

'*Meweeha*,' they said, clapping their hands together in appreciation. 'Thank you.'

As we drove out to camp on the sandy track, with lights on full beam to ensure we didn't run into an elephant, the women chattered to each other in the back seat. The conversation was loud and I could smell something weird in the car. It was pungent and sour. Looking in the rear-view mirror, I noticed that one of the women had a swollen black eye.

'I think they've paid a visit to the local pub,' Jen said.

We'd passed quite a few local shebeens selling cheap liquor in Tsumkwe. I had little doubt that they made a killing out of people like Half Ear's family, who I'd just paid for putting up the tents. Tragically, I realised, most of that money, if not all of it, had probably gone on booze. I immediately felt responsible.

But what could I have done? *Not* paid them? I couldn't control what they did with the money, but that didn't make it any easier to reconcile.

When we got back to camp, everyone was talking over the top of each other, some of them yelling to be heard. The woman with the small baby held it out to Jen and I heard her say in Afrikaans, '*Jy betaal*?' You buy?

The baby began to scream blue murder.

The men were laughing, but she was insistent. '*Jy betaal*? *Systag*?'

'She's asking you to buy her baby,' I said to Jen.

'Oh my God,' Jen exclaimed. 'You're kidding, right?'

'Nope. Sixty dollars. Going cheap.'

Jen paused, shocked. 'That's a little too much reality, man,' she said, shaking her head.

I pointed to the woman with the black eye and tried to ask her what had happened. She replied by hitting her fist into her other palm. Someone had thumped her.

Sitting by our campfire a little later, Jen and I remained a little shaken by the whole baby-selling escapade. Had they been kidding? It was possible. Even so, it wasn't funny. Booze made people do crazy things in any culture. With the Bushmen, they were so peaceful and gentle normally, the contrast when they were drunk was disturbing.

'You can't help feeling sorry for them,' I said. 'I read that the Bushmen in Namibia are now living in just fifteen percent of the area they used to roam over.'

'It was even more than that. They were the first ones in Africa. They used to roam over the whole of southern Africa until Bantu-speaking tribes arrived with their domestic stock.'

'And look at them now. I mean, these people have always been nomadic hunter-gatherers. Living in permanent villages like this has only happened in the last few decades . . . Their culture is steadily being destroyed. How do you stop it, though? It's inevitable that influences from outside are going to intrude.'

'It's heart-breaking. You know, they're kind of like elephants, the Bushmen. Both used to cover large tracts of Africa. Both are now being forced into smaller and smaller areas, having to change ancient patterns of behaviour in order to survive.'

Jen was right. The Bushmen, just like elephants, were becoming an endangered species.

FIVE

On my next field trip to Bushmanland a few weeks later I met a killer. Her eyes were filled with such raw, cold malice they made me shiver. She would have disembowelled me if she could.

'Kssssshhhhh!'

Behind the metal bars of the small cage, covered by a green tarp to keep her calm, the leopard slunk into the far corner away from our prying eyes, cussing and spitting ferociously.

She'd been living the good life for the last few nights, preying on the reverend's goats. I guess even leopards have those days when they can't be arsed putting any effort into dinner. She'd taken the fast food option – one McGoat burger and fries, upsized, if you please – and it had backfired. The reverend wasn't happy about losing his goats and had called on Dries to remove the culprit. Dries set a cage trap and baited it with a live bleating lamb, leaving it there overnight. It can't have been very nice for the poor little lamb, but it did the job. In the morning, he found the irreverent cat in the cage, wild with rage.

'It happens fairly often,' Dries said. 'Young leopards that aren't so good at hunting yet . . . she sees some easy prey . . . of course she's going to go for it.'

In Namibia, human-wildlife conflict isn't restricted to elephants. People living in rural areas have to deal with threats to their livelihoods from many other species too. Concomitant with the growing populations of wildlife – something the conservation community is celebrating – are increasing incidents of human-wildlife conflict. In 2005 over 3000 problem animal incidents were reported in Namibia. Almost a quarter of the conflicts involved elephants, but a good half were caused by predators (hyaenas, jackals, leopards, cheetahs and lions).

Namibian legislation provides for communities to apply to the government to have a problem animal identified and destroyed. But this isn't as easy as it sounds. Poor people living in the middle of nowhere with no communication often have to walk a very long way to get this message to the local warden, then it can take up to six weeks for the order to be signed off, by which time the community has lost the best part of its livelihood and is a lot less likely to want to conserve the local wildlife.

You can't blame these folks. When it's the lives of you and your family on the line, it's hard to have much sympathy for the animals that are the threat. Rural people in Africa are no different from farmers in America who shoot at wolves and coyotes, or Australians who wiped out Tasmanian devils and decimated dingos to protect their stock. In Europe, it was wolves, bears and big cats like the Iberian lynx. In India it was tigers, now perhaps the most endangered big cat in the world. All around the world, top-order predators are under serious threat, often because they threaten human livelihoods.

In Bushmanland, this made Dries's job as the protector of the game a challenge. He knew that if the people weren't happy with the wildlife, it would be the animals that came off second best. Keeping people content paid off. Sometimes it was easier and smarter to bypass the bureaucracy, take an African approach and 'make a plan' to fix a problem yourself. In the case of the leopard, Dries side-stepped the official route and took the initiative of catching and relocating the leopard himself. This was a far better option for the leopard than being declared a problem animal and shot, even if its chances of survival were only about fifty-fifty in its new terrain.

My friend and a former sponsor of my research on black-faced impala, Warren Tapp, had flown across from Australia to help me on my second field trip to Bushmanland. A successful businessman with a kind heart, Warren had seen the pleas for financial support for my work in Brisbane's *Courier Mail* newspaper back in 2001 and got in touch to help. Successful businessmen with kind hearts are not all that hard to find, but ones that put their money where their mouth is are. This was my chance to repay Warren for his support and it was also great having his company.

It was springtime in Bushmanland and a cornucopia of acacias blossomed with all sorts of flowers, resplendent in garbs of bright yellow pompoms or fluffy white baubles. The air hummed with engorged insects sick on the sweetness of copious pollen. Rust-coloured pods rattled like Christmas tree decorations upon a leafless limb as a lilac breasted roller launched itself off. It swept through the air onto another branch to pierce the heart of an unsuspecting basking lizard with its spear-like beak. The bush was beginning to come to life again, literally buzzing in anticipation of the wet season a few months away.

Warren's visit coincided with the arrival of a BBC film crew who were to join us and Dries and Stacey on a trip into Khaudum National Park to investigate the human-elephant conflict situation there. Khaudum is so remote and inhospitable that you can't go in there on your own. It is a rule of park entry that there must be two vehicles travelling together at all times, so that if one breaks down, the other can go and get help. The reasoning behind this is quite clear. Khaudum has a booming population of elephants and considerable numbers of large predators, and if you break down there, it could be days before you are found. By that time it may only be your bones that are left as a miserable testament to your stupidity at being there on your own.

Fortunately for me, I was going to Namibia's wildest park with not just any other vehicle and its driver, but the warden himself and his well-equipped Landcruiser, as well as a third vehicle belonging to the BBC crew. But first, before entering the park, we had an important job to do. We had a leopard to release.

Warren and I followed Dries and Stacey to a waterhole in the far northern part of the conservancy, quite close to the border of the park. I parked our Hilux about thirty metres away from where Dries had parked his Cruiser beside a medium-sized tree. The leopard inside its cage on the back of the cruiser continued to lash out and hiss as Dries set up a rope to hoist the cage door. He needed to be able to do it from inside his vehicle.

'Whatever you do, don't get out of the car,' Dries ordered. 'If you do, this cat will kill you.'

As if in support for the warden, the leopard hissed menacingly.

Warren looked over at me, his eyes smiling, and said, 'Doesn't mince his words, does he?'

We had no objections to staying right where we were.

It took about half an hour to prepare the device for the release. Dries slung a rope from a tight knot at the top of the cage door over a strong tree limb so that he could lever up the door through a narrow opening in his car window. It was quite an operation just setting this all up and by the time he was done we were all sweating. It was the kind of thing you could imagine going horrendously wrong in the blink of an eye if you didn't get it absolutely right. The leopard's favourite food is baboons, so they know exactly how to kill a human quickly through disembowelment.

'Okay!' Dries called out, signifying that he was going to lift the door.

I gave Dries a thumbs-up through the windscreen.

The metal door of the cage must have been quite heavy, as Dries's face contorted with the effort of pulling it up. It wasn't lifting. Dries swore in Afrikaans, almost as tense as the leopard by now. He got out and walked around the back of the car to rearrange the rope a little. The leopard launched itself at him as he passed her, then recoiled to the back of the cage. *Remind me never to corner a leopard*, I thought. At that moment in time there was no one that cat wouldn't strike the entrails from if given half a chance. Dries had barely flinched.

Back inside his car, he pulled on the rope again. It tightened and the heavy door began to lift up. With a screech of metal on metal the cage was open. A millisecond passed. During that fraction of a second the leopard leapt out of the cage, off the back of the Cruiser and vanished like a flash of lightning into the long grass.

She had moved too fast for my camera to capture her moment of freedom.

'Shees! That was fast! Did you get a shot?' I asked Warren.

He grinned and showed me his picture. It was a magnificent shot – of my leg.

The small BBC crew joined us at Sigaretti Camp at the entrance to Khaudum. The rundown office with its bedraggled thatched roof clearly didn't see too many tourists. A man in a tattered uniform appeared, looking surprised to see us. Dries told us he hadn't been able to get a message through to let them know we were coming; the phone and radio were dead.

'Sigaretti . . . That's an interesting name,' I said, thinking it must have some deep significance. 'What does it mean?'

'Cigarette,' Dries replied, stubbing his out.

Will West, a tattooed, tall Englishman, was the all-in-one director, interviewer, cameraman and sound expert from the BBC, and I immediately felt completely comfortable with him. That was important because for the next three days Will would film pretty much everything I did in a day's work. I had to try to forget that he was wielding a camera and pretend I was just having a chat with him, which was easier because he was such a genuinely nice guy.

As our convoy of three vehicles catapulted into Khaudum, I wasted no time putting the Hilux into low ratio to plow through the thick sand. The car would stay in four-by-four for most of the next few days. The same tall, broad-leafed trees that typified the habitat in Nyae Nyae were in Khaudum too, but the bush was more open, a sign that there were more elephants here.

Elephants *owned* this place. The sandy vehicle tracks were covered in endless trails of dinner-plate-sized elephant footprints, large piles of elephant dung and tree branches that they had pulled across the road. Driving over these roads was like going for a spin in a cocktail shaker. Trees some twenty metres high had been completely knocked over by elephants and smaller ones had been debarked or debranched by them.

Elephants are believed to play an important role in the natural conversion of woodland savannah to grasslands. In Khaudum, as in other parts of southern Africa where elephant populations are growing, you could almost see this transition happening before your eyes. It was as though the elephants were trying to reclaim this place for themselves. They had even gone to the trouble of pushing large trees right across the road, making them impassable in some places, essentially serving as boom gates. I could imagine a sentry bull standing to attention there in baggy pants with trunk held high trumpeting, '*Thou shalt not pass!*'

The population density of elephants was higher in Khaudum than in Nyae Nyae, most of them probably immigrating in from the Caprivi region north of there, and perhaps some from Botswana, the country with more elephants than any other. With no people or villages, just signs of elephants everywhere, it felt incredibly wild.

It was September, not yet the height of the dry season. Nonetheless, the temperatures neared forty degrees Celsius at midday. The sky was white with the smoke of fires burning all over north-eastern Namibia. Dust formed a constant blanket around us, coating every surface and invading every orifice with a fine layer of dirt. I could taste and smell it constantly, sticking to the back of my throat and clogging my nostrils. Thick clouds of it trailed each of our vehicles, so we had to stay a few hundred metres apart in order to see the road.

We pulled in at a waterhole called *Tsao*, which means 'lion'. Curiously, as we drove through the clearing that led to the waterhole, two lions slipped away into the long grass. In typical big-cat fashion, they were invisible almost immediately. Will and I got out of the car to take a look at the long concrete crib that provided water for the animals. It was about five metres long and a metre across, rectangular in shape, with concrete sections dividing it every couple of metres – 'to stop calves falling in and getting stuck,' Dries said. Water trickled into the crib at one end and overflowed into a large muddy dam beside it, providing the perfect place for an elephant to wallow.

Dries had been right about the hot dry season being the time to see elephants. The season had changed and with the heat came thirsty elephants to the man-made waterholes, whereas before they were finding water naturally in the bush and so weren't nearly as visible. Later in the morning, at another waterhole, several herds of elephants came together, about fifty in total, all of them competing for space at the crib. Roan antelope, a species that is incredibly rare in Africa, hung around the fringes waiting for a chance to drink. With their shaggy brown coats and long, large ears, roan antelope weren't going to win any beauty contests. Nonetheless, they were one of the most expensive antelopes to buy at game auctions, valued at about $50 000 per animal at the time. I didn't like this small herd's chances of getting a drink with literally tonnes of elephants lining up for one first.

It took us most of the day to get to Khaudum Camp in the northern part of the park. Khaudum National Park is a long rectangle of land that borders Botswana to the east and Caprivi to the north. The habitat and animal compositions changed considerably as we passed into the northern part of the park, where the rainfall was higher. We seemed to have passed through a natural ecotone.

The most blatant difference was that there were vervet monkeys. This may not sound very exciting, but the majority of Namibia is too dry for primates. Only the toughest of baboons can survive in most of this thirsty desert country, but you don't find any primates other than humans until you hit the areas with higher rainfall and rivers in the north-east. I can't tell you how happy it made me to see some monkeys. It was like seeing old friends. And it was just the reassurance I needed that I'd found my place of tall trees and plentiful water.

We arrived in camp about an hour before dark, looking forward to a cold beer from the car fridge and a little comfort after the long bumpy drive. Dries had told us to bring at least twenty litres of water because there was no water in camp and very few tourists stayed there. I knew I wouldn't get a shower for three days, but I wasn't worried about that. It hadn't twigged for me that the reason we needed to bring our own water was that the camp itself was a war zone.

The four chalets (if you could call them that) of Khaudum Camp were made of wooden planks with thatched roofs that had been under attack by monkeys and, as a result, had gaping holes. Chicken wire lined with torn mosquito gauze did a poor job of enclosing the windows. Gecko dung speckled the floor and there was a shrivelled snake skin in the corner of one chalet. A couple of forlorn springy single beds with ripped mattresses sat inside one of the rooms like haggard prisoners of war.

'These are the VIP bungalows,' Dries said, chuckling.

The communal ablution block, made of the same materials, leaned at a diagonal. The wooden walls had been knocked over and one of the toilets was on its side. The metal basin was heavily dented in the middle and had been pulled out from the wall. Chunks of battered wood were scattered all over the concrete floor and pipes were pulled literally right out of the ground, jutting like jagged antennae. Behind the ablution block there was a large hole in the ground where the septic tank used to be.

'You see, Tammie,' Dries said, 'this is what your elephants get up to.'

I was shocked. The camp had almost been destroyed.

'They even got into the septic tank,' he went on, his voice tired in a seen-it-all-before kind of way. 'Sucked it dry. It's not worth fixing the pipes. The staff here have given up on that. The elephants just come back every night and pull them up to get at the water. If an elephant's thirsty enough, he'll do anything to get a drink.'

Will and I took a careful walk around the camping ground and found further evidence of destruction by elephants. Large holes in the sand had been dug up where elephants had tried to get the water pipes out of the ground. Their enormous wrinkled footprints were everywhere. Few of our own footprints fell on sand where elephants hadn't trod before. One of my boots made up less than a quarter of one of their footprints. Elephants owned this place just like they owned the park. I felt like the elephants had taken over and we were now the intruders on their turf.

We took a walk down the hill on which the camp was set, across the open grasslands to the Khaudum waterhole. I couldn't understand why the elephants would make such a mess of the camp to get water when they had a waterhole a few hundred metres away. There had to be an explanation for it.

When I saw the waterhole I realised what that was. A tiny trickle of water oozed from the pipe onto a small slab of concrete that was no bigger than a birdbath. When it filled up, it flowed over the top into a large mud hole, much like the one we'd seen earlier in the day. It made for great mud, perfect for mud-bathing, but it didn't make for good drinking.

One thing I'd learned about elephants simply through watching them in places like Etosha was that they really like clean water. They'll always go to the source of the water for a drink, taking it straight from the pipe if they can. Sullied water is not an elephant's cup of tea. Individuals will compete for prime position at the source of the water, waiting for the clean water to flow out rather than settling for some that is slightly dirty. Fusspots, yes. But you really can't blame them, can you? Would you drink dirty water?

Unfortunately, looking at this waterhole, it was obvious that there was not enough clean water flowing out to hydrate a couple of elephant bulls, let alone a number of herds. A full-grown African elephant bull can drink a hundred litres of water a day. Dries told me that he was pumping 800 000 litres of water every day in Khaudum and about 300 000 litres in Nyae Nyae at this time of year. That's a heck of a lot of water, but not much when you consider that at the time there were thought to be about 5000 elephants in the area. The waterholes had to provide enough water not only for the elephants, but for all of the other game in the park, including Namibia's largest population of roan antelope. The hotter it got, the more the animals needed to drink and the more likely it was that elephants would damage pipes and other installations in order to get at the precious water.

It had been a devastatingly hot, dusty day, typical of the late dry season in Namibia. A raw red sun throbbed over the *omarumba*, the low-lying stretch of land that became a river when it rained but now was a dust bowl of suffocating heat. I was pretty thirsty myself. I couldn't imagine ever feeling fully hydrated at this time of year. No matter how much I drank, I always needed more. My throat itched from the caking of dust. I could understand the desperation these elephants must have been feeling in order to cause such destruction in the nearby camp. They must have been mad with thirst.

While pondering this, I saw movement out of the corner of my eye. It was an elephant bull walking tall and fast – thirsty – headed our way. Will and I were squatting right at the source of the water. He was about a hundred metres away, but we had a large clearing to cover before we were in the safety of the camp. Then again, was the camp really safe, considering the elephants were now the landlords? Either way, we had to get out of there in a hurry and give him some space. We could take about four steps in the time it took for the bull to cover one.

Will continued to film as we walked briskly away. The elephant stood even taller as he approached the water, a show of dominance at the two relatively small figures hightailing it out of there. He shook his head, making a loud slap as his large Africa-shaped ears slammed against the side of his head, creating a halo of dust around him. From the relative safety of the hill, Will and I sat puffing behind some bushes and watched the bull drink. Sucking it up into his trunk directly from the water pipe, the bull sprayed it carefully into his mouth, not wasting any of the precious liquid. He was drinking straight from the pipe.

'That's why we're building cribs, Tammie,' Dries said later, by the campfire. 'This is why I wanted you to see Khaudum. With cribs, more of them can get a drink of clean water at the same time. Without them, well . . . you get situations like this camp.'

Dries's expression as he stared into the flames was concerned. Every so often I saw another side to him, a softer side that he guarded closely.

'How many cribs have been built in Khaudum so far?' I asked.

'There's quite a few now. About half of the waterholes have cribs. But it's Nyae Nyae where we need them. At least there's no people in Khaudum. In Nyae Nyae it's a different story and we're seeing more elephants there every year. It's just a matter of time before another person gets nailed.'

Despite the evidence of their destructive natures, on more than one occasion in Khaudum I found myself very close to elephants without feeling in any way threatened. That was the weird thing about elephants. They were such a contradiction. The world's largest land mammal could be the most gentle, social animal on earth, but it could also be a terrifying vandal and a killer.

The next day, while Will filmed, I stood behind a dirt mound about thirty metres from two bulls drinking at a waterhole. I was amazed that the elephants were so tolerant of my proximity. They were well aware that there was a small group of humans close by. They raised their trunks to smell us and undoubtedly they could hear our voices.

When one bull began to walk towards us during the interview, I stopped mid-sentence and said to Dries, 'Are we all right?'

He nodded, his dark eyes observant, his jumbo-killing 4.16 rifle slung over his shoulder. The elephant took another step towards us. We all knew the bull could have crossed that distance in no time and we were about fifty metres from the vehicles. But all he did was lift his dexterous trunk into the shape of a cobra and smell us. He was curious, not aggressive. It was humbling to be so close to these peaceful giants, having seen firsthand the havoc they could wreak if they chose to.

On our way back to the south of the park we stopped at a waterhole called Tsoana, where we came upon a tragedy. Every day the weather seemed to get a little hotter, and as the temperatures increased, so too did the concentrations of elephants at the waterholes. At Tsoana, during the heat of the midday sun, we found almost two hundred elephants.

We climbed a high wooden hide encircled by a deep trench to get a better view. There were several breeding herds of females and young, with a couple of bulls loitering on the fringes. The vast majority of the elephants hovered around the crib, trying to get at the clean water. A couple stood in the mud wallow, hurling mud over their backs to protect their skin from the sun. A few stood in the shade of trees.

To one side, out in the open, a cow stood over a young calf. Dries estimated that it couldn't have been more than three years old. It was lying on its side, squealing and crying out, trying to stand up. Something was wrong. The mother stood over it, shading the small elephant from the searing rays of the midday sun.

It was suffocating in the shade, but truly scorching in the direct sunlight. Even under the shade of the hide, sweat was streaming down my back. The cow was tense and roared at any other elephant that came near, except for a teenager who hung close by, her older daughter perhaps.

There were several herds intermingling at the waterhole, more than sixty of them in total, and the place was buzzing with squealing, roaring, rumbling elephants of all sizes. I wished I could understand what they were saying to each other. As one herd left, another came in, so there was a constant flow of elephant herds materialising from the bush.

We couldn't work out what was wrong with the infant. It was trying unsuccessfully to lift its head and legs, but it couldn't even roll over. I wondered how long it had been there. Over and over again, the mother tried to help it onto its feet with a gentle push with her foot or trunk, but the baby wouldn't rise. The teenage elephant tried to help too, but it was hopeless. The baby was distraught, literally crying out in high-pitched shrieks. It seemed to us as though its back were broken.

We watched this awful scene for many hours. The cow flapped her ears constantly, trying to cool down with air fresh out of an oven. It would have been little respite. One herd stood in the shade of the trees a few hundred metres away for all of the time the mother was standing over the calf, baking herself in the sun to shade it. Other herds came and went, but this one stayed. We could hear rumbles coming from the tree line fairly regularly. It had to be her herd. They were waiting for her. Once or twice she screeched what seemed to us to be a reply. She was desperate. It seemed like her herd were telling her that they had to go and that she had to go with them. Was she saying back, 'How can I leave my baby here to die?'

It was heartbreaking. The herd wouldn't leave, but I

wondered how long they would wait for. Elephants need to cover large distances every day just to get enough food to survive. They can eat up to two hundred kilograms of food a day. That's a lot of vegetable matter. What this cow was doing was not in the best interests of the herd. In nature, everything I'd ever seen demonstrated that it was always every animal for himself. It was intriguing that the herd seemed to be showing tolerance, possibly even compassion, for the female. She stood stoically over her calf, trying to save it from the sun's rays in the vain hope that it might stand. And all the while we could see that the baby was losing strength, no longer crying out as often, but still flapping its small ears to cool down. But she wouldn't give up on it.

Although I had no children of my own, I could feel this mother's anguish. Scientists aren't meant to anthropomorphise animals, but it was impossible to distance myself from this situation. I knew that the little one wasn't going to make it. Left alone at the waterhole, if it didn't die of dehydration first, it would certainly be taken by a predator after dark, eaten alive by hyaenas or lions. The mother knew that. But there was nothing she could do for it if it couldn't join the herd. Tragically, its young life was over. She was simply refusing to accept it.

I wondered if this wasn't a product of the growing numbers of elephants in the region competing for limited resources. It was quite possible that the youngster had been hurt in the jostle between the tense elephants trying to get a drink at the waterhole. A small elephant could easily have been crushed or knocked over. Dries told me that the population growth rate of elephants in this area was ten percent, twice that of elephant populations in other parts of southern Africa.

After three hours of hoping the elephant would move off on her own so he could put the baby out of its misery, Dries said, 'That cow's going to charge. I can't get in there.'

He radioed Doyo, one of the park staff in this area, to come and take over the wait. Until the cow chose to leave the calf, park staff couldn't get close enough to end the young one's life. An hour later Doyo arrived and, with heavy hearts, we left the harrowing scene.

Just after sunset, Dries got a radio call from Doyo. The mother had finally moved off and joined her herd, giving the men a chance to end the baby's life. I tried not to think too hard about the reality of that. It was too awful. It was probably a blessing for the baby. Considering all the ways you could die in Africa, a single shot to the head was one of the better options.

As I got into my swag that night, it wasn't the baby I was thinking about. It was the mother. She had made an impossible decision that day, the choice to leave her baby.

I had fallen into elephant research by accident to some extent, but now I was beginning to understand why the people who worked on elephants were so obsessed with them. Watching the mother standing over her baby I could feel her pain as if it were my own. It was easy to feel like that among elephants; the more I got to know them the more I realised that they were a lot like us. The baby's awful cries and the mother's distress were – dare I say – human. Or was it that *we* were simply more like elephants than we realised? I felt like a friend who could do nothing to help, a bystander with nothing but sympathy to give, and it simply wasn't enough.

From a purely human perspective, based on what I had already seen of Khaudum and Nyae Nyae, elephants were making a real mess, causing expensive damage to infrastructure that people in this part of the world couldn't afford to fix. But the story was different if you looked at it through elephant eyes. Long before there were national parks, conservancies and farms, this was elephant country. Names and lines on maps were irrelevant to elephants. Their migration paths wove through the once thick bush where fences and farms now blocked the way, changing age-old patterns of habitat use that had been handed on over many generations.

These woodlands and savannahs provided sustenance for babies, mothers, grandmothers and grand old bulls. Entire family histories were formed here over thousands of years. These were lands where elephants had long memories of births and deaths of their families. Little ones had grown up here and learned the ancient routes from the old ladies of the herds, who had learned it from their own grandmothers.

These were beings that learned from and looked after each other in tight groups of relatives. To elephants, family was everything and loyalty was essential to their survival. They seemed to feel emotions like grief upon finding the bones of their own kind, as if remembering the soul that they had once known. They showed excitement and pleasure when approaching water after a long day in the sun, in the same way that children do at the sight of the ocean. I was starting to really like elephants. In so many ways, they were just like us.

SIX

I wanted to understand more about what the Bushmen thought of elephants. It was one thing to see the conflict and to understand the problem from a western point of view, but that didn't automatically give me a solution that worked both for elephants and the Bushmen. I was pretty sure that the solution – if such a thing existed – was tightly linked to the lives of the Bushmen. I had a feeling that the answers might even come from the people themselves.

A social survey of the local community's perceptions of elephants was an important part of my research, but I had no idea how to construct one, let alone where to find a sociologist in Namibia. I broached the subject over a beer one Saturday while watching the rugby at Dries's place. The pack of dogs had generously shared their lounge with me, allowing me a small space squashed up next to the arm. A puff of dust and musty dog smell rose as I sat down on the black vinyl.

'You guys don't know of anyone who knows a bit about social surveys, by any chance?' I asked.

Dries slammed his beer on the table and shouted, 'Arrrgh! These fucking Australians are cheating! Did you see that? Arsehole!'

'Well, yes,' Stacey said demurely, ignoring her boyfriend, 'I did my Masters in Sociology.'

'Really?'

Again the beer slammed down. 'Awww, fucking ref! He must be Australian too!'

Oblivious to the outburst, Stacey said, 'Yeah, if you like, Tammie, I'd love to help you.'

A deathly stare from Dries was shot my way as the Wallabies scored again. 'You know that if the Australians win you're not welcome here any more.'

I laughed, 'And if we lose?'

'Then you *must* stay so I can abuse you.'

Mysteriously, it turned out that Stacey was not only a goddess, but also a godsend. Over the next week, she and I developed a survey to find out more about local perceptions of elephants. We wanted to ask questions like: What do you think of elephants? Are they good or bad? If you had the chance to have no elephants in Nyae Nyae, would you want that or not? Are there any good things about elephants? Have you personally experienced any conflict with elephants?

I met the son of Chief Bobo, the young man who had been recommended by Stacey as a potential translator for my social surveys, and was delighted when he accepted my offer of employment. Leon had worked with John Marshall, the American film-maker, helping translate for his films, and now as a tour guide in the conservancy. His English was good and a brief conversation with him was enough to convince me that he was perfect for the job.

There was no time to waste. Over the next couple of months, Stacey, Leon and I drove out to as many villages in the conservancy as we could. At each one, Stacey spread a blanket on the ground under the shade of a tree and set to work. She asked the questions in English, then this was translated by Leon and we took notes on his answers. I spent most of the time listening to the magical clicking language of the Bushmen, not understanding any of it but just enjoying its lyrical sound.

Leon was a patient and humble soul. He was tolerant of my western ignorance without being patronising and he seemed to know where we were coming from, so that he was able to ask the Bushmen our questions in a way that got answers. You would think that getting answers to direct questions would be easy, but it wasn't. The Bushmen are incredibly shy, particularly the women. It took a patient and warm person they were comfortable with to elicit answers from them. Leon told the people that our study had the support of his father, the chief, and that we were trying to find solutions to the problems with the elephants. This usually got people talking.

The older women were fascinating. Their eyes twinkled with humour and they laughed as they spoke. Some of them were so animated that I found myself laughing with them even though I had no idea what they were saying. Their faces were furrowed with wrinkles that mapped the story of the road they'd travelled in their lives.

I began to change my opinion on wrinkles. The society I came from told me that they were ugly and to be avoided at any cost. The anti-aging industry placed youth at the pinnacle of human existence, making it synonymous with beauty. Insistent messages blared from every TV screen, magazine and bus stop in the faces of air-brushed supermodels with impossibly beautiful features. It was no longer a case of a little bit of lippy and a haircut to keep up with the beauty train; now nips and tucks were becoming commonplace.

If I applied those rules in this place, then the whole of Bushmanland needed a big batch of Botox. Here, everything had wrinkles and they were *magnificent*. I couldn't imagine anything worse than removing them. There was beauty in the wrinkles of this ancient place, in the deep crevasses in an elephant's leathery trunk, in the ample folds of its droopy haunches. It was there in the fine creases of an old Bushman woman's smiling eyes, lines that reached down to meet the curved furrows in her cheeks, like wrinkles holding hands. In the grooves and warts of the aged bark of a giant baobab tree, there was beauty too, with limbs gnarled and arthritic arching over the land like a wise elder.

I wanted that kind of wisdom, the kind for which wrinkles were badges of honour. While westerners like me clung to self-help books, burned incense and learned about Buddhism in the search for internal peace, these old grandmothers of the Bushmen just seemed to have it naturally. They weren't religious but they were deeply spiritual. After all, it was the singing of the women that was the trigger for the trance state, which the Bushmen say is as close to dying as you can get without actually snuffing it. The strength of these women elders seemed to come from a strong interconnection with nature, their families and the community. They were of the earth, these women, tied to the stars and the moon and the soil on which they trod in bare feet to collect water every day. Like chameleons, they blended with the colour and the pulse and the seasons of the land, moving with it and adapting. They belonged here.

I thought about my own journey to this far-flung land. Where did I actually belong? I felt a strong sense of home in Africa, but could I really stay here forever? Now approaching thirty, I had gained a few wrinkles of my own lately. Observing the new fine lines beside my eyes in the mirror at my flat in Windhoek just a few days earlier, I'd had my first glimpse of age in my reflection.

'Oh my God, I'm almost thirty,' I said to the pug, who was sitting on the bathroom mat at my feet.

He cocked his little flat face, folded over and over with multiple rolls of skin, and farted decisively.

'You're right, pugster, I'll take that as a vote of support,' I said, then applied a healthy scoop of moisturiser to my face.

Thinking about those fine lines now, watching the old lady speak to Leon, I thought to myself, *I'm going to wear them with pride*. Goddamn it, I'd earned those wrinkles!

One thing was clear from our conversations with the Bushmen. Elephants were bad. *Very* bad. Old men, young women, children, pretty much everyone we spoke to said that elephants were bad. Even the odd goat dashing through a village seemed to be bleating 'Baaaaaaaaaaad!' Elephants broke precious water installations, competed with the people for bush foods, chased them and even killed them. So they were bad. The way Leon translated the word 'bad' with so much feeling in it, almost spitting it out, we were left with no doubts as to how people felt.

I was surprised at this. Call me slow, but weren't the Bushmen meant to be the ones who lived in harmony with nature? Didn't they set the standard for sustainable living off the land? Weren't they the ones who ran down an antelope for hours after shooting it with a bow and poisoned arrow, then knelt beside the exhausted animal and thanked it for feeding their families? Weren't the Bushmen meant to *love* animals?

Well, it turned out it wasn't that simple. The Bushmen did have a huge respect for nature, but there were so many elephants coming into their area now that they had become a real threat to their livelihoods. One old man told us there were never this many elephants in the area when he was a child. But something else had happened to create this problem, something that was a consequence of people and politics, not growing elephant populations. No longer nomadic, the Bushmen of Nyae Nyae had become sedentary.

Namibia was first colonised by the Germans in 1884 and then by the South Africans as part of the British Empire from 1915 until 1990, when Namibia gained independence. A product of the South African colonial regime was the Apartheid-style designation of homelands to each of the ethnic groups in Namibia. If you were an Owambo, you were forcibly settled in Owamboland. If you were a Damara, you lived in Damaraland. If you were a Bushman, you no longer roamed freely across the country. You had to live in Bushmanland, an area just fifteen percent of your previous range. It was a way for the then government to divide up the land so that the best freehold land went to the white farmers (about forty-three percent of the country's land).

During the independence war, the South African army moved into the area and established Tsumkwe as a military base. They took advantage of the Bushmen's excellent tracking skills to hunt down the enemy, Namibia's liberation movement, the South West African People's Organisation (SWAPO). A consequence of this, and one that had a severe bearing on their culture, was that many of the Bushmen moved away from a traditional hunter-gatherer lifestyle to one in which they were dependent on the army for a wage. Hard cash was introduced to a previously egalitarian and moneyless society and with the army came the bottle shops. Having barely been touched by the outside world until then, the delicate social structure of the Bushmen was shaken to the core.

Finding Bushmanland torn apart by crime, alcoholism and prostitution in the 1980s, film-maker John Marshall initiated the Nyae Nyae Development Foundation, focusing on self-help farming projects to try to improve the quality of their lives. Boreholes were drilled throughout the area to provide water for stock, most of them in the south bordering Hereroland. I heard that this was to prevent the famously farming-savvy Hereros encroaching on Bushmanland by establishing a presence in the southern part of the region. The Bushmen built small villages around the boreholes, which was one step further away from their former nomadic lifestyle.

The drilling of boreholes also meant that there was now a ready source of water all year round for elephants in Nyae Nyae, whereas before there had only been natural pans, which filled during the rains and dried up for the rest of the year. Inevitably, elephants drawn to the area by the reliable water were coming into conflict with people. The issue wasn't only that the population of elephants in southern Africa was growing, it was that the demographics of the human population and the consequent provision of water had fostered favourable circumstances for an elephant invasion.

Marshall's heart was probably in the right place in that he was trying to move the Bushmen away from a dependency situation to one in which they could live independently again. But, unlike many of the other tribes in Namibia, in general the Bushmen aren't natural farmers. It simply isn't their way.

The Bushmen of Nyae Nyae remained among Namibia's poorest and most marginalised people. Things didn't get better for them after Namibia gained independence. Having supported the South Africans during the independence struggle, when the war ended in 1990 they were not popular with the new government, which treated them with detached ambivalence.

Things continued to look bleak for the Bushmen, but many believed that wildlife offered them hope for a better future. In 1997, the Nyae Nyae Conservancy was registered, Namibia's largest and first communal conservancy. The designation of a conservancy meant that the Bushmen had legal ownership of their wildlife and could derive income and employment from wildlife-based enterprises. Elephants were now literally paying their way, through trophy-hunting fees to the conservancy.

While the vast majority of the Bushmen we spoke to felt that elephants were bad news, most of them said that they had value in the conservancy because of the trophy hunting operation and the opportunity it offered for tourism, and thus for jobs, meat and income. Only fourteen percent said that they'd rather not have elephants in the area at all. Leon framed the question in his own inimitable style: 'If the President came here to Nyae Nyae and said he would shoot all the elephants, would you want that?' Most people said no.

There was no question about it. Elephants were dangerous and a serious threat to livelihoods in a place where most people were malnourished and really had more than enough to worry about just trying to survive. But you couldn't deny the benefits that came from Namibia's growing wildlife-based industries. The question was how to find a way to continue to let people benefit from the presence of elephants, while reducing the cost.

As we interviewed more and more people, I began to understand where they were coming from. Elephants were important in their culture. The Bushmen of Nyae Nyae performed a traditional healing dance known as the elephant dance.

One small boy told us that elephants were an important part of nature because they helped disperse seeds.

'If an elephant come here to Nyae Nyae and he go to Grootfontein, you will see a tree that was growing here and it will be there then,' Leon translated.

One old lady, a chief in her village, who had been chased by elephants while collecting roots and tubers in the bush, said that it was fine for us. *We* didn't have to live with elephants. She told us she rarely went out to collect bush food any more. Her eyes were no good, she said, laughing self-deprecatingly, a hilarious cackle that came from somewhere deep inside her chest. Her eyes were milky with cataracts and her face was a maze of wrinkles. A bright scarf was tied around her head, and her neck and arms were circled by rainbows of coloured beads.

'She say if an elephant come here now,' Leon translated, chuckling, 'you can stay here, but she will run!'

She was right, of course. We really had no idea what these people dealt with on a day-to-day basis. The history of the Bushmen was hard enough to comprehend, let alone the present.

It was only a few hundred years before that there was a price on the heads of the Bushmen. Dries told me that the word San, which some people still use for the Bushmen, means thief, which is exactly how they were seen for a long time. In 1792 a bounty of fifteen rixdollars was set for every Bushman captured alive. 'Wild' Bushmen children were captured by colonists and 'tamed' to be servants. The term Bushmen came about from the seventeenth century Dutch word *Bossieman*, which means outlaw. It referred to people who lived off the land and had no domestic stock, which gave them low status. They were literally treated like animals and considered to be vermin. I'd seen shocking pictures of Bushmen hung by the neck from trees.

Not unlike the leopard that Dries had translocated for making an easy meal of the reverend's goats, the Bushmen hadn't seen hunting of domestic stock as stealing. This didn't go down too well with the Bantu-speaking tribes and, later, with the white folks who depended on agriculture for their living and treated the land that the Bushmen had once hunted as their own. For the Bushmen, the idea of ownership of animals or land was absurd. The land and animals, including the sheep and the goats, belonged to everyone. The Bushmen had just been doing what they had always done, but now certain things were illegal, punishable by death or jail. Africa was changing. By the 1800s, Bushmen independence was over and many saw them as a dying race.

But they didn't die out. Resilient to being shot at, hanged, trapped and enslaved, they adapted. Sadly, things didn't get much better for them. Even in modern-day Bushmanland, with benefits starting to flow in from the conservancy, people still battle diseases that most of us in the west get vaccinated against as children. Tuberculosis is the big one. Toma, a young man who stood in for Leon as my translator one day, coughed constantly as we did our social surveys. Once, after a cough, I saw him wipe fresh blood from the side of his mouth with his handkerchief. HIV/AIDS is on the rise, as it is throughout Africa, leaving children without parents and families without breadwinners. As most people are malnourished, they are susceptible to all sorts of things that wouldn't harm a healthy person.

One day, during a social survey at a village called Xamsa, I spotted an old lady lying face down near her hut. A violent hot wind whipped dust through our 'office' on a blanket under a tree, where Stacey was asking questions of a villager. She clung to the papers to stop them blowing away. Three little boys stood watching us from behind a large tree nearby, snickering and giggling just like small boys do everywhere in the world. A forlorn donkey with hobbled front legs hopped painfully past us, followed by a herd of scrawny goats. A metal bell around the neck of one of the goats clanged with every step. The slow, building, heat was gradually strangling the energy out of me. The skin on my face felt tight where it was exposed to the dry wind.

My friend Kisa Baldwin, an Australian vet, had arrived a few days before to help me with my next couple of field trips. Kisa and I had been house mates while studying at the University of

Queensland. We had shared many a late-night study session over midnight munchies and plotted the adventures with animals we would have in Africa when we graduated. Almost a decade later, Kisa had finally made it to Africa. Still jetlagged from the long flight, she was, I'm afraid, thrown in the deep end straightaway with a heavy dose of 'too much reality'.

When the interview was done, I asked our translator, a man called Twee who was filling in for Leon, if he could find out whether the old lady was all right. She didn't look well and I thought that maybe we could give her a lift to the clinic in town.

The four of us walked over to the hut. An old man sat on a plastic chair beside where his wife lay on her stomach on the ground. She was wrapped in a dusty, red chequered blanket, her arms sticking out like skinny chicken wings and her tiny, gnarled feet exposed heels up. Her forehead rested in her hands and her eyes were closed. She barely moved as we approached her, too weak even to sit up. Twee conversed with the old man.

'He says she hasn't eaten in months,' Twee said.

In Bushman time I knew that didn't literally mean months, it simply meant a long time. Mind you, she was such a sack of bones that it *did* look like she hadn't eaten in months.

'Her throat is very sore,' Twee went on. 'She cannot take any food.'

'Tell her you're a doctor, Kisa. Maybe she'll let you help her,' Stacey suggested.

'I'm an *animal* doctor, Stacey,' Kisa objected.

'I know, but just see if she'll listen to you.'

'Can't hurt, Kise,' I said.

Stacey said to Twee, 'Can you explain that this lady here is a doctor? She wants to know if she can help.'

The woman shuffled slightly and, with a quiet word, acquiesced.

Kisa squatted down next to the skeletal woman. She gently placed her hand on her bony shoulder.

'She's very dehydrated,' Kisa said. 'She needs to drink. Can't we take her to the clinic in Tsumkwe?'

But the old man told us they'd already done that. The clinic had sent her away with a Panadol and advice to see a traditional healer.

'You know what that means,' Stacey said quietly to me, 'she's dying. There's nothing they can do.'

'It could be throat cancer,' Kisa said, her eyes full of concern. She seemed unable to pull her hand away from the woman's frail shoulder.

The old woman spoke then, quietly but forcefully.

'She does not want to go to the clinic. She wants to stay here with her husband in the village,' Twee said.

The old woman's eyes spoke of pain and suffering. Her hair was ash grey. Few people reached her age in this part of the world. The World Health Organisation put life expectancy of people in Namibia in 2006 at about forty-two, but it was probably lower than that among the Bushmen.

There was nothing we could do but accept the old woman's wishes. She wanted us to leave her alone and wasn't happy with the attention. No one in the village seemed overly worried about her. Her husband had been smiling, not anxious at all. It was the kind of acceptance of death that I'd seen in people in other parts of Africa where it is a regular visitor.

As with all the villages who participated in the survey, we left them a couple of plastic bags full of groceries like mealie meal, cooking oil, sugar, tea and tobacco. We also gave the old man some more Panadol and rehydration salts for his wife. The village seemed satisfied, but the small gesture of thanks didn't lift any of our spirits. No matter which way you looked at it, we were leaving that old woman there to die. It was a poignant reminder of just how precarious life in this place was.

So times had changed for the Bushmen, some for the better, some for the worse. Life went on. But what did this mean for the elephants? How had their life histories changed?

I was beginning to see that the futures of the elephants and the Bushmen were inextricably intertwined. The elephants were dependent on the Bushmen for their conservation. Without the conservancy and an economy based on wildlife, this land could easily be cleared and converted to agriculture like much of the region south of it. The Bushmen depended on the elephants to draw in income, jobs and provide meat. Elephants were this community's best chance of becoming financially self-sustaining.

Like Jen had said on our first field trip, as a result of Africa's history the Bushmen and the elephants had both come off second best. Both may once have numbered in the millions but were now reduced to a fraction of that. Both had been marginalised, hunted and forced to live in smaller and smaller chunks of land. Now, in Nyae Nyae, both needed each other to survive.

SEVEN

'How many do you reckon, Kise?'

'I'd say . . . well, with the extra four that just climbed into the back, maybe twenty?'

'Hmmm . . . yeah, by the way the Hilux feels I think you could be right. Maybe twenty-five.'

'I think you may have broken the record of how many Bushmen you can fit in one double-cab Hilux.'

It was dark, a sliver of moon providing decoration rather than illumination. We were driving back from Tsumkwe to Klein Dobe camp, a journey of about twenty kilometres on thick sand. There was a village half-way between, where we dropped off half our load of people, only to have even more climb in.

'*Ek moet ry!* I must go!' I said to an old lady and man standing beside the road. '*Ons is vol.* We are full.'

I was starting to panic about the sheer number of people in the car. We were very overloaded. The Hilux was groaning under the weight of us all and I didn't fancy my chances of reversing quickly if charged by an elephant on the way to camp.

The old woman pleaded with me.

'I'm sorry,' I said, shaking my head.

I actually had no idea where she would fit anyway. Did she want to sit on the roof?

The women and children in the back seat were all talking over the top of each other and a baby was wailing. In the back of the Hilux, I counted at least a dozen men squished in like fish fingers. I couldn't imagine how they could even breathe in there. A lot of them were drunk. Everyone was shouting.

That was the moment the old woman cursed me. She went berserk, pointing a crooked finger at me and yelling aggressively in words that I could not understand. My usual translator from Klein Dobe, Xao, was too drunk to translate.

'Just go!' he said. 'Go!'

In the passenger seat, Kisa's eyes were wide. This was her first trip to Africa, a place she'd always dreamed of visiting, and I was quite sure this wasn't what she had expected. There was the magic of Bushmanland and then there was . . . well, *this*. The reality. Too much reality, as Jen had once described it. The social decay of the villages near Tsumkwe was like the ugly brown froth that laps at the shore during an oceanic algal bloom. Only by diving right in through the froth could you see how beautiful it was in the water.

I drove off, leaving the cursing woman behind, in a Hilux as heavily laden with Bushmen as my stomach was with self-blame.

The next morning, a stray dog wandered into camp. She was a mess. The only bit of her body with any flesh on it was her teats. Sharp ribs jutted out through sunken skin that was covered in lice-laden, patchy fur.

'She's feeding pups,' Kisa said.

The dog skulked around the fringes of camp all morning looking for some food to scavenge, but was too scared to come within twenty metres of us. My veterinarian friend's heart broke at the sight of this poor bedraggled creature. Whenever Kisa walked towards her she dashed away into the bush. Kisa left some milk for her in a bowl, placing it far enough away so that she would drink it. The dog lapped it up as though she'd never had such a feast in her life.

Some strange thoughts started going through my head as I watched the dog drink. I'd been in Africa a long time, over a decade on and off, and I loved it. Life in Africa had become more normal to me than life in Australia, but it hadn't always been kind. Sometimes it had been downright abusive and I'd walked away bruised and battered by its brutality. But it was always so damned seductive that I could never let it go. One sideways glance and it could always rope me back in. I didn't know quite how to live without it.

Having Kisa there, a friend I'd known since university, I realised with a sudden clarity just how much I'd changed. Some of those changes were good. Others were not. I didn't know if I could ever go back to my old world again. I wasn't sure that I wanted to.

Seeing that poor, skinny dog I barely felt anything. I felt numb. I know how awful this sounds, but it wouldn't have occurred to me to give her some milk. I recall thinking, *Why bother? How is that helping? She might live another day or two, but she's doomed anyway. That's Africa. Get over it.*

I had become hard. I'd surrounded myself with so many protective barriers to keep from being affected by things that I had almost stopped feeling anything at all. In retrospect, I guess it was a coping mechanism. This must be what people working in refugee camps become like in a much shorter time frame. In Africa, every day you are there, you are surrounded by poverty. Some people choose not to see it, but it's always there. Suffering is always close by and death is a regular occurrence.

The whole time I was in Bushmanland, more so than anywhere I'd worked before, I felt constantly torn by the way this place made my heart soar one second and break in two the next. There was so much raw beauty and yet so much unspeakable pain. It seemed trite to dwell on my own response to the poverty because, after all, I had enough food in my belly. I really wasn't the one with the problem. But I could see now that I'd become so obsessed with trying to fix conservation problems while remaining scientific and emotionally unattached, that I'd forgotten that caring for individuals was important too.

Each day Kisa left some milk in a bowl for the stray dog, putting it closer and closer to our tents. The dog put on a little bit of weight before our eyes. After a few days, she let Kisa pat her. She was still skittish and prone to spontaneous bolting, but the way she looked at Kisa, with eyes filled with utter vulnerability and gratitude, it was clear that the dog had never known so much love in her life.

I felt my own barriers dropping away along with the dog's and a solid brick of guilt settled in the pit of my stomach. I felt awful. There was never a bad time for compassion. I couldn't believe that just a few days before I'd felt like *reprimanding* Kisa for wasting our milk on the dog. Thank God I'd held my tongue. What on earth was wrong with me?

Kisa had noticed it too.

'You've changed, Tam. Remember the reason you fell in love with Africa? It inspired you . . . I know it's tough here, but don't forget that. It wouldn't take much for this place to burn you out.'

She was right. The problems in Bushmanland were starting to get to me. On more than one occasion I'd wondered how I was really helping by being here. After all, the explorers, the missionaries, and others with the best of intentions, had all tried to help before, and what did the Bushmen have to show for it? Although I was bringing a small income to some of the villagers at Klein Dobe, every time I paid them they headed into Tsumkwe and got drunk. Sometimes the women got beaten up as a result. By my very presence there I was having an impact. Whether it was positive or negative, I couldn't say.

I remembered Dries's words often, 'What are you going to do for *us*, Tammie?'

Sitting on a log and writing in my diary during the heat of the day, I listened to the wind shake the acacias, littering the ground with millions of tiny leaflets. Then I heard a mighty roar. Before I could get under cover, a dust devil raged through camp and I was right in its path. Seconds later I was in the thick of it. I put my head in between my knees and wrapped my arms around my head as it hit, letting it batter me with its angry slaps. Leaves and sticks and dust flew through the hot air in the violent winds.

What? I wanted to yell. *What are you trying to tell me?*

The furious whirlwind passed. I shook the leaves and twigs out of my hair, brushed the dirt off my diary and resumed writing.

I thought I was doing the right thing, but hadn't the explorers and missionaries thought that too? Was I, simply by my presence in this place, making things worse for these people, adding another factor to diminish their culture? Was I thinking too hard about this? I couldn't say for sure. My perspective had become completely blurred through immersion. It was impossible to see out. That's when old friends like Kisa became invaluable. She reminded me who I was and why I had come here in the first place.

For the first time in my life I realised that I couldn't do this kind of work forever. A little self-preserving voice somewhere deep inside me was getting louder. Elements of working in the bush in Africa were incredibly nurturing, like being among nature and wild animals, experiencing the kindness and generosity of very poor people and watching the sunset over the savannah with a cold beer. But other parts of it wore me down. Annoying little things that once I would have laughed at and said of them 'That's just Africa', I now had no patience for. Sometimes it felt like I was all 'give' and not much 'get', but at the same time I could never really reconcile to myself how much I had compared with the local people I was working with. When poverty is in your face it's impossible to let it go. The changes I wanted to see in Africa wouldn't happen in my lifetime, even if I gave everything I had to them. Things took time here – African time. The more I thought about how big the problems were, the more wrecked I felt. It was like running on a treadmill and going nowhere even though you were dripping with sweat.

Kisa and I drove back to Windhoek, as I was committed to some work for Wilderness Safaris, and we left the dog behind to fend for herself. When we came back a week or so later she was nowhere to be found. Half Ear said he thought she had gone back to where she had come from, but we never really knew for sure.

A South African friend, Ron Swilling, who managed camps for Wilderness Safaris, had a week off and decided to help us form a team in Nyae Nyae's annual waterhole game count. On the drive to Nyae Nyae, cruising along in the Hilux at a hundred and twenty kilometres an hour, an enormous kudu bull blasted out of the bush in front of us, heading straight for our bonnet. In the millisecond that I saw him I could tell that he was a big bull, standing at least one and a half metres at the shoulder. But he seemed much larger because of the huge full set of spiral horns on his head. I knew that hitting an animal that size could roll the car and kill us all.

I slammed on the brakes and yelled, 'Hold on!'

I knew he was going to hit us, no matter what I did, so I just kept braking to slow us down and reduce the inevitable impact, not swerving but gently pulling the car to the right onto the other side of the road to give him more space. Thankfully there were no cars coming in the opposite direction and it was a long straight road ahead. Just before the impact, from the corner of my eye I could see both the front and back passenger windows entirely filled with the tawny brown fur of the kudu. Ron and Kisa were just inches from him. I held the steering wheel hard and braced myself, praying I wouldn't kill us all.

I had slowed down to about eighty when the kudu hit the Hilux side on, causing the car to heave. He seemed to bounce straight off it and for a second I thought he would go in the other direction. But he must have had too much momentum because the next thing I knew he was jumping clear over the bonnet in slow motion. Still braking, I watched the kudu glide through the air in front of me, land on the bitumen, then gallop into the bush on the other side of the road, apparently unaffected by the whole experience.

When we arrived at Klein Dobe that night, we were all shaken by our brush with death, but grateful to have escaped unscathed. We had been very lucky. While the girls cracked a Tafel lager, I made my excuses and retired to my tent early. In typical Cancerian fashion, dwelling too much on all of my worries about the Bushmen, the elephants, my future, exacerbated by the scare with the kudu, had quickly translated into a bad case of the flu. It had started with aches and pains that morning and grown progressively worse all day. You never knew in this part of the world if something was really flu or cerebral malaria, so, curled up on my swag under a mildly comforting duvet, I contemplated whether or not I might actually die.

I didn't get much sleep that night and woke up looking like hell. Ron, who, it turned out, was a trained reiki practitioner, told me to lie down on a mattress under the veranda outside my tent and proceeded to assess my chakras. I don't know exactly what she did, but at the end she pronounced, 'I can feel a burning around your heart chakra. You're giving too much, Tam. You don't take enough back. You need to accept some love.'

I thought back to the week before when my favourite pilot had come up to me at the pub with his bedroom eyes, begun stroking my lower back with warm, artist's hands and whispered in my ear, 'I really want to bite your shoulder.'

At the end of the night, he kissed me on the cheek in a way that we both knew lingered too long. My heart had been racing.

I said to Ron, 'What about if I just *imagine* getting love? Does that count?'

'Come on, Tam, that's like saying you can get love from watching *Dirty Dancing*,' Kisa interjected.

'What about if I get love from the pug?'

'Tam!'

'Okay, okay . . .'

The problem was, much as I would have liked to be welcoming some romance back into my life, there really wasn't a lot of spare time to go looking for it. My life was very full. Every couple of weeks I was up in Bushmanland, and in between I was travelling out to the camps doing environmental assessments for Wilderness Safaris. I hadn't had a day off in weeks. Although I thought I wanted the French pilot, I knew that, despite his sizzling sex appeal, he was not what I needed. I knew I needed some nurturing, but had no idea how to make it happen.

I'd just been to my regular hairdresser in Windhoek, a lavishly made-up Afrikaans woman called Daphne, who believed that good hair, husbands and God were the answers to everything.

'How are you, Tammie? Have you got a boyfriend yet?'

Straight up.

'No, not yet.'

'Oh, *shaaame*,' she gushed, with genuine pity for my sorry state. 'Well, at least we will make your hair nice, hey?'

'It's really okay, Daphne. I'm doing fine on my own.'

'*Shame!* Of course you are, darling,' she said, tut-tutting at my obvious ignorance of my own misfortune. Not only was I single, I was clearly also stupid.

Oh well, at least I had good hair to fall back on.

'Oh dear, did you know you have a lot of grey hairs here?' Daphne said, her face filling with dread for my future.

'How many? More than three?'

'Oh, *ja,*' she exclaimed. 'Quite a few!'

'Thanks, Daphne.'

'My pleasure.'

The writing was on the wall. Although I loved working in Africa, it was giving me grey hairs. And now, lying in the foetal position in my tent in the oppressive daytime heat of late September, it all seemed a bit too hard. I was glad that the game count didn't start until the next day because I really felt like I needed a day to recover (code for wallowing in my own misery).

On top of that, a strange experience earlier that day had made me wonder if I wasn't starting to lose it completely. In the heat of the day, after shovelling the Hilux out of a deep sand bog, I'd driven around the bend into camp and seen a man sitting on the campchair outside my tent.

'Who's that?' I said aloud, before the trees obscured the tent from view.

When I got to the tent, there was no one there. I swore I had seen a man, and the silhouette suggested someone taller in stature than a Bushman. I didn't mention it again to the girls, worried they might fear for my sanity.

Later in the day, people from all around the conservancy started to arrive in camp for the game count. I met Raymond from Namibia's WWF LIFE program, who co-ordinated the counts in Nyae Nyae every year and volunteered myself, Kisa and Ron to count animals at the waterhole right next to camp. Counting at a nearby waterhole seemed the easiest option, given that I felt like death warmed up and wasn't sure how I was going to stay upright to count animals anyway.

Raymond had kind eyes and a gentle smile. Square glasses framed a contemplative face that was masculine and warm.

'Ah, so, the famous Tammie!' he said, smiling as he reached out to shake my hand. 'Everywhere I go, people are saying to me, "Have you met Tammie?", "Haven't you met Tammie?", and I say, "No, I haven't met Tammie. Who is this Tammie?" and they say, "You haven't met Tammie? You must meet Tammie!"'

I laughed, sensing a kind soul in the wilderness, not someone in the boys' club.

'Really?' I replied, 'That's funny because wherever I go people say the same thing about this guy called Raymond.'

Kisa, Ron and I stuck around while he gave the game counters a briefing; they were largely Bushmen men from all around the conservancy and a few government workers in MET uniform. Most of them had done it before. The annual count would last three full days and nights. Our team of three girls would work the midday to midnight shift, while two men from the conservancy would work the midnight to midday one. Raymond explained the rules. There could be no fires, voices must be quiet at all times, and we had to count everything we saw and record it on the standard monitoring forms.

'*Daar is slang an olifant*. There are snakes and elephants. *Jella moenie hardloop*! You mustn't run!' Raymond said, which sent the men into fits of hysterics.

Kisa gave me a look that said, 'Why is that funny?' and then laughed anyway.

We parked the Hilux about a hundred metres back from the waterhole and the girls stayed on duty while I lay in the back on a mattress waiting to die. Not one animal appeared for eight hours from midday. It was a long eight hours. Then, finally, a small herd of elephants came in, providing us with some light entertainment as they sprayed water over themselves in the dam.

After dark I sat in the driver's seat, just in case we had to make a quick getaway. I'd promised Kisa's mum and her fiancé, Greg, that I'd make sure she was returned to Australia safely. Mind you, I wasn't much use in my current state. Come eight o'clock, my head was pounding so hard I rested it on the steering wheel and, lulled by the constant background whirr of the generator pumping water, promptly fell asleep.

Around eleven, Kisa tapped me on the shoulder and whispered, 'Tam! Two elephants! *Right here!*'

Groggily I looked out my window to see two gigantic bulls walking ponderously beside the car about twenty metres away. In the eerie light of the full moon they seemed bigger than any elephant I'd ever seen, ghostly in the shadows of the moonscape. One bull's stomach rumbled as he walked past, headed for the waterhole where a herd of females and young were drinking. Pearly ivory glinted in the moonlight like enormous swords. They knew we were there, but we were largely ignored. The second bull rose even taller than his incredible height and, like a king, he turned his head towards us and looked down on us, making us feel like meek dwarfs at his service. A wall of about fifty elephants jostled at the waterhole, screeching and competing for space at the source. These two bulls cleared the area, taking pride of place immediately.

At midnight some elephants were still at the waterhole, so I switched on the engine without putting the lights on. There was enough moonlight to see without headlights. We drove back to the camp carefully, vigilant for predators and elephants that might require a rapid reverse in the Hilux. We picked up the two men who were to take over from us and dropped them back at the waterhole. They didn't have a vehicle to sit in, so earlier that day they had built a small shelter of sticks and branches.

I thought these men were incredibly brave to sit out at a waterhole with nothing but branches for protection. All around Nyae Nyae Conservancy, others were doing the same. They didn't even have a fire as a deterrent because it might disturb the natural behaviour of the animals in the game count. If a lion or an elephant came along, they couldn't drive away. They would have to climb a tree.

Tucked up in bed about twenty minutes after dropping them off, I heard a man's voice. I thought I must be dreaming. *Oh, it's you, God . . . Did Daphne send you?*

'Hello?'

There it was again. It didn't sound Godly this time. Maybe I didn't have flu, maybe it was cerebral malaria. Perhaps I was delirious.

'Yeah?' I said, wondering if I was talking to myself.

I sat up in bed and saw the two men I'd just dropped at the waterhole standing in front of my tent. We'd forgotten to give them the folder with the data sheets and they'd walked a couple of kilometres in the dark through elephant-infested bush to get it. I quickly dressed and dropped them back out there. I'd thought they were brave before. Now I thought they were superheroes. There had been lions at the waterhole just a few days earlier.

Overtired and still feeling like crap the next morning, I decided to try a traditional medicinal technique that a Himba research assistant of mine had once recommended for flu – elephant dung. I picked up a bolus of dried dung and threw it in a boiling pot of water on the gas cooker. As it bobbed around in the bubbling water, dozens of desperate insects began to crawl or fly out of it, some of them plunging into the boiling water to their death. The hotter it got, the more critters squirmed out of it and the quicker they squirmed.

'Are you sure this works?' Kisa asked, an eyebrow raised.

'I have no idea. Savimbi told me it does. He's a Himba. They're experts in traditional medicine.'

'Look at all those insects. Oh my God, Tam, you're killing an entire ecosystem!'

'Okay, I'm going in!'

I'd gone this far, now I had to go through with it. I threw a tea towel over my head and held it over the smoking dung, then inhaled a great big breath of boiling elephant dung. I almost choked on the intense smell. I hate to say this but it really was like inhaling very hot shit.

'What's it like?' Kisa asked, giggling. 'Smell good?'

I took a few more deep breaths, then threw off the towel. My face felt flushed, and streamed with sweat and condensation.

'So?'

'That is the most disgusting thing I've ever done.'

Kisa burst out laughing.

'You've got a flying insect stuck to your forehead,' she managed to say in between fits of laughter.

I blew my nose and various green things flew out.

'Maybe it takes a while to work,' I said. 'I still feel like shit.'

'There could be a reason for that,' Kisa said. 'You've got it all over your face.'

That afternoon I asked Half Ear if he had ever heard of this treatment for flu. His crinkled face contorted into laughter and he shook his head, giving me a look that said blatantly, 'Idiot'. He showed me a leadwood tree and indicated that they used its bark to help with head colds. Elephant dung? No self-respecting Bushman would even dream of sticking their head in a boiling pot of *that*. Never trust a Himba . . .

After three days and nights of counting animals, we joined Raymond for a few beers at sunset. The next day we would head back to Windhoek. I was almost well again (no thanks to my Himba friend's advice), and was certainly well enough for a beer.

Born and bred in Rehoboth, a town south of Windhoek, Raymond had spent a lot of time in Nyae Nyae over the years with his work for WWF. I asked him how he coped with the problems in this part of the world, how he stopped it engulfing him so he could get on with the job at hand.

'You know, Tammie, the Bushies can look after themselves perfectly well. They were doing fine before we got here. They'll be fine after we leave.'

'But it's so hard to ignore the problems. I mean, the alcoholism, the social issues . . .'

'*Ja*, sure, but show me one society that doesn't have that. England, America, even your Australia! The world is changing and they have to adapt to it. Don't worry about them. They don't need your pity. They probably pity you more because you're a woman without a husband!'

We all laughed. It felt good to laugh. I felt some of the Catholic guilt slipping off my shoulders. I wasn't responsible for the horrible history of the Bushmen, only for my actions here and now. I couldn't fix everything that had happened in the past, nor could I repair the social problems, but maybe I could help them sort out their elephant problem. Whether I made a positive or a negative impact was up to me. I'd made a promise to Chief Bobo and I intended to keep it. My role was only small, but I had become a tiny part of the narrative of this enchanting place and I wanted it to be positive.

I realised that I hadn't been laughing enough lately. Despite their problems, the Bushmen were always smiling and laughing. They found humour in everything. I'd been taking my life far too seriously and I really needed to take a leaf out of their book.

'When you don't have much, little things mean a lot,' Raymond went on. 'That's why I always give the Bushies lifts in the car, because it's a little less they have to walk . . . and I pay them in cash, not food, because they have the right to decide how to spend it. That's not for us to decide.'

'That's true,' I conceded.

'You know, this place really is magical. I know they've got their problems, but it's still magic.'

Driving back to Windhoek I got a text from my friend Sal in Australia. She said she kept having a vision of a tall, dark-haired man next to me, his eyes were full of mischief and humour. She wondered if I had a new love interest. And, in an instant, I knew who it was that I had seen sitting outside my tent earlier in the week. It was my friend Mike Hearn, a wonderful young man who had dedicated his life to black rhino conservation in Namibia. Jen and I were writing up the data Mike had collected for his doctoral research, because he had passed away in tragic circumstances several months before. Although I sensed him around me at other times after that, and he contacted Sal many times, the only time I ever saw him was that one time in Bushmanland.

Raymond was right about this place. Bushmanland was so dysfunctional at times that it was hard to see the magic. But that didn't mean it wasn't there.

EIGHT

Ever since I was little I've always been surrounded by animals. I grew up in a town of 130 000 people in North Queensland. My dad was mad about the outdoors, so I spent my childhood fishing and crabbing in the Horton River, snorkelling with sharks and corals on the Great Barrier Reef and camping in the outback of central Queensland. At home, my mum ensured we had a menagerie of pet guinea pigs, cats, dogs and birds. For a little while, my sister even had a pet rat. I'm sure this influenced my decision to become a wildlife conservationist and I know it was pivotal in my younger sister, Kek, becoming a vet. My younger brother, Davo, works in the city, but he has a natural knack with training stud cattle and border collie dogs.

Animals are natural healers. Whenever I was feeling down about anything as a kid, I always found an animal to play with. Scientists tasked with the job of treating people with depression call this 'pet therapy' because of the positive effect that animals have on emotional wellbeing. Let's face it, the unconditional love of a dog is pretty hard to beat (hence my comment about the pug earlier – I was only partially kidding). I've always found that some time with wild animals in the bush has the same effect on my psyche.

The thing about working on human-elephant conflict is that there are two parts to the issue and they're both of equal importance. Up until now I'd been heavily focused on the human part of the story, ensconced in the problems facing the Bushmen. What I needed was some quality time with the elephants so I could see things better through their eyes. When Dries offered Kisa and me the chance to join his team on the Khaudum game count in October I couldn't believe our luck. I knew that some animal time was just what I needed to regain my energy.

Kisa and I met Stacey and Dries at Sigaretti, but just as we were about to set off to our designated waterhole for the next three days and nights, Dries realised there was an emergency. He'd forgotten the vodka. In a mild panic, he told us to head for Tari Kora waterhole and to take Stacey with us. He'd follow us later.

It was great to be back in Khaudum, blasting through the bush over rough sandy tracks covered in elephant dung. I was so happy to be back in the wild I barely noticed the bumps. I followed the signs to Tari Kora and we were there within a couple of hours. Well, that is to say, we were *nearly* there. We could see the camp on the other side of a large waterhole, but we couldn't get to it.

In front of us was a rather large mammalian roadblock. It was a breeding herd of elephants and they weren't moving. Flapping their ears to ease the heat, they didn't seem in a hurry to go anywhere. At the waterhole to our right about fifty elephants were drinking. Yet another herd loitered in the open bush about thirty metres away, raising their trunks in serpentine shapes, smelling us.

I didn't turn off the car, just enjoyed the moment for a little while. It was about eleven in the morning and already close to forty degrees Celsius. It was suicide season, the hottest, driest time of year, when Khaudum gets its famously high concentrations of elephants at waterholes. Dries told me that in last year's count they saw three hundred at just one waterhole and over a thousand there during the course of the three-day count.

We waited, idling for about twenty minutes, thinking that sooner or later the herd would move away or that Dries would come along and help. But the herd had no intention of going anywhere. Every time I eased the Hilux forward a little, the matriarch raised herself up and shook her head at us. With every minute that passed, it was getting hotter. There seemed to be more elephants at the waterhole already; at least sixty now.

'There's Dries,' Stacey said, pointing over to the camp.

Perplexed, I watched his Cruiser pull in under the large acacia trees.

'How did he get there?'

'There must be another road,' Stacey thought out loud. 'I wonder if he can see us.'

She leaned out the window and sat on the door, then began waving her red bandana in the air at him.

'Dries! Over here!'

Although we could see him, Dries was a long way off. There was no way he'd be able to hear us or see Stacey's red bandana.

'Is it a good idea to be waving a red flag when there's this many elephants around?' Kisa whispered.

'Um . . . I wouldn't recommend it,' I said, now beginning to feel tense.

After another twenty minutes, unable to go forward because

of the herd, another lot of elephants emerged from the bush behind us. We were surrounded.

Now, when I said I wanted some elephant time this wasn't exactly what I'd envisioned. An inspiring situation had quickly turned into a frustrating one and could easily become life-threatening. I had been thinking of sitting under a tree with a whiskey and ginger ale watching elephants at a waterhole at sunset from a safe and mutually comfortable distance. There was nothing comforting about this. We were very close to these elephants and they didn't want us there any more than we wanted to be idling there.

I couldn't understand why Dries hadn't spotted us and come over to help. Couldn't he see we were trapped? I watched him through my binoculars. The camp was very basic. It had a wooden hide with two levels built by Raleigh International volunteers and a humble fence made of old railway lines. The latter was to stop the hide being damaged by elephants scratching their butts on it, but it wouldn't have kept any other animals out. I watched Dries casually setting up camp, throwing swags out of the car and putting out camp chairs.

I tried to appear calm, because fear is contagious, but inside I was beginning to panic. If any of these elephants decided to give us a rev, we could only go backwards or forwards into another herd of elephants. The bush on either side was too thick and thorny to drive through. All we could do was to be patient. Unfortunately, I am one of the least patient people in the universe. I am the person who wants everything done yesterday so I can tick off the box and get on with the next thing. I am one of those people who doesn't know how to have a normal holiday because I get bored sitting on a beach for more than a day. Waiting drives me crazy.

But the elephants didn't care about my personal peculiarities.

We were on elephant time now and as far as they were concerned we would have to wait. More and more herds were arriving. As the day heated up, I knew that even more elephants would come to the waterhole for a drink. This problem was going to get worse with time, not better. And we were right in their thoroughfare, parked on an elephant trail.

Waterholes are tense places for breeding herds of elephants. Lions frequently hide nearby, waiting to kill animals when they are drinking and vulnerable. Many different herds come together at waterholes, so there's always lots of greetings and social action. It's where bulls often loiter to look for females in oestrus and their presence among breeding herds can be quite disruptive. By the time elephants get to the waterhole they've walked a long way and they're thirsty. Dehydration makes elephants grumpy, just like people. It must have been frustrating for them not being able to get a drink straightaway because there were others there dominating the source of the water. We were tense, and so were the elephants.

On top of that, I knew that many of the elephants in Khaudum came down from the Caprivi strip, a place of intense conflict between humans and wildlife. Up until just a few years ago, the Caprivi had been embroiled in yet another bloody war started by rebels seeking independence from the Namibian government. Wars are almost always catastrophic for wildlife. Animals may be shot to feed armies or just as easily become amputees from landmines, as villagers do. Who knew what these elephants had experienced in their lives?

Unlike the elephants in Etosha, where there were lots of tourists, the Khaudum elephants' experience with humans was limited and may not have been positive. I felt insecure with these elephants. They could be wary war veterans. I didn't know how to judge them. A hard ear flap was usually enough of an indication that you were too close. A head shake was a warning too. A charge meant you'd overstepped the line. But there were plenty of grey areas when it came to judging elephant behaviour and I was still very much a novice.

After about an hour of waiting for an opportunity to drive through, my impatience got the better of my fear. The elephants behind us had cleared off, but judging by the map it was a long way back to go around the way that Dries had come in. It would take us another hour and a lot of fuel. Fuel was always an issue in this part of the world because the nearest place you could buy it was Grootfontein, almost four hours from Tsumkwe. Just to go and get fuel and come back took about a third of a double tank.

'What do you reckon, girls?' I said, not feeling as brave as I sounded. 'Should we risk it?'

Hesitantly, they both agreed. I edged the Hilux forward. The matriarch slapped her ears and gave me a look that said, 'Don't mess with me'. She thought about it for a second, but I held my ground. Then, to my amazement, she moved slowly off the road. The herd followed her lead. They were still close, just a few metres away, more than close enough to swipe us if they wanted.

'Hold on!'

I revved the engine and put it into second gear, then charged down the road towards them. My heart was beating frantically. The tension in the car was palpable. The huge proboscideans loomed large to the left of the vehicle as I charged past them, but I didn't even look at them. I just focused on the road and held my breath.

'Woohoo!' we all cried out as we made it to the other side of the herd.

But a second later, as we rounded the corner, there was more trouble.

'Oh shit,' Kisa said.

A large bull loomed ominously to our left as he walked out of the bush, striding fast towards the waterhole. He was headed straight towards the road in front of us. If I drove fast I could beat him to it.

'Hold on!' I said again.

I revved the Hilux up and plowed over the rough calcrete tracks at forty kilometres per hour. It was a bumpy ride, filled with expletives. The bull raised his shoulders and shook his head at us as we passed him within a few metres, then carried on along his path to the waterhole. He was more concerned with chatting up the elephant ladies than he was with us.

After the long, tense wait for the elephants to let us pass I was euphoric.

'All in a day's work, Tam?' Kisa commented.

I laughed. My heart was still beating at a million miles an hour.

When we pulled in at Tari Kora, annoyed with Dries for not recognising that we needed help, he didn't pick up on the vibe.

'What took you girls so long?' he said. 'I've done all the hard work setting up camp!'

For the next three days and nights we lived at Tari Kora waterhole. Dries and Stacey slept in a small tent on the ground, while Kisa and I threw our swags on the upper level of the hide and enjoyed a view of the stars. Someone was always on duty, counting animals coming to the waterhole. During the day this was easy and we all looked forward to new animals coming to drink. Nights were harder, particularly the shifts between midnight and four in the morning when all sensible primates should be tucked up in bed.

Tari Kora was the place of the elephant bulls. Males dominated this waterhole, hogging the water like schoolyard bullies, and as a result not many breeding herds bothered to even try to get a drink there. The bulls were afraid of nothing and no one.

During the heat of the day, six bulls stood under the trees that shaded our camp at the hide, just twenty metres away. They rested there for hours, slowly fanning themselves with their ears, their eyes half closed in a Zen-like meditation. They weren't in the least bit bothered by us, treating us just like another inconsequential herd of antelopes. The three- or four-tonne bulls could easily have broken the loose railway wires that separated us from them. Dries told us they'd been scratching on them, which is why the wires were droopy. I sat in the shade, watching the bulls and allowing their restful mood to permeate that of our whole camp. As the afternoon cooled down, the bulls moseyed off one by one, trudging heavily within metres of where we stood inside the psychological boundary of the wire fence.

One came a little too close for comfort, just two metres from the car, approaching more out of curiosity than aggression, I thought. Having dented the Hilux a few weeks earlier when the kudu hit it, I had visions of it also bearing the imprint of an elephant tusk through the bonnet. Dries stood up, held his rifle in the air and took a few confident steps towards him, yelling loudly at him to back off. The bull immediately took a step back, surprised but not alarmed by the outburst of the insignificant human creature. I imagined the elephant chuckling in ultrasound, the sound frequencies that elephants regularly communicate in that are too low for the human ear to detect. Perhaps he was thinking, *You're not worth it, but you're quite funny to watch . . .*

'You almost lost your car, Tammie,' Dries said, chuckling.

Camping out in the park, watching the herds come and go from a single vantage point, gave me a good sense of the utter dependence of elephants on waterholes. The heat in October was overpowering and it created a kind of tension that simmered continuously. Everything was harder in the heat. Walking, talking, even breathing, seemed to take more effort than usual. During the middle of the day, when the sun was at its most vicious, we followed the elephants' lead and rested in the shade, saving our energy. From an elephant perspective, anything that got in the way of a drink of precious water was literally an impediment to survival. And under the strain of the season, when the sun was at its zenith, patience was in short supply for the elephants as much as it was for the people who lived here. No wonder this was when most of the human-elephant conflict seemed to happen.

At dusk on the second day a young roan came in to drink. It was alone, which was odd, and in poor condition. It was too young to be on its own.

'That's food for the lion, that one,' Dries said.

A few hours later we heard the lions making a kill, their roars slicing through the still night like sharp knives.

'Poor little guy,' Stacey said.

The next morning, I woke at four to the sound of Kisa's voice.

'Tam? Lions.'

It was time for my shift and I had lions and dawn insects for company. I peered out from my swag on the first level of the hide, about five metres off the ground. I loved this time of day. Watching the full moon sinking behind the tree line just before the sun rose opposite in a halo of dusty pink, for a few moments I felt as though I owned the whole world. This time belonged to me and Africa alone. The early morning air was crisp and fresh. Francolins, rowdy chickens of the African bush, began squawking. Doves cooed. Four silent lionesses lay near the waterhole while a young male lapped at the water. They looked relaxed and full. A herd of roan barked their displeasure, standing back from the waterhole, waiting for the lions to move off.

I had slept lightly, as always, in the bush, ready to wake in a flash in case we had animal visitors. All night, in random bursts, blacksmith plovers had been going berserk, signifying that something was near their vulnerable nest on the ground near the waterhole. I thought I heard spotted hyaenas giggling maniacally at one stage in the night. All of these sounds of the animal world merged into my subconscious, so that I couldn't tell dream from reality. Later in the morning, Kisa confirmed that a hyaena had come in around three in the morning.

The close proximity of the lions made morning ablutions interesting. I snuck off behind the cars to a termite mound about thirty metres away to pee. That was as far as I was prepared to go in the near darkness with big cats around. Ants desperate for moisture scavenged madly at the wet patch I'd just left on the ground as if they'd found heaven.

A couple of hours later, the rest of the camp woke up. Somehow Stacey emerged from the tent looking like a supermodel, despite none of us having showered in three days in forty degree heat. My skin felt caked in dust and sweat. I had covered my oily hair in a cap that I didn't intend ever to take off in public again.

'Has she got a silent hairdryer that runs on batteries in there?' Kisa whispered.

'I don't know, but I'd kill to have the secret.'

A few hours later, after breakfast of cornflakes and long-life milk, Dries grinned wickedly and announced, 'I want to see that kill. Come with me, kittens.'

Kisa and I gave each other a look that said, 'Is he kidding with this whole kitten thing?'

Before we had left Tsumkwe I'd heard Dries speaking to a mate in Afrikaans on the phone, not realising that I could understand. Roughly translated, he had said, 'You've got to help me, man, I'm going to Tari Kora for game count with three women!'

as if he had been cursed. But his initial trepidation about being in a remote camp with the three of us had faded quickly to a recognition of the perks. Now we feared his status as the lone male had gone to his head. But we all piled obediently into his Landcruiser to see if we could find the lion kill.

Dries charged down the track in the Cruiser, dodging potholes and mounds of dung. An elephant bull moved off the road to let us through, then shook his head at us as if to say, 'Hey, slow down, you almost killed me, you maniac!' We left the car on the road and followed Dries on foot across a grassy clearing in the direction of a group of vultures he'd spotted in a tree. The elephant bull watched us from a distance of about fifty metres. I was well aware of the risk we were taking by walking up to a fresh lion kill. I'd done the same thing in Etosha not so long ago and found myself the target of a pride of lions that had seen me as a threat to their carcass. I knew what it felt like to be prey and it wasn't fun. The grass in the clearing we were now walking across to a fresh kill was man-height in places, perfect for hiding big tawny cats the colour of dried grass. Dries didn't seem worried, clutching his 4.16 by his side.

'What are you going to do if the lions come back?' I asked him.

'Well, there's three of you and one of me. I've got the gun. So I thought I'd offer one of you as bait.'

'Which one?' Kisa asked.

'I haven't decided yet.'

A flurry of avian scavengers had gathered at a point not far from the tree with the vultures, picking with their strong beaks at what had to be the carcass. There was nothing left of the roan but the skin and the bones of one leg with the hoof still attached.

'You know, I burned my finger on a marshmallow last night when I was toasting it on the fire,' I said to Kisa. 'It really hurt.'

I paused for effect.

'It's still sore . . .' I went on, 'but, you know, this kind of puts that into perspective.'

'Well, yeah . . .' Kisa gave me a quizzical look.

There's nothing like some quality time in the bush in Africa to give you a healthy dose of perspective. Between the elephants and the lions and the melodramas with marshmallows, life was looking up again.

NINE

'Hello. I am pleased to meet you. You are welcome here. I am Lina Chipalunga and I am *beautiful*. Don't you think I am beautiful?'

The large African woman pulled me into the ample folds of her enormous bosom and squeezed me tightly. After what seemed like a long while later, my face emerged from her cleavage in a film of sweat.

This was how I met the Ministry of Education's representative for the village schools of Bushmanland. And, indeed, she was beautiful in the African way; that being, the larger you are, the more attractive. Resplendent in a bright lime green dress that ballooned off her voluptuous curves and swallowed her neck in a feminine frill of white lace, how could I disagree?

'I have been here eleven years and let me tell you something, lady. What is your name again?'

'Tammie.'

'Tam-mie. I like it. Very beautiful,' she paused, contemplating the sound of my name as she eased her vast bulk into a comfortable lounge chair. The cushion made a loud farting sound as she sank into it, but she didn't seem to notice.

'Tammie, most of these San children, they are afraid of Tsumkwe. They haven't even been to Grootfontein. This is why we have the village schools. If there was no village schools, these San children would be getting no education. They are afraid.'

'Afraid of what?'

'Tsumkwe.'

'You mean, of the bigger children?'

'Ja . . . many things. If you want to take them to this environmental camp you are talking about, this will be making me very happy, but you must be taking their teachers too, okay? Otherwise, these San children they will be too afraid.'

After four months my fieldwork was almost complete. I had visited all of the sites for which there was a record of human-elephant conflict in the last five years and recorded the appropriate data. With Stacey and Leon I had surveyed most of the villages in the conservancy, obtaining interviews from about fifty people, men, women, adults and children. Now came the harder and less fun part – statistically analysing the data and finding out the results.

It was just in the nick of time because my work visa with Wilderness Safaris was about to run out and Dave wasn't confident that he'd be able to get me another one. That meant I didn't have much of a choice. Even though I would have loved to stay longer I wasn't prepared to remain in the country without a valid visa again. Without a visa after the middle of December, I would have no job and no income. Whether I liked it or not, I was being forced to move on. I tried to look on the bright side. I knew I would be back and in a sense the timing was good. I had to return to Australia because my first book, *Dry Water*, was being released. But there was one more thing I had to do before I left.

As Dries had pointed out the first time we had met, plenty of researchers who work in Africa get their data, have a wonderful time and then return to their own country with a sparkly new qualification, but the people in Africa never see the results or get any benefit from it. I was determined to ensure that my research had real outcomes for the Bushmen.

I had some leftover funding that I had decided early on that I would put towards environmental education for the children in Bushmanland. If we could get the next generation of Bushmen thinking positively about the opportunities that elephants offered rather than just the problems, then I figured that could only be a good thing. Jen and I had co-written a children's book on the life of a baby elephant growing up in a conflict zone, and a pilot friend, Flo Kohl, formerly a graphic artist, had provided the colourful illustrations. We called it *An Elephant's Tale*. I put the extra funding I'd secured into printing enough colour copies of the book for every child in Nyae Nyae's five village schools.

While I was working for Wilderness Safaris, I had learned about a program they ran twice a year called Children in the Wilderness. The program took groups of kids affected by HIV/AIDS or poverty, aged between seven and fourteen, literally into the wilderness to learn about the environment and build their confidence. I suggested to the Children in the Wilderness team in Namibia that they might like to take a group of Bushmen children on the next camp. If they did, I would help pay for the kids' transport to and from the camp with the last of my project funding. To my delight, there was a camp being run in December and Wilderness Safaris agreed to my suggestion.

Now that I had Mrs Chipalunga's approval, it was arranged for ten children from Nyae Nyae to take part in Children in the Wilderness at Wilderness Safaris' Palmwag Rhino Camp in Damaraland. Jen and I decided we would join the program for a few days to see how the Bushmen children went, taking with us lots of copies of our children's book to use in the activities. There were ten children from Nyae Nyae, aged between ten and thirteen, none of whom had ever travelled further than their nearest large town, Grootfontein. These children rarely went further than their own village, only very occasionally to Tsumkwe, so, as Mrs Chipalunga had said, this was a big deal for them. Travelling to the opposite side of the country into the red, rocky desert of Damaraland was like going to another world.

The Bushmen kids were joined in the camp by ten children from the Kavango Region north of Bushmanland. They were the same age but a lot bigger. Traditionally, Kavango people bullied the Bushmen and I was told this still happened in the primary school in Tsumkwe. But there was none of that on this camp. Many of the children who were selected were orphans or HIV positive and had never known such generosity. As the kids from Bushmanland had no shoes, some of the girls at Wilderness Safaris had thrown a fundraiser involving large quantities of cocktails so that they would have something to put on their feet. For the whole week all of the children were treated like royalty.

Over the course of the week, the five-star luxury camp was completely closed off to tourists and the children were guided by topnotch Wilderness Safaris guides. They piled into game-viewing vehicles usually reserved for high-paying tourists, drove through exclusive wilderness areas, and were taken up close and personal to animals some of them had never seen before.

Many of the children had been terrified of elephants, because of what I now understood to be their terribly *bad* reputations in the villages. But now, seeing elephants up close in broad daylight, feeding and drinking and being quite peaceful, they saw a different side to them, a side that was awe-inspiring. The children saw black rhinos for the first time in their lives and learned the names of the desert plants they ate. They learned about the holes in the dry riverbeds that elephants dig to get water, helping other animals to drink too by providing access to underground streams. They learned the differences between elephant and rhino dung by the texture and the types of partially digested plants they contained. They talked with the guides and with each other about the problems with these animals and shared their fears. Most importantly, the guides showed them how wildlife tourism could help in a place like this so that wildlife and people could live together and benefit from each other's presence.

'Why are we needing to shoot the elephants?' the camp director and safari guide, Sunday Nilenge, asked the kids in his lively, expressive way, throwing his arms around like a music conductor.

Sunday was a ball of energy, jumping around the group with his long bandy legs, breaking into cackles of laughter often, his eyes wide and kind as he listened to the children and gave hugs randomly to whoever was standing close by. He told stories with his whole body, using his legs and his arms and his face to express the words with so much enthusiasm that at times it seemed as though he might self-combust. The children were captivated by him, and the best thing was, he'd grown up the hard way, just like them. He was a Namibian who'd worked his way up from the bottom and now he was a role model.

'The elephant . . . He is just like you and me! He is needing water and food and personal space, just like the people. He is showing the other animals where to find water. Ah yes!

The elephant! And *remember*, the tourists are coming to see the elephants, so you see, guys like me and Kapoi and John are all having jobs.'

We sat in small groups one afternoon going through our elephant book with the children. Many of them couldn't read English, but the pictures told the story of a small elephant, Ilala, who had grown up in a place where she did all the things that human children do – eating, drinking, playing. When her mother, the matriarch, was killed by men wielding guns and spears, the herd ran away until they found a place that was safe (a lot like Nyae Nyae Conservancy). In this safe place, people came to see the elephants and everyone lived together happily. It sounds a bit corny telling it like this, but the book was so popular in Nyae Nyae's village schools that recently, Trine Wengen, a Norwegian friend and dedicated community worker who lived in Tsumkwe, had these books translated into Ju/'hoan.

The Bushmen were exceptionally shy compared to the other kids, rarely asking questions or making direct eye contact. But when it came to elephants, a couple of them spoke up. Mr Haikera, the principal, translated what a little girl said.

'She is from the village where the woman was killed by elephants in 2002. She says that the MET didn't get the right elephant. They shot the wrong one. The killer is still roaming around trying to get people.'

Before I could answer, another child spoke, a small boy.

'How can you know if an elephant is a killer?' Mr Haikera translated.

'Well, not all elephants kill people. It's only when they feel threatened by people or sometimes when the males are in musth, when they are looking for mates, they can become aggressive. You can tell this by the stink and by the moisture dripping from the side of the bull's face. But that doesn't make him a killer.

Elephants don't like to hurt people. They eat plants, not meat. If you give them lots of space, there is no problem.'

A few of the kids nodded, but even to me my answer sounded inadequate. I knew perfectly well that while humans and elephants shared the same environment, a space that was becoming smaller and smaller, some conflict was inevitable. It was no wonder these children felt afraid.

Towards the end of the camp, the Bushmen began to open up a little more. Whereas at the beginning they were extremely shy and hesitant to participate in the activities, now they were jumping around in their oversized shoes and singing raucously with the best of them. The Children in the Wilderness camp would be something these children would remember forever. Their experiences would be discussed around the campfires with their families for months afterwards. And maybe, just maybe, some of these ten would go on to be leaders in the conservancy, responsible for the management of their wildlife in the future.

On the last night, Sunday asked everyone to write a wish on a small piece of paper. Everyone formed a circle around the campfire, holding hands. I had a little Kavango boy on one side and a Bushman girl on the other. One by one, everyone walked to the fire at the centre and threw their piece of paper into the flames.

When everyone was done, Sunday became sombre, his eyes earnest.

'Now, everybody,' he said in a low, deep voice, 'the big man up there is listening to us.'

He paused, letting the gravity of that sink in. Not a peep could be heard. A number of the children looked up to the sky, where the stars glittered the way they do only in the middle of the desert.

'Let's all have two minutes of silence while your wishes are being considered.'

I felt goose bumps prickle my skin as a blanket of stillness descended upon the gathering and I found myself praying for every one of these children's wishes to come true. I prayed for their happiness, for their lives to be successful, for them always to have enough food in their bellies. I prayed for them to get educated beyond grade four (the standard level in Bushmanland, if they were lucky) and I prayed for their culture to survive the bombardment of outside influences that was bound to increase over time. But above all, I prayed for them to remember what they'd learned about elephants, to see them not as a threat but as an asset to their communities. Like Sunday had said, elephants were just like them. If these children could take that message home with them, who knew what it could achieve.

Looking at their small faces illuminated by the flickering flames, I imagined all the wishes of these children rising like silver halogen balloons into the desert night, the silent heartfelt pleas held within. My own wishes rose with theirs. I felt more hope then than I'd felt in my entire time in Bushmanland. This was the future. Right here, in this camp, was the difference between elephants being seen as the problem or the solution. My heart swelled with emotion.

I knew it was absurd, but standing around that campfire I felt truly *connected*. Connected to what, I wasn't sure. But definitely connected to *something* in this place and with these people. Something strong and deep. Something that went back a very long way. Maybe I was feeling the ancestors. Perhaps all our combined prayers had drawn in some higher power, and whatever it was, I felt very sure that it was listening to our wishes that night.

I felt so grateful to have been a part of the world of the Bushmen, if only in a small way and for a short time. I would never forget them. They had become a part of my world more than I had become a part of theirs. To them, I would be less than a pinprick in their long and complex history, a past that had known more exploitation and deprivation than my tribe ever had. When I'd made my promise to the chief the year before, he'd been smiling knowingly. Perhaps he already knew back then that it would be me who would be smiling later.

I didn't want my conversation with the Bushmen to end. I felt as though I'd only just picked up the receiver and started listening properly. But it was too late. An operator with an Australian accent was butting in.

'Your call has been disconnected. We apologise for any inconvenience. Goodbye.'

'If you want to meet a man, Tammie, Sydney is not the place to do it. The good ones are taken and the rest are gay. Trust me.'

I was sipping chardonnay at a plush restaurant on Sydney Harbour with my new book publisher, editor and publicist, and yes, you guessed it, the conversation had switched from Africa to men already. I was staying at a five-star hotel that overlooked the famous Harbour Bridge and the distinctive arches of the Sydney Opera House. It was a dazzling sight. The water on the harbour shimmered with luminescent reflections of the city lights. High-rise buildings towered over us, aglow with office lights and red neon signs. Sydney is a city that literally glitters.

Despite my publicist's well-meant advice, I wasn't here to meet a man. There wasn't nearly enough khaki and stubble in Sydney for me. I was here to sell my book.

'Surely the pickings must be better on that front in Africa?' my publicist went on.

'That depends,' I replied, 'on how much you like khaki.'

A gathering of teenage girls wearing the latest in cocktail

dresses was posing for cameras nearby. They leaned provocatively over the rails, pouting like sex kittens.

'They're from *Australia's Next Top Model*,' my publicist said; then, recognising my blank look; 'You know, the television show.'

Of course.

The next morning I was scheduled to do an interview and photo shoot for a Sunday magazine. I hoped they didn't want any pouting like that out of me. My publicist had lined up a daunting schedule of radio interviews, book launches and signings all over eastern Australia to coincide with the release of my book *Dry Water*. All I had to do was be myself, she said, and tell a few stories from the book, preferably the ones that involved me nearly getting eaten by lions.

The next few weeks passed in a dazzling array of fancy hotels, radio studios and photo shoots. My boots and boyangs were replaced by stilettos and stockings. The loose khaki shorts became tight skirts or dark jeans. Instead of spending my days with the Bushmen under a baobab talking about elephants, my time was spent with gushing PR people proffering piles of books to sign. It was very flattering to be the centre of attention, and believe me, I wasn't complaining. It just seemed a little odd.

I knew what a privilege it was to have a book published and a publisher willing to publicise it. I was immensely grateful for that. But, in truth, I think a lot of the experience was wasted on me. I was in culture shock.

The sheer wealth and luxury of life in Australia compared with rural Africa was overwhelming. What started as guilt for having so much more was soon became replaced by anger. It just wasn't fair. Why should people living in the west have such a high standard of living when people in Africa had so little? No one gets to pick what family they're born into. It's just the luck of the draw whether you're born in a famine in Ethiopia or in a fancy Beverly Hills hospital. How could governments allow this to happen? How could we all ignore it?

How could I throw money away on cappuccinos and cheesecake when the Bushmen were lucky if they got enough mealie meal to make pap? I watched people complaining about our hospital system on the news and thought of the old lady dying in her village in Nyae Nyae, who'd been turned away from the clinic with a few Panadol tablets. I saw people dropping out of university degrees that the government gave them a loan for *up front*, when most of the Bushmen weren't even going to make it through primary school. My stomach always churned over the twisted dichotomy of unchosen fates when I came back to Australia. This was nothing new. Once you've seen the great divide between the west and the rest, it's hard to forget it. But my discontent with life in Australia got even worse after Bushmanland.

I think I finally realised that for all our luxury, we weren't really any better off in the west. People weren't all that happy. Rural Africans living on less than $1 a day seemed to laugh more freely than we did. In Australia, I knew too many people with depression and several whose lives had been touched by the suicides of friends or family. I heard that more people died due to suicide than to road accidents. We had everything we needed in a material sense. We had big cars, bigger houses and went on holiday to the South Pacific, but we *still* weren't happy. What was it going to take? When would we have enough? We had so much food that we had issues with obesity and diabetes. How on earth does *that* happen in a world where millions of people still die of starvation?

I remembered a conversation I'd had with Leon not long back. He told me he had been to America twice to translate John Marshall's films. I tried to imagine my quietly spoken translator, the son of Chief Bobo, standing in the middle of New York looking up at the high-rises and flagging down a taxi.

'Did you try a McDonald's burger?' Kisa asked him.

'*Ja,* I did, but this hamburger, I couldn't eat it,' he laughed. 'It was too big!'

I had a vision of this little Bushman trying to shovel an American-sized meal into his mouth.

'Those people in America, they were crazy!' Leon exclaimed, laughing from the bottom of his belly.

It seemed to me that the *ease* of life in the west was slowly killing us. My wise friend Sal once said that even the word 'disease' seems to suggest that ease could be an ailment: dis-ease. Could it be that apathy was just a symptom of a culture overtaken by all the wrong priorities? How did it come to be that we now had a malaise born of excesses of all the good things in life? If the television was anything to go by, Australia wasn't alone. This was a phenomenon in much of the western world.

On the rare occasion I broached this with people it came out sounding all wrong. I could imagine them walking away thinking, *It's okay for Little Miss Piety to go live in the middle of nowhere in a tent then come back preaching, but I like my three-bedroom house and sports car and I* ain't *giving them up, sister!* The thing was, that wasn't my point. I liked those things too (well, maybe not the sports car; I'm more of a Land Rover kind of girl). I wasn't suggesting we should throw away all the good things that human development has brought into our lives and go and live as monks in Nepalese caves. No siree. I was all for my comfortable bed, dishwasher and designer shoes. I didn't want to throw any of that stuff out. It was just that it seemed to me that we all needed a little less stuff and a bit more perspective over here. *We really had nothing to be complaining about.*

I moved in with my friend Shelby on the Sunshine Coast in

Queensland. Shelby, a fellow zoologist, had worked with Aboriginal people in Kakadu National Park and had a great passion for their welfare. We'd known each other since university and she knew more than most how hard it always was for me to adjust to life back in Australia. It had taken her a while, but she now had an active social life at the coast and, while she missed the Northern Territory, she felt grounded in her new home. It gave me hope that if Shelby could adjust back to a normal life, in time I might be able to as well.

I threw myself into it with as much enthusiasm as I could muster. During the week I publicised my book and worked on a novel that I'd started years before. At weekends we hit the pubs and the beaches. At twenty-nine, like me, Shelby was recently single. Her good looks, vivacious personality and fun-loving streak meant that she was always attracting adventure and more than her share of eligible bachelors.

'We're getting old, Tamsticks! We have to get out there and make it happen. No one else is going to do it for us. Here, put some lippy on! We're going to a house party.'

At the party in a high-rise overlooking Mooloolaba's Alexandra Beach, the girls looked like supermodels in glamorous short dresses and stiletto heels. G-strings poked provocatively above tight hipster jeans. Fake breasts bulged from low-slung tops. The boys were surfers, bronzed and fit, clearly enjoying the view. There were a lot more girls than guys. Shelby flitted in and out of the crowd like a magnificent colourful butterfly and, feeling like a lost moth, I trailed her. I downed a glass of white wine quickly and grabbed another.

'Tam, this is Rachael. She owns this place,' Shelby introduced me to one of the cocktail glamour girls.

'Hi, Tammie! Shel's told me all about you. I've always wanted to go to Africa,' the girl said. 'You have to meet Pete. He was just there last month.'

Rachael led me by the hand across the pounding dance floor to a veranda where a group of guys was leaning over the rails drinking beers. I glanced back and saw that Shelby had disappeared into the crowd.

'Dare you to puke on the next person that walks by,' I heard one of them say.

'You have to see this, Rach!' I heard someone call from inside.

I felt the woman's grip on my hand loosen then slip as she was dragged back into the house.

I stood there at the edge of the veranda, wondering which way to run. The decision was made for me. A drunk person fell against my back from the writhing dance floor, pushing me into the crowd of boys. I felt my wineglass slip from my grip and the liquid flew across the room, soaring through the air and right into the middle of the gathering of guys. The unintended victim saw it coming. He closed his eyes as the wine splattered across his chest in what seemed to me to be slow motion, but other than that he didn't flinch.

'Oh geez, I'm sorry,' I blurted.

One of them came up to me, put his arm around my shoulder and said, 'You know, you should never, never waste alcohol. It's a cardinal sin.'

I could smell the beer on his breath, heavy and humid in my ear. I felt nauseous, like I was going to throw up.

'Hey, you look a bit white. Are you gonna spew?'

I felt the world spinning. One of them pushed me down onto a plastic chair. I put my head between my knees and let the spinning subside. Someone passed me another glass of wine, but I pushed it aside.

'What's wrong with her?' I heard someone say distantly.

God, if only you knew, I thought. *I'm a foreigner in my own land. That's what's wrong. I don't belong here. I wish it was different, but it just isn't. I don't want to be standing here pissed with no idea what to say to anyone. I want to be sitting around a campfire in Bushmanland listening to the drums.*

In Africa I'd always had a strong sense of purpose because I was always fulfilling some dream or other. Back in Australia, I had everything I needed and nothing I wanted. Without a mission, I felt lost and aimless. But much as I wanted to, I couldn't just up and go back to Namibia yet. All of the doors that had been open to me there a year ago had closed for the time being. I had no visa and no job there. I was being forced to re-enter my old world, whether I liked it or not.

I got a job as a waitress, working in a café in Buderim, a quaint town in the Sunshine Coast hinterland full of retirees, and worked nights serving champagne and canapés to wealthy socialites hosting parties for their friends. I embarked on a mission to reintegrate with Australian society. I mean, it couldn't be that bad, could it? I should have been loving this. The weather was fantastic. The beaches were magnificent. The surfers were hot. Sooner or later the balmy, hedonistic beach atmosphere was bound to rub off on me. I would forget that I'd ever been to Africa and I would just be normal.

The problem was, no matter how much I tried to act normally, no one saw me that way. I went to dinner parties and pubs with lots of other singles my age who were caught up in the almost-thirty panic. Most of them had ticked a few of the necessary boxes already. Some had a house and a mortgage or enough savings for a house deposit. Some had the man but not the ring on their finger. Some had the kid but not the man. A few had done a bit of travelling. But I was definitely the only one who hadn't ticked *any* of the most important boxes. No house. No savings. No man. No kid. Not even a proper job or a financial plan. Things were grim. At best, at I was a novelty item at dinner parties. At worst, a complete failure.

My younger sister, with a five-year-old daughter, a fiancé and a full-time job, had once been the rebellious one in the family. Now it appeared that without even trying I was the one who had slid off the rails of acceptable society. My mum sent me an email with a proverb about apples. I can't remember it exactly but it said something along the lines of the last apple on the tree being the best one of all. It was well meant, but *ooooouch*. It was a stark reminder that by the standards of regional Australia I was running the risk of becoming the weird family spinster who handed out orange socks and expired chocolates at Christmas. When your mum sends you messages about apples, you know things are serious.

I'd never had any regrets about spending the best part of my twenties in Africa working as a conservationist up until then, but now, single, broke and without a home to call my own, I began to catch the almost-thirty panic that had gripped a number of my friends like a contagious virus. I wondered, had the wrinkles really been worth it? In this world they weren't badges of honour but shackles of shame. Over a decade in Africa and what did I really have to show for it other than a good tan and a pair of well-worn boots? After all, tans always fade and sooner or later you've got to throw the boots away.

TEN

Then again, some boots never need to get thrown out. The more scratches and scuffs and holes in them, the more you like them. You know the ones I mean? They may not have much grip left on the soles, but they still do the job. Wearing them is a whole lot better than wearing in a new pair.

After a few months at the Sunshine Coast, the opportunity came up to do some research for the Namibian government, investigating potential reintroduction sites for black-faced impalas in the communal conservancies of the Kunene region. It took all of two minutes for me to decide that I'd put my boots on again and head back to the desert. I spent three weeks in Namibia's arid north-west looking at the habitats in each of the conservancies, considering their potential to support small populations of black-faced impala sourced from Etosha's growing population. Camping out in tents with my new assistant, Munekamba, and James Watson, a friend and ecologist from Australia, we did a lot of driving over enormous distances in search of good habitat with reliable, permanent water and the right shrubs for black-faced impala to eat.

It was here, on my very first night in the desert, before James arrived, that Munekamba and I were paid a visit by those two elephant bulls, one of them almost standing on top of my tiny pup tent. For the first time I understood what it was really like to live with elephants, to be truly afraid of an animal that could crush a human in an instant. And after that, although I was focused on impalas for the job at hand, elephants remained at the forefront of my mind.

For one thing, we were seeing a lot of them. Despite the aridity of north-west Namibia, there were plenty of elephants around, breeding herds and bulls tracing the dry riverbeds as part of their migratory routes. On the way to visit a remote Wilderness Safaris camp on the Hoanib River, which my old mates Sally and Jeremy Henderson were managing for a few months, I watched tall bulls shaking the pods out of giant Ana trees. The pods that fell provided nourishment not only for the elephant but for the oryx antelopes and baboons waiting nearby for the left-overs. I marvelled at yet another example of the elephant's role in the ecosystems of Africa. Sal told me an old bull was hanging around the camp like a sentinel, a presence she found comforting rather than confronting.

Elephants looked different here. They seemed dwarfed by the stark, gigantic environment of the north-west Namibian desert, astounding for an animal that weighs several tonnes. They blended in perfectly, in contrast to my white Hilux, which was more cockatoo than chameleon, as I negotiated the thick sand tracks along the dry riverbeds. These desert-dwelling elephants were tough, adapted to a life of extremes in which the respite of rain was fleeting and limited.

I couldn't help but notice that people in the Kunene region also had problems with human-elephant conflict. As in Nyae Nyae, concrete enclosures had been erected around boreholes and windmills and large round cement cribs had been built to provide water. I wondered whether these methods were reducing their problems.

At the end of my impala work I grabbed the chance to return to Bushmanland. I had a cardboard box full of *An Elephant's Tale* to hand out to each of the village schools and a couple of versions of the final report from my study. I wanted to deliver the findings in person to Dries, Chief Bobo and the conservancy chairman, Kievet. It was just the excuse I needed to go back to Bushmanland.

It was early August, the middle of winter and excruciatingly cold at night. Sleeping on the ground in a small pup tent, I shivered all night in the Kalahari chill. But it was worth it. It felt like coming home.

It turned out there were a few simple things that could be done to reduce human-elephant conflicts in the region. Some of them were already being done. Since the first couple of 'bombproof' enclosures made of concrete and rock had been erected to protect water installations near villages in 2004, human-elephant conflicts had begun to reduce. Most of the conflicts in the last five years happened in the hot dry season, just as Dries had said, and the majority were caused by small herds of elephants, most likely bulls. The data suggested that conflicts were less likely to happen when villages and water sources were further apart. Concrete cribs like the ones we'd seen in Khaudum seemed to help reduce the amount of conflict.

It wasn't rocket science. Keep the drinking places for elephants far away from villages so that they don't go into villages to get water, and make sure that elephants have enough clean water where they drink. I didn't need to spell it out in complicated scientific language. I just needed to let Dries, Chief Bobo and Kievet know that they were on the right track with the protection of water installations and the cement cribs. I had to let them know that our social survey suggested that people were happy to have elephants around as long as they were getting benefits through the trophy-hunting operation and tourism. Opportunities for sustainable incomes and employment through wildlife were the way forward, and I needed to encourage the leaders to keep this going.

During the game count in Khaudum, I had told Dries how I'd been hesitant to take on an elephant project because of the egos associated with working on them. One well-known elephant researcher had already replied to an email of mine in such a condescending fashion that I determined never to speak to him again (mature, I know). Another simply refused to talk to me full stop.

'Well, fuck 'em, Tammie. You've got my support,' Dries said, with surprising conviction.

It was the closest thing I ever got to an acknowledgement that just maybe he had recognised me as being on the same team as him (provided the rugby wasn't on).

'You know,' he went on, 'simply going out to the villages and talking to people will get them talking to each other and saying, 'Why are they asking us about elephants?' It makes them realise elephants are important. So this is already raising awareness in the community, which is probably more valuable than any research anyone has ever done here.'

He was probably exaggerating, but even so, I was touched.

After giving Dries an official copy of the report, he put the word out to find the chief. As usual, it wasn't easy. After roaming all over Bushmanland, I finally found him at his family's house in Tsumkwe. His scrawny royal buttocks were perched on the dusty back step of the small prefab building, surrounded by an assortment of old and young women. He was so thin I wondered if a strong gust of wind might blow him away like a lightweight plastic shopping bag. His clothes hung off a frame too skinny to be healthy. This was a sign of the reality for the Bushmen, that in stark contrast to every other fat chief in Africa, theirs was a slither of a man without even a paunch.

He coughed often. I wondered if he, like so many of his people, was suffering from TB. There was nothing about the old man that wasn't shrivelled. As he closed his eyes for a moment, I noticed that even his eyelids were wrinkled. And yet, skinny and coughing, perched on a dusty step, he had the regal presence of a chief. On his head he wore his famous felt navy blue cowboy hat brandishing a purple feather. I had never seen him without his hat, glued to his head like an extra appendage, a crown for the king of the wild west.

A demented August wind was whipping through Tsumkwe, vehemently hurling clouds of dust down the street in choking waves. I sat in the winter sun on a wobbly, old, cracked plastic chair and spoke to the chief through a translator named Beesa. Renegade strands of hair thrashed around my face in the wind, refusing to be tamed. Wind drove me crazy, but it didn't seem to worry Chief Bobo. I wondered if he would be quite so peaceful and mellow if he had straight unruly hair like mine that the wind used like monkey demons to torment me, and not sensible, stable peppercorns. It was yet another example of how much better adapted these people were to the land than we westerners.

I asked Beesa to ask the chief if he remembered me.

He shook his head, nonplussed.

Slightly embarrassed on my behalf, Beesa said he did not.

Feeling mildly disappointed, I reminded him about the

elephant project and the work I'd done the year before with Leon, his son, trying to find some solutions to the elephant problems.

Recognition lit up the old man's haggard face and he became suddenly animated, as if the mention of his son had triggered a lost memory.

'*Ja, ja! Ek viet!* Yes, yes! I know!' he exclaimed.

I tried not to show my relief, which was difficult, being one of those people who wears their feelings on their sleeve. The chief spoke with Beesa for a moment in Ju/'hoan. When he'd finished speaking, slowly and crookedly he rose to his feet and stood there, slightly stooped.

'What did he say?' I asked, thinking I must have offended him.

'He says he has some business to do in town, but he wants to talk to you. Can we come back in two hours?'

'Yes, yes. Of course.'

We agreed to meet at his house a little later, knowing that two hours could mean two days. I wondered if he was going to the clinic to get some medicine for his cough. In the meantime, we went out to Kievet's village.

Kievet looked even smaller and older than Chief Bobo. He lived at Baraka, a village about twenty kilometres east of Tsumkwe and home of the old conservancy office. Kievet peered at me with crinkled Mongolian eyes that were light blue and cloudy. I wondered if he could see me at all. His head was covered in black peppercorns flecked with grey. We sat around on a circle of old plastic chairs, several men from the conservancy listening in too, and I had the floor. I handed Kievet a copy of the report for the conservancy's records. I didn't think he'd be able to read English, so the gesture was more symbolic than anything

Kievet was incredibly gracious and humble. He smiled as he took the report in his arthritic hands and said, '*Meeweeha*'.

ANDY RIDLEY

Elephant watching from a boat in Chobe National Park, Botswana.

The textured old face of an elephant, rich with character and wisdom.

TAMMIE MATSON

TAMMIE MATSON

Malvern Karidozo (left) of the Elephant Pepper Development Trust pays a local lady for the chillies she has grown and picked at a Zambian village. The Trust provides a guaranteed buyer through affiliated company African Spices for chillies grown by local villagers.

Mr Kanga proudly shows off his chilli plants on his land, an Elephant Pepper Development Trust demonstration farm, at the outskirts of Livingstone, Zambia. The farm is protected by a chilli fence (seen in the background).

ANDY RIDLEY

Getting a better view of South Luangwa National Park savannah from on top of a landrover in Zambia.

TAMMIE MATSON

Chilli briquettes: a combination of dried elephant dung and chillies mixed together. A hot coal is placed on top and the burning briquettes are placed around the perimeter of a crop. The strong chilli smoke is what helps keep elephants away.

TAMMIE MATSON

This Zambian woman allegedly used to 'rat' (survive on rats) for a living with her infant daughter, but now spends her days earning a better living picking chillies in Livingstone.

TAMMIE MATSON

Fiery red chillies ripening in Zambia – the humble chilli is one weapon being used in the fight to reduce human-elephant conflict.

TAMMIE MATSON

An elephant calf in Chobe National Park takes in the smell of a car of tourists.

TAMMIE MATSON

A thirsty herd of elephants thunders down to the water of the Chobe River for a drink and a bath. The excitement of a herd approaching water on a hot day is something to behold.

TAMMIE MATSON

An elephant calf digs for salt, an important natural supplement in elephant diets.

TAMMIE MATSON

A temperamental bull in musth charges the car in Hwange National Park, Zimbabwe.

TAMMIE MATSON

An amazing picnic lunch on an island in the Zambezi River near Ntwala Camp, just moments before Andy proposed in May 2008.

Camera set up – TAMMIE MATSON

Andy and I in Zambia.

TAMMIE MATSON

Elephants drink and bathe in the cooling waters of the Chobe River in Botswana on a sunny autumn day.

Dries Alberts (left), Stacey Main (centre) and I play cards while waiting for animals to come to the waterhole during the annual October 72-hour game count in Khaudum National Park, Namibia.

KISA ASHBOLT

Jen tucks into some lunch on the back of the Hilux in a break from exploring Nyae Nyae Conservancy.

TAMMIE MATSON

Leon (right) and I interview Chief Bobo (centre) as part of their social survey of the Bushmen on human-elephant conflict in Nyae Nyae Conservancy.

TAMMIE MATSON

TAMMIE MATSON

A springbok catches some shade on a hot day at the Nyae Nyae pan. During the dry season the salt pans dry up, but in the wet, flamingos, wattled cranes and many other migratory water birds flock to the temporary wetlands they provide.

Elephant bulls are generally more approachable than breeding herds of females with young. This bull in Khaudum approached the group curiously until they decided he was close enough and retreated.

TAMMIE MATSON

Elephants congregate around a crib on a hot day in Khaudum in September, while others wait in the background for a turn to drink.

There's something about baobabs that makes you want to talk to them. Here, Kisa, Ron and I are dwarfed by a giant tree (though not the biggest in the region).

TAMMIE MATSON

During the Children in the Wilderness camp, the kids explored Damaraland with experienced safari guides, learning about the animals and gaining confidence in their own abilities.

TAMMIE MATSON

TAMMIE MATSON

Two children from Half Ear's family jump in the back of my Hilux to see some elephants coming to drink nearby at the Klein Dobe waterhole.

Sunday Nilenge and a young boy from Bushmanland share a joke next to an ancient welwitschia in Damaraland during the Children in the Wilderness camp.

TAMMIE MATSON

Children at Klein Dobe camp gather excitedly around Kisa as she shows them photos of themselves.

TAMMIE MATSON

Kievet, the chairman of Nyae Nyae Conservancy, looks at the children's book about elephants that I produced with Jennifer Lalley and Flo Kohl for the conservancy's village schools.

Leon (left) and Stacey (centre) conduct an interview at a village in Nyae Nyae Conservancy, seeking to better understand how people feel about elephants.

TAMMIE MATSON

Eye to eye with an elephant bull.

TAMMIE MATSON

A tea garden in Assam where women work tirelessly to prune and harvest the valuable leaves. Assam produces most of India's tea.

TAMMIE MATSON

Bicycle load by bicycle load – this is how the forests of Assam are now disappearing. First it was the clearing of forests for tea gardens, then for commercial logging, now it is to provide wood for impoverished families.

TAMMIE MATSON

Kunkies and their mahouts patrol a recently harvested rice paddy at dusk, preparing to drive any wild elephants away from the crops. Elephants typically raid crops at night under the cover of darkness.

TAMMIE MATSON

A less than comfortable sight: the shackled leg of a captive elephant in India. Mahouts chain elephants to trees when they aren't occupied with their work.

TAMMIE MATSON

A mahout gets a leg up onto a *kunkie*'s back.

TAMMIE MATSON

Greater one-horned rhino, Kaziranga National Park, Assam. This male may have been attacked by another rhino, judging by the bleeding gash on his flank.

NAFISA NAOMI

Villagers in north-east Assam share their human-elephant conflict problems with me.

NAFISA NAOMI

These are the boxes of firecrackers and guns used to deter elephants from crops at night in rural Assam.

Andy and I ride a majestic captive elephant bull called Anendan in Kerala, India – seeing the world from an elephant's point of view gave me a different perspective.

A Forestry Department staff member rides an elephant on patrol in Kaziranga National Park, Assam, India.

Thank you.' He listened to me explaining the results of the study, translated intermittently by Beesa, and several men in the circle nodded and grunted. I showed him the children's books we were delivering to the village schools. His face lit up when he saw the pictures and he laughed with a youthful vibrancy that contrasted sharply with his ancient appearance. And like Chief Bobo, when he spoke it was with the gravitas of an elder.

'He thanks you for coming here and doing this work. He is grateful. He says it is good that you are coming to give feedback. Most researchers do not do this,' Beesa translated.

Tentatively, we agreed on a few of the waterholes in Nyae Nyae that would benefit from having cribs in the near future. They were those my study had identified as high-conflict zones, where the need was greatest.

Back at Chief Bobo's house later in the morning, I went through the same explanation with him, with Beesa translating.

'When you come back,' Beesa said, 'he would like to invite you to come to his village. He is very happy that you have come to see him with this feedback. Maybe, when there are more of these cribs, there will be no more problems with the elephants now. He says it will be very good if you can help make this happen.'

It was a huge honour to be invited to the chief's village. I thanked him and said that I would like that very much. As I left him there, slouched on a plastic chair covered in dust, I doubted that he would remember me next time I returned. Somehow, that didn't seem to matter at all.

Delivering messages about the need for cribs and water installation protection was one thing, and these steps would certainly help to alleviate the conflict, but I knew they were only band-aid treatments. The real solution lay a bit deeper than that, in the benefits the people were getting from elephants. Elephant populations would continue to increase. If Bushmanland could take advantage of the economic benefits that the elephants could bring, then I was confident their future together would be prosperous. I left Bushmanland feeling positive and pleased that I had been able to provide feedback to the conservancy elders, but also disappointed that I couldn't help them take it forward. The report made suggestions, but it didn't implement the results. With no money left in the bank, I couldn't do any more than that.

I was also beginning to realise that the situation in Bushmanland was a small part of a much bigger problem. Back in Windhoek for a couple of days before I returned to Australia, I met one of the gurus of elephant conservation in southern Africa, Dr John Hanks. I knew of John's reputation and I was nervous about meeting him. After all, I was only a humble impala researcher on an elephant sabbatical. I still had a lot to learn. John was Cambridge educated, but had lived most of his adult life in Africa as a conservation leader for organisations like WWF and the Peace Parks Foundation. At a restaurant in Windhoek, he put me at ease instantly with his old-fashioned English charm and promptly ordered a good bottle of wine.

'Have you heard of the KAZA, Tammie?'

I shook my head.

'It stands for Kavango-Zambezi Transfrontier Conservation Area. It will be the largest conservation area for wildlife in the world,' he told me. 'There's a whole lot of options on the table to manage elephants. Translocation, contraception . . . and, of course, culling is still on the agenda. But nothing comes close to the effectiveness of transfrontier conservation areas. They're all about allowing elephants to move back to their historic range across country boundaries, while providing local people with wildlife-based benefits.'

The KAZA TFCA was to be one of several transfrontier

conservation areas, or 'peace parks', being established across country borders all over southern Africa. TFCAs were large, multi-use zones that included existing national parks and protected areas, communal conservancies, freehold and communal land.

The great thing about this concept was that it took into account the fact that elephants ignore country borders. For instance, elephants living in north-eastern South Africa and Kruger National Park can today cross freely into Mozambique and Zimbabwe. This now forms part of the Greater Limpopo Transfrontier Conservation Area. One of the most challenging aspects of the idea was that it meant several African governments needed to work together to make them work, hence the alternative name – 'peace parks'.

The KAZA TFCA, encompassing almost 300 000 square kilometres (imagine a place the size of Italy, minus the red wine and pasta), was at the interface of five African countries. It contained the largest contiguous elephant population in the world. That was Botswana's 150 000 elephants, as well as those in southern Zambia, north-western Zimbabwe, the Caprivi of Namibia and south-eastern Angola. This area was elephant heaven, full of rivers, savannahs and big trees. It was also full of people living on the poverty line.

'There are more than half a million elephants in Africa and a large proportion of them are in southern Africa. As you know, it's not poaching we have to worry about down here, although that's still a problem in parts of central and west Africa. But on the whole, African elephant populations have grown at an astonishing rate. There are plenty of people now who believe we actually have an elephant problem.'

'Here it's a case of too many elephants, isn't it?' I said.

'To some extent, yes, but I think it's ridiculous that some people refer to the elephant situation here as "overpopulation".

How could it be? What is the reference point? There used to be millions of elephants in Africa. It's just that there's not enough space for everyone any more. The question is how to allow people to make the most of their elephants. You know from your time here in Namibia how successful conservation has been in communal conservancies. Giving people jobs and income from wildlife makes an incredible difference to their attitudes.'

John's voice had a British lilt and an eloquence that resonated much like David Attenborough's. I learned later that he had his own radio show in South Africa, *Talking of Nature*.

His words made sense. I'd seen the clash for resources between people and elephants with my own eyes in Bushmanland. Elephants could represent jobs and income and meat to local communities if the economy was based on sustainable development, integrating industries like ecotourism and trophy hunting as key components. People may still have thought that elephants were a pest and a problem, but in Nyae Nyae at least some of the cost of living with them was traded off by the benefits. Why couldn't this model be applied across the elephant range? The approach, referred to by conservationists as CBNRM, or community-based natural resource management, was already working well in Namibia.

Khaudum and Nyae Nyae were just inside the border of the KAZA and thus would benefit from the presence of the TFCA. But from what John was telling me, human-elephant conflict wasn't nearly as serious where I had been working compared with places where densities of elephants and people were higher, such as in Namibia's Caprivi region, Zimbabwe and northern Botswana. There, people were using all sorts of innovative but simple techniques to keep elephants off their crops.

'There's this group called the Elephant Pepper Development Trust. They were based in Zimbabwe but they've moved to Livingstone in Zambia because of the trouble in Zim. They're using chilli to keep elephants out of crops. The villagers grow the chilli and get a cash crop out of it, but it also keeps the elephants away. Elephants seem to find chilli *distasteful*.'

The way John said 'distasteful' made me smile. It was as though he could taste the hot peppers himself as he said the word.

'They grow them around the edge of their maize and vegetable crops like a buffer. They use these things they call chilli briquettes. They're made of chilli and elephant dung mixed together, dried into a brick shape. Then they put a hot coal on top and the smell of the chilli seems to keep elephants away. It's really quite impressive.'

I listened intently as we leaned over John's laptop looking at photographs of human-elephant conflict in other parts of the continent. The conflict scenario in many other parts of Africa was focused on crop protection, rather than centred on water as had been the case in Bushmanland where there was very little agriculture. This was a whole different kettle of fish. I began to think about the problem beyond Bushmanland, to the wider context of elephant populations that moved in and out of countries, belonging to all and none. Even the elephants I had seen in Khaudum and Nyae Nyae probably migrated beyond Namibia's Caprivi strip into neighbouring countries. The local problems I had seen there were part of a much bigger picture.

'We don't know how well these techniques are working, though. For example, no one's actually done a rigorous scientific assessment of the impact of chillies on elephants. I mean, what happens when the wind is blowing the wrong way? How much chilli do you need for every kilogram of dung? What's the right ratio? Do chilli fences work better than briquettes, or do you need both? There are still a lot of unanswered questions.' John paused for a moment to take a sip of wine, giving me time to let what he was saying sink in.

'Tammie, what we need is someone to do a strategic study of the different chilli-based deterrents to get a good sense of what works best so we can start applying it all across Africa. Is this something you would be interested in?'

Was I interested? Was he kidding? I was blown away by John's passion and enthusiasm for both conservation and poverty alleviation. I couldn't have been more thrilled to be offered the opportunity to get involved in the KAZA work. It felt as though this had all been written in some greater celestial plan for my future. I would finish my project in Bushmanland, only to have a bigger project waiting in the wings that was even more exciting. It seemed perfect. I returned to Australia feeling hopeful and inspired, certain that I would be able to return to Africa as soon as the funding rolled in for the chilli project.

But Africa, my dear bloody Africa. It never lets anything go to any sort of plan other than of its own random making. Back at Shelby's place at the Sunshine Coast, my excitement faded as months passed and there was delay after delay in the funding due to politics related to the establishment of the KAZA. John was as frustrated as I was. He knew I couldn't wait forever. I continued to work on my novel, paying the rent by working in the café in Buderim and pouring champagne at wedding functions. I read scientific paper after paper about the use of chillies to deter elephants from crops, growing increasingly fascinated by this simple yet effective solution.

Six long months later, with my bank balance nearing zero, the five governments finally signed the memorandum of understanding for the establishment of the TFCA, but we realised that it would be even longer before the funding would be released. I couldn't wait any longer. I was flat broke and sick of making cappuccinos. I started applying for other jobs. The kind that paid. The kind that would give me some financial security but would also hold me ransom to civilisation. The kind I'd avoided my entire life.

But first, I had to go back to Bushmanland just one more time. I couldn't let it go. In my heart I knew it wouldn't be the last time I ever visited Bushmanland, but the way things were going I feared it would be a while before I would return again. I would help take thirty young Australian volunteers to Namibia with a group called Oz Quest. As part of their expedition, they would spend a couple of weeks with me in Bushmanland helping build concrete cribs for elephants. This was my chance to help the conservancy start implementing the results of my research project.

In late November, the week before I flew out, WWF Australia granted me a job interview for a position I had applied for on a whim, not thinking I had a remote chance of getting it because of my clear lack of experience with Australian threatened species conservation. I flew to Sydney for the interview, literally shaking in my stilettos, and stumbled my way through questions about local fauna and flora that I had absolutely no clue about. It was awful. *Phew*, I thought. *There's no way I'll get that job and have to move to Sydney now.*

At Singapore airport en route to Namibia a few days later I checked my email. There was one there from Dr Nicola Markus, my interviewer at WWF Australia. *That was quick*, I thought, thinking they must notify the unsuccessful applicants first. I clicked on it, anticipating a rejection so definitely that I almost felt relieved in advance. So I just about fell off my chair when I read that I was being offered the job.

What on earth was I thinking, going for that job? Why in heaven's name were they offering it to me? Surely there were a million other conservationists in Australia with better résumés and much more experience than I had? How could I go and live in a big city like Sydney after so long in Namibia? How could I go from elephants and impalas to kangaroos and koalas? How would I talk to people in business suits and ties after months of tentative Afrikaans and sign language with the Bushmen? I could barely *speak* Australian any more. When I got back to Australia, I would have two weeks to pack my few possessions, drive two days to Sydney and find a place to live. I was terrified. I had the next month in Bushmanland to come to terms with it.

In December, early in the wet season, Nyae Nyae was a boiling cauldron of bubbling heat. I had never seen it like this and it was incredible. Moody pregnant skies churned with angry, dark grey thunderclouds, which threatened to explode all afternoon before bursting with cold, heavy drops that fell in colossal lost cities of rain. Jagged lightning sliced the sky like it was a soft tsama melon, followed by deafening thunderclaps that shook the tents with their ferocity.

In the forty degree heat, we worked in the searing sun to collect rocks, make cement by hand with shovels and build walls solid enough to hold in water and withstand elephants stepping on them. It was back-breaking, sweaty work. The Australian volunteers worked alongside a half-a-dozen men from the conservancy, Bushmen who worked at twice the pace with half the sweat.

Bushmanland was a different place in the wet season. The baobabs, leafless for most of the year, now had green leaves and giant white flowers with golden stamens dusted in copious yellow pollen. The flowers spun out of the sky like delicate golden-haired ballerinas pirouetting in white tutus. When they landed on the canvas roofs of the tents they made a loud thump, as if they weighed as much as a ground squirrel. The hum of wild bees was constant during the day as hundreds of insects feasted on the sweet pollen. Whereas before the baobabs had looked old, grey and wise, their limbs twisted and arthritic, now they looked like they were all dressed up for a cocktail party in a finery of green robes with bright white baubles.

We camped under a baobab to build the first crib. Though the setting was beautiful, the camp itself was rough. There was no fridge and we all largely became vegetarians, living on cream crackers with Marmite (for lack of Vegemite), beans and the occasional tin of tuna. Despite the heavy work, it was so hot that no one felt much like eating during the day. Some of the volunteers dug a hole in the bush to serve as a long-drop toilet. Everyone's tents leaked when it rained at night. The shower was a canvas bag of water hung over a tree branch and surrounded by a tarp. By day it swarmed with bees desperate for moisture, so those who wanted to wash had to do so at night-time or risk a nasty sting. At night we sat on logs or rocks, chatting by the campfire. Tiny black scorpions, drawn by the heat of fire, crawled around by our boots. Spotted hyaenas cackled not far away.

One night one of the Bushmen asked if an Australian woman could marry a Bushman man.

One of the guys answered, 'You wouldn't like Australian women, mate. They don't want babies. They want to work.'

They spoke in Ju/'hoan for a moment among themselves, then one said, shaking his head, 'Why would you want a woman who doesn't want babies?'

Everyone laughed, but they were serious.

He went on, 'It doesn't matter if a woman is ugly or beautiful. The main thing is she must produce children and work hard. These are the most important things.'

I imagined a television show contrasting what men want in Bushmanland with what men want in the west. I couldn't imagine a western man saying that beauty was not important or even demanding that their girlfriend bear children.

One of the Bushmen declared, 'I want to marry a woman with a cell phone and a double-cab car.'

I watched the faces of the young Australians sitting around the fire and I remembered how it had been for me on my first trip to Africa at the age of fifteen. That was fourteen years ago now. I wondered if this experience would open their eyes and change their lives for the better, as it had mine.

On days off, we all just enjoyed being in Bushmanland. This was a new experience for me too, because taking in the sights was something I'd never really given myself time to do when I was conducting my research there. Nyae Nyae Pan, dry and glary for most of the year, now shimmered with temporary water and migratory birds. Hundreds of flamingos formed a wavy pink haze on the horizon. All over the conservancy, waterholes that were small springs for most of the year became large muddy pans. Elephant bulls waded ankle-deep through the water, ripping up nutritious green grass with dexterous trunks. The fresh kill of a group of African wild dogs – a steenbok – was devoured in less than half an hour, then left for the vultures to pick out its eyes. Maribou storks stood over the bones like garish undertakers, their crusty red heads poking out of old black tuxedos.

After a rain shower one afternoon, some of the Bushmen took us on a walk through the bush, showing us the foods that could be eaten. The air was crisp and fresh after the shower. Raindrops had left tiny pockmarks in the soil and the leaves still dripped with tears of rain. The men pointed out all sorts of plants and trees that were useful in one way or other. Some could be used in love potions or to aid fertility. Others could be used to break up a relationship, 'if you want that woman for yourself'. Some bright yellow berries on one bush could be mixed with some other ingredients to make the poison for the arrows they used to kill game.

On another day Dries showed the group some of the treasures in his official storeroom. Salted skins of lions and elephants shot as problem animals, vegetable juice-stained tusks of ivory and the heavy horns of a Cape Buffalo bull were just some of the specials on offer. The room smelled of old meat and salt, pungent and overwhelming. He brought out a couple of his rifles to show the group, something that few of them, having grown up in the city, had ever seen.

Stroking the wooden butt of one gently he said in the low voice of a lover, 'Beautiful . . . just beautiful.'

'You need to get out more, mate,' one of the volunteers joked.

Dries smiled good-humouredly and I watched the girls in the group melt.

'Is he single?' one of them asked me later.

By the end of the month I was exhausted and had lost several kilograms from the diet and the hard physical work, but I was on a high. It felt good to be fit, tanned and fully alive in Africa. I felt a million miles away from civilisation and I had no desire to go back to it. But life doesn't always work out the way you want it to. A job in the big city now had my name on it and I was too broke to say no.

On our last night in the bush, we joined the Bushmen at a nearby village for a night of dancing and singing. It started with one of the young men using a plastic jerry can as a drum, his hands creating loud, rhythmic beats in the quiet night. Our group and the women from the village sat in a circle on the dirt around the fire. The women began to clap and the children joined in too.

I tried to keep up with the round the women were clapping in, but it was so complicated, with all of them clapping to separate beats that somehow integrated into a single rhythm, I couldn't work out how it was synchronised. I stopped trying and just let myself float on their chanting voices, the hollow beating of the drum and a dozen rapid clapping palms. *I don't want to leave this place. I love it here. I don't want to move to Sydney.* My mind buzzed with thoughts I didn't want to have.

An old man wearing only a duiker-skin loincloth came into the circle and began dancing, a movement that involved a lot of jumping with both feet at the same time. His feet thumped the ground hard and heavily as if he were trying to wake the earth from a deep sleep. The contagion of the dance overtook all inhibitions and self-consciousness. Soon everyone was up on their feet, doing the hopping dance in a line around the fire, the volunteers, the children and the women, all following the old man's lead.

Impulsively I grabbed the hands of two small children. There was no resistance or fear. They both clung tightly to my much larger hands, holding on as we jumped around the fire in unison like well-synchronised kangaroos. When the singing stopped they looked up at me with eyes that were at once vulnerable and trusting. The light of the half-moon reflected in their dark brown eyes and seemed to fill these tiny beings with a kind of radiance. Unable to speak my language, they just smiled. Then they let go. And it was time for me to do the same.

PART TWO

ELEVEN

It was the week before I moved to Sydney and I hadn't slept properly in days. Anxiety clutched my every thought with sharp, demonic claws. Shaking with fear at the prospect of living in a city of four million people after so long in Namibia (a *country* of two million), I loaded my little Holden Barina (Barry the Silver Bullet) and clattered south with all my worldly possessions (a torch, a few recently purchased business suits, some bedding, an African wall hanging or two and some biltong). Barry seemed to share my resistance as we chugged along together at a top speed of ninety kilometres per hour. My trusty chug-along was powered by a croaking four-litre engine that sounded more like a motor mower than a car. I wasn't a hundred percent sure he was going to get me there.

The drive from south-east Queensland to the grand metropolis of Sydney was about a thousand kilometres and would take two days. The last time I'd covered this distance in a single stretch was when I'd driven across the Kalahari Desert from South Africa to Namibia in another little car, a Chico Golf. Back then the journey had been in search of adventure and a new research project after Zimbabwe had turned to hell.

I'd plunged into that desert land knowing only that it was a place of undulating sand dunes, strange arid-adapted animals, and Germans who regularly committed fashion sins like socks with sandals. I had no choice but to cross my fingers that things would work out at the other end because I really had no idea what I was getting myself into. Similar thoughts were running through my head now. Again, I had no idea what this journey would bring. I had been less scared back then. The prospective of adventure had spurred me on. Excitement and youthful blind courage cloaked fear so that I hardly felt its wintry chill. This time, launching into another great unknown, I wished I felt as brave.

I wound down my window and let the summer breeze blow back my hair, cooling the sweat dripping down my spine. I took in the sweeping views of the east coast beaches and the endless blue sky, the grey woodlands of swaying gum trees that lined the highway and the cackling kookaburras perched on powerlines. I sighed. *You can do this.* I sighed again.

I passed yet another speed camera. In Australia everything was so regimented and organised, so utterly averse to any kind of near miss or mild-mannered calamity; I wondered if I might fall asleep at the wheel on my long, hot journey south. The roads were wide, tarred and free of potholes. There were no barefoot, ragged urchins running down the street begging for sweets, no women walking along the road with heavy loads of firewood balanced on their heads and babies strapped to their backs with colourful sarongs, no soldiers with AK47s standing on the corner by the convenience stores. Not that any of that was a bad thing, really. Australia's safeness is one of its greatest attributes and the reason why many flock here from foreign shores to live. For me it had just one fatal flaw. It wasn't Africa. And I wasn't sure I was ready for this level of, well . . . tameness yet.

Road signs blared warnings every few hundred metres. The police even warned drivers with flashing signs saying, *Slow down. You are approaching a speed trap*. I mean, it made you want to speed up just for a little adrenaline rush. In Africa, no one bothered to check anyone's speed unless the policeman wanted a bribe. I recalled the time in Botswana when I had been flagged over by some cops I was convinced were going to give me my first African speeding fine, but instead of fining me the policeman grinned and handed me a small packet.

'Go well, madam! Be safe!' he exclaimed, a gold tooth glinting. 'Welcome to Botswana!'

I opened the packet to find a half-a-dozen condoms. In Africa, the police had bigger things to worry about than speeding cars, such as a population with an HIV/AIDS rate of twenty-five percent.

I knew I had to take some of my own advice and get a little perspective on my worries. But it was hard, because everyone around me was equally concerned about how I would adapt to this epic transition to life in the big city after so long in Africa.

'You'll never last in Sydney,' my dad had said, grim-faced and sombre before I had left the farm.

I was pretty sure he was right. Dad and I shared a lot of genes; he usually knew me fairly well.

'I just can't imagine you there, Tam,' Shelby said on the phone, 'but I'm sure it'll be great.'

I could hear the niggle of doubt in her voice, suggesting what she was too nice to say to my face – that she expected me to be right back in Africa within a month.

'Just look at it as temporary until your next lot of Africa funding comes through,' Mum said.

Mama Matson was being falsely (but I'll grant, generously) optimistic because I knew she was secretly wishing that wouldn't happen. It must be a mother's worst nightmare having a daughter who lives and works in Africa, especially a mum like mine who couldn't understand why anyone would want to up and leave a wonderful place like Australia for kicks. Mum didn't like my love affair with Africa, but to her credit she always tried her best to be supportive.

Then, more adamantly, she went on, 'Who knows? I think you'll meet a man down there. I bet you find a husband at WWF!'

Of course! There *was* hope! Mum smiled in that way that mothers do when they are having a rose-coloured vision of their daughter's future standing in a church before a priest in a veil and ivory gown. I wished that I could find it in my then tortured soul to humour her, but that was the last thing on my mind. I was just thinking about *survival*.

No matter which way I looked at it, I always came back to the fact that I was going into a regular nine-to-five job in civilisation, far from the megafauna that I loved. I already missed hanging out with elephants. Waking up on the farm in the few days after I got back to Queensland, I sometimes forgot where I was, sure I could hear trumpeting coming from the hills, only to realise that it was the moo of a cow, not an elephant at all. It all felt so wrong. Taking the job in Sydney felt like selling out, a selfish move purely to make money. I knew full well that Africa's miserly capacity to save its species contrasted markedly with the vast number of well-educated, experienced conservationists in Australia. I mean, seriously, in a country with ninety-nine percent adult literacy that spent billions of dollars on the environment every year, how bad could their conservation problems be?

I met my new flatmate, Gabby Shaw, online. A Sydney girl all her life, she did yoga, liked hiking and had done a fair bit of travelling abroad. She sounded like the sort of person I would have a lot in common with and she had a great flat overlooking the ocean at Bronte Beach. Thankfully, not knowing any of my peculiarities, Gabby agreed to have me.

I must have looked like the kind of person who would get swallowed up and spat out by Sydney because on my first day at work, my new flatmate walked with me to the train station and literally took me all the way to the WWF building, only drawing the line at holding my hand as we crossed at the traffic lights. She worked just down the road from WWF at the ABC, so it wasn't much out of her way, but nonetheless I was so grateful to be adopted by this fabulous woman I almost kissed her.

'Good luck,' she said with a kind smile, leaving me on the pavement looking like a lost child.

If Gabby had dropped me in the middle of the Namib Desert with nothing but a scarab beetle for company I would have felt more comfortable. But, as it was, I was at the base of a towering high-rise and there was only one way from here – up. *God give me strength* . . . I pressed the number thirteen button in the lift and entered the concrete jungle.

My first week at WWF passed in a blur that I would come to know as very much typical of working there. It was fast-paced, riven with unspoken hierarchies and, its workforce being two-thirds female, thick with oestrogen. The Sydney office had the slightly maniacal atmosphere that you might expect to find on the inside of an ants' nest, workers scurrying backwards and forwards in a flurry of busyness. No one ever had enough time for much more than a two-minute conversation in the corridor. They spoke in a language of acronyms and Australian idioms that were foreign to me, so I did my best to be a chameleon, blending with my surroundings, nodding and smiling as if I knew exactly what they were talking about.

Quite sensibly, Human Resources put me into a one-day leadership course in my first week. I sat in a stuffy boardroom with the entire executive team of WWF and the leaders of all their conservation programs, trying to look and feel the part. I was Tarzan's Jane in the concrete jungle, Crocodile Dundee in New York, Amy Winehouse in a nunnery. A song from Sesame Street kept playing in my head: *One of these things is not like the other*. . .

At the head of the table was Greg Bourne, the CEO, a man in his fifties who seemed to operate on a battery of boundless energy. On my second day at work he had taken me out for a coffee for a friendly welcome chat and I noticed that he took the time every morning that he was in the office to walk down the corridors and say good morning to everyone. Completely bald, fit as a fiddle and bursting with enthusiasm and passion, he was clearly someone who lived life to the fullest.

There was Ray Nias, the conservation director and my direct boss. Our first conversations had passed in a combination of long awkward silences and questioning looks on his part, usually following embarrassing moments of ignorance on mine. I was sure he thought I was a complete idiot. Dr Ray, as he was known to the staff, was one of those uncanny scientists who retained vast amounts of information on just about everything. You could ask him about the endocrinology of sloths or the sex drive of sperm whales and he'd have a viable answer for you. "Ask Dr Ray" was the most common response to questions in the building. To say the least, it was a little intimidating.

Among my colleagues in the leadership course, there was

a charismatic ex-Labor political advisor from Queensland, a Harvard-educated Welsh woman who was obsessed with sharks and sea cucumbers, an ex-lawyer with a dry wit and strong opinions on sustainability, a bearded man who spent half his time on a wooden dugout in the South Pacific, and a genuine man of the bush who was so in love with WWF that he had a collection of panda paraphernalia. The head of marketing was there too, an important job in an organisation that depends on donations from the public to stay afloat.

Ten minutes into the course, two men walked in.

'Sorry we're late,' the first one said, looking slightly sheepish. Noticing the new face in the room, he reached over, smiling warmly and shook my hand to introduce himself as Charlie.

The tall, broad-shouldered man behind him was wearing a suit and carried himself with the confidence of a soldier going into war. He had striking blue eyes shielded by funky square glasses and lots of spiky dark hair. Ray stopped talking as the men walked past him to the two spare seats near the end of the long table. The one in the suit sat next to me.

'Ah, Mr Ridley,' Ray said, raising an eyebrow in a pretence of reprimand, 'good of you to join us.'

When the man spoke it was in an English accent with a daub of humour. 'Thank you, good doctor. I always like to make a fashionable entrance.'

Everyone in the room laughed, including my boss, and the tension in the room dissipated. With a single sentence, the enigmatic Englishman had completely lightened the atmosphere.

As the day went on, the underlying current of gently brewing human egos, territoriality and hierarchical power plays that I had already begun to pick up on, relaxed a little as the leaders of WWF learned how to become better managers of people, better listeners and more respected human beings. I was trying hard to be taken seriously, because I was the youngest in the room by about ten years and one of only three women. But my professional façade fell apart when I was paired up with the Englishman in an exercise about listening.

'Andy,' he introduced himself, with a cheeky grin and a strong handshake.

I recognised his voice because the day before I had heard him gleefully exclaim in a mock Crocodile Dundee accent, 'Punchin' shaaaaaarks!' in response to a newspaper headline. An abalone diver had been seized by his head by a Great White shark, just off the coast of New South Wales. With his head inside the giant shark's mouth, the man had punched it in the eye with his abalone chisel until it spat him free.

There was mischief in Andy's eyes, which the glasses couldn't conceal. He struck me as the type of guy who had once charmed girls like me into letting him copy their homework.

I learned that Andy was head of communications. He was behind what was then WWF Australia's largest awareness campaign to reduce the impact of climate change, a night planned for a couple of month's time when all the lights would go off in the city for an hour. Everyone at WWF was talking about it. It was called Earth Hour. Self-consciously he rubbed at his upper arm, where a Nicorette patch was just visible through the white shirt.

Andy turned his chair around to face me directly and leaned forward. As part of the exercise, I listened as he told me about his favourite holiday. My job in this exercise was to remember as much of it as possible and relay it back to him. He spoke about being twenty-one and on the bow of a wooden boat on the Nile in Egypt. On a break from working for his uncle in Hong Kong he ended up in the land of pyramids on a solo holiday. He remembered floating down the oily brown Nile on the bow of a felucca, a traditional Egyptian sailing boat. Watching the flowing water rush by as it had for thousands of years, the river's serpentine path fringed by reeds and palm trees, Andy felt on top of the world. For days he had admired the ancient pyramids in the scorching desert heat, their triangular structures built before the time of Christ and constructed as tombs for great pharaohs. Surrounded by ancient buildings built with the blood, sweat and tears of thousands of human slaves, he had sat at the bow of that boat and felt truly happy.

I knew that feeling. It was how I felt in Africa. I recall thinking, *This guy's interesting. He's an Englishman living in Australia. He lived and worked in Hong Kong and he's been to Egypt.* And as he told the story, I remember giggling – a lot.

Then he had to listen to me and the topic was 'Your worst staff management issue and how you dealt with it'. Struggling to keep a straight face, and never having had a 'real' job, I did the best I could. I told Andy about an issue I had in north-west Namibia on the border of Angola at the magnificent Epupa Falls. My translator had been talking to some very traditional Himba elders about where we were most likely to find some black-faced impalas in their area. They didn't want to talk to a woman, but my translator didn't want to tell me that. Instead, while I sat there trying to ask them questions through him, he conducted the interview himself, leaving me out of it entirely. Not knowing that he was trying to protect me from embarrassment, I had been furious with him for what I saw as male dominance with the men of his tribe at my expense. Then he got upset too and we both refused to talk to each other for an hour. Earlier in the day, as we had been setting up our tents, a snake had literally dropped out of the sky and landed in the dirt beside us. I had wondered if it was a curse. In the end, I called on my friend James to mediate and we sorted it out.

Andy listened to this story intently, the glint of amusement never leaving his eyes. But this reaction was nothing compared with mine. I didn't know what had come over me. I couldn't stop laughing just from being in this man's presence. On the other side of the table, a colleague had just burst into tears telling her obviously quite traumatic staff management story. And here I was, in my first week, with tears and mascara running down my face too, but they were tears of laughter. This really wasn't the professional, serious impression I was trying to make. It was all this charismatic Englishman's fault.

But there was plenty of time to make up for it. Over the next few months I saw more of Australia than I ever had before. I learned that, far from having everything under control, we had the worst rate of mammalian extinction in the world. In spite of all our human capacity, all the billions of dollars spent on the environment, more and more species were being added to the Australian threatened species list every year.

I travelled to Tasmania, where the last bastion of Tasmanian devils was fighting for survival against a disease so harrowing it belonged in a childhood nightmare or a horror movie. An infectious cancer was spreading like wildfire through the already endangered population. It was impossible to stop because it was spread by the mating behaviour of devils, which involves biting of the neck. The disease created ugly red open sores on the face and head, and was fatal to the animal within three months of its appearance. I met with Professor Hamish McCallum, a former university lecturer of mine, now working on the Devil Facial Tumour Disease at the University of Tasmania.

'This is really, *really* serious, Tammie,' he told me. 'The way this disease works is quite unusual. Two-thirds of Tasmania already has infected devils and it's just a matter of time before the rest get it too. I'm not being overly pessimistic about this. My conservative estimate is that the devil will go extinct in Tassie in twenty years unless we find a cure, and that's unlikely.'

Hamish was not the sort of guy who exaggerated. It was a sickening thought, though, to know so surely in advance that we were going to lose a species.

'Is it too late then? I mean, surely we must be able to do something?'

Hamish shook his head. 'The only way we're going to save them is if we translocate them to islands off Tasmania, or even to the mainland, and then later, when the disease is gone from here, bring them back.'

I tried to imagine how farmers like my father would react if he were told they were returning Tassie devils to mainland Australia. There was a reason why they were exterminated from the mainland in the first place. Like the Tasmanian tiger, or thylacine, the devil competed with a nation hell-bent since its colonial inception on creating a world-beating agricultural sector. Predators like dingos, Australia's wild dogs, and Tasmanian devils were a direct threat to farmers' sheep and calves. And we Australians were known for our tenacity. If we wanted something, we usually got it. Sometimes you've got to be careful what you wish for. We had become exceptional farmers, but our wildlife had paid the price.

Conservationists were debating whether to translocate a population of devils to an island off the coast of Tasmania, but some said the side effect of that would be to diminish populations of other species there, as they would become prey for devils. It seemed a balancing act of poor scenarios. Sooner or later there would have to be a compromise. The alternative was too awful to contemplate: yet another extinction, this time of one of the world's most charismatic creatures.

I saw the agricultural landscapes typical of southern Australia, where great swathes of former wildlife habitat has had to make way for human development over the last two hundred years. Sheep and cattle grazed open grassy paddocks where wallabies, cockatoos and koalas used to live in old woodlands of native trees. Steadily sprawling cities engulfed a little more habitat every day, so that species like bandicoots and flying foxes had no choice but to became urban dwellers too, creating a whole new set of problems for both animal and human residents.

I drove west from Perth into the wheat belt and saw the tiny pockets of habitat on the sides of roads that are all that is left for endemic species like black cockatoos to feed, sleep and raise their young. I realised with horror that this was all we had left them, just a few leftover trees on the sides of roads that we couldn't be bothered clearing. South-west Australia was globally recognised for its biodiversity, largely due to the plethora of endemic plants, but it was just as degraded as the rest of southern Australia.

The continent was crawling with another threat that had only emerged since colonisation – feral animals. European foxes and domestic cats gone wild had decimated Australia's small mammal populations. Feral pigs, goats, cane toads and camels were exacerbating the effect, destroying natural ecosystems and making life impossible for native fauna and flora.

I saw a bilby for the first time in Western Australia at a captive breeding centre called Dryandra, a few hours west of Perth. The tiny creature was the size of a small rabbit, with long, skinny ears, and a pointy nose designed for eating seeds and insects like ants and termites. It was so delicate and gentle in every movement, its fur so fine that it looked like it was made of millions of tiny grey feathers.

The fragility of this creature touched me. I wondered how on earth *any* of them had survived the presence of cats and foxes. These stealthy European predators had landed in Australia to find the perfect niche for themselves and a country crawling with a hopping feast of small wallabies, bandicoots and bilbies. They must have thought they had found heaven with so much naïve food presented to them on a platter of future extinctions. I learned that the Lesser Bilby had gone extinct within fifty years of its discovery. Now the Greater Bilby faced the same fate. It once covered the majority of Australia, but was now restricted largely to the arid centre in just twenty percent of its former range.

How bad were things, really? Well, pretty bad. Of all the extinctions of mammals that had occurred worldwide in the last two hundred years, forty percent of them had been in Australia. How's that for an embarrassing track record? I had thought we were *advanced*! I realised with a rude awakening that in fact it was southern Africa that was ahead of us. The fertile training ground I'd had as a budding conservationist in Namibia hadn't been backward at all, but the greatest gift I could have had. The guys in southern Africa were getting it right where we Australians were failing.

The major damage had been done to mammals in what scientists called the 'critical weight range' species (35 to 5500 grams), otherwise known as perfect mouthfuls for foxes and cats. Wiping out Australia's natural predators – thylacines and devils – and reducing dingo populations opened up all sorts of exciting possibilities for these stylish European immigrants to take the native predators' places. Once they were established, they were almost impossible to remove permanently. It was a disturbing revelation to me when I heard one federal government official talk about them as 'uneradicatable'. The best we could do was manage them and keep their numbers low, and now that task would go on forever.

As I discovered more about the plight of species in southern states, I grew more and more depressed. The words 'They're buggered . . . they're buggered . . .' kept filtering through my head, like ghosts of extinct mammals, keeping me awake at night. In each state, I saw how committed my team in the Threatened Species Network (TSN) was, how passionate and dedicated they were to working with community groups to save Australia's species, and I wondered how they managed to stay positive.

I still missed elephants and I was sad they were no longer a part of my life. But I found myself getting wrapped up in the problems facing Australian species in a very short space of time. Suddenly it was late March and I had almost passed my three-month probation period at WWF. During that time I had travelled to almost every state in Australia, seeing more of the country than I had ever dreamed I would in my life. The more I learned and saw with my own eyes about the state of Australia's environment, the more overwhelmed I became by the scale of anthropogenic degradation we had wrought in just two centuries.

Was this what I had come back to civilisation for, to try to fight for species in a place where agricultural, urban and industrial development was more important than anything else? At least in southern Africa they recognised the economic value of their wildlife. Human livelihoods were linked to conservation, and in Namibia tourism was the fastest growing industry. There, people were poor but they had recognised that their natural assets were the most valuable of all. They weren't perfect either, of course, but the proof was in the pudding. Namibia's threatened mammal populations were growing. Australia's, on the whole, were not.

TWELVE

The thing about hope is that it's fickle. Just when you think it's completely shrivelled up and not worth hanging onto even a shred of, it fills up you up again like hot air in a balloon, lifting you off your feet until you are buoyantly floating into a blue sky of optimism. Hope and I had almost parted ways when our tenuous relationship was saved by a field trip to Darwin in the Northern Territory, to meet Jarrad Holmes, TSN coordinator for the north.

Jarrad, a quietly spoken, humble chap about my age, and I bonded over barramundi fishing and beers on the Adelaide River one Sunday afternoon in March.

'If we're lucky, the barras'll be biting. If we're not – well, at least the beers are cold,' Jarrad said in the laidback way of people in the north.

He cast his line across the murky brown water near the reed-lined bank with practised control. The bait whirred through the air and landed with a heavy plop. Sunscreen melted off my forehead and stung my eyes. The humidity was oppressive combined with the early afternoon heat.

The ridged bumps of a crocodile's head emerged close to the boat in a smattering of pink lilies, its sinister yellow eyes assessing our potential as food. It wasn't the first time I had been sized up this way by a predator. I'd felt the same way in Etosha, staring into the feline eyes of a hungry lioness, and more than once at the Sports Bar in Maun, where packs of lecherous safari guides lurked.

'How would you like your eggs, darling?' The words of a drunken guide in Botswana filtered randomly into my consciousness. 'Poached, fried or fertilised?'

The crocodile sank under the water and disappeared as silently as he had arrived.

'Don't worry about him, he's only a baby,' Jarrad said. 'He won't worry us.'

I estimated the croc had to be almost two metres long. *That's a pretty big baby*, I thought.

'It's the full-grown ones you have to worry about, the kind that turn over boats this size.'

'Oh . . . excellent.' I scanned the small dinghy, feeling somewhat less confident than I had before.

'Another beer?' Jarrad proffered.

I accepted the chilled can willingly. It did little to reduce the sweat streaming down the side of my face but it still felt good. I held the can against my warm skin for a moment, relishing its coolness, and then tossed the liquid down my throat in large thirst-quenching gulps.

Jarrad was from Sydney originally, but he had been in the Territory for several years and considered himself almost a local. My guess was he'd earned social acceptance through being an exceptionally good listener and probably a very good drinker. The Territory was the sort of place where you could never really call yourself a local unless you were born and bred there. It was angry and raw, sizzling with oppressive humid heat and big, strong personalities that matched the extreme seasons. In many ways, the remoteness and frontier feel of the north reminded me of Namibia.

Jarrad decided to initiate me into the north by arranging a special visit to the Tiwi Islands. The Tiwis are made up of two islands, Bathurst and Melville, just off the north-western part of the Northern Territory, eighty kilometres from Darwin. They are owned and managed by the Tiwi people, who have lived there since long before colonial times and now number a couple of thousand or so. They're famous for their football skills (AFL), allegedly having the highest rate of football participation in the country per head of population.

The Tiwi Islands are a shining beacon for biodiversity in the north. There is nowhere in the Northern Territory that comes close to it in terms of the number of species, including several plants that are not found anywhere else in the world. Unfortunately, the intact rainforests that harbour these species were under threat from a forestry company that had a mandate to clear big chunks of the Tiwis' forests for woodchips. The cleared land was being used to grow monocultures of acacias. The community was getting some benefits from the forestry company, including jobs for the locals in forestry and for a team of rangers employed to protect biodiversity on the islands.

And they needed those jobs. Crime, domestic violence and alcoholism were rife, and many people were on government unemployment benefits. But most shocking was that the Tiwi people had an extremely high rate of suicide, with, allegedly, one in four people having tried to kill themselves. Forestry was bringing in jobs and income, which meant self-respect in a culture fighting for its own survival. Naturally the Tiwi Land Council saw the benefits of an economic industry as good.

But it was more complicated than that. Jarrad told me there were rumours that the forestry company was breaching environmental laws and green groups were up in arms about it. No one really knew what was going on because the Tiwi Land Council was refusing to allow anyone from an environmental group onto the islands. An exception was made for us because WWF hadn't lambasted them in the media and because we were funding the salary of the Tiwis' ranger coordinator. Jarrad advised me not to take photos from the air.

We boarded the six-seater aircraft shortly after dawn with our escort, Kate Hadden, a representative of the Tiwi Land Council. The balmy heat of northern Australia had already resulted in large sweaty patches under my arms even though the sun had only just come up. Fresh sweat slithered snake-like down my spine and simmered in the hot creases behind my knees. Inside the claustrophobic plane the heat was oppressive.

'There it is,' Jarrad said, after half an hour or so, indicating a large green land mass in the Arafura Sea.

Looking at the tanzanite blue waters below I imagined all the marine animals that called it home. With a much lower human population, Australia's northern oceans had been less heavily impacted by fishing than elsewhere. Here, dugongs and turtles munched on seagrass beds near the shore, crocodiles basked on sandy islands and sharks gorged themselves on the multitudes of fish. It was a kind of paradise.

That's why the contrast when we flew over the Tiwis was so striking. As the plane flew low over the islands, we saw where swathes of forest had been cleared. From the air the scars of forestry seemed more devastating, the clearings standing out like skin grazed down to the bare muscle of the earth. It didn't seem right, and it probably wasn't, but the people of the Tiwis were desperate for a decent livelihood and this was the best option they had at the time. I couldn't help thinking that if this had been Africa, and the forests were filled with megafauna like elephants and rhinos, this community would have been rich on the proceeds of ecotourism or trophy hunting. But the closest thing they had to megafauna was a few common wallabies.

On the ground, we roared over wide red roads, muddy after recent rainfall, and drove through armies of ancient trees. It was boiling hot and the humidity sucked the life force out of me. The forest buzzed with the voices of a million singing insects, a dizzying cicadean cacophony that left a ring in my ears long after we left.

We joined a government botanist called Dave to look for endemic plants, plunging into the thick rainforest on foot with reckless abandon. My boots slid hazardously down slippery mud ravines and long, strangling vines tried to trip feet more conditioned to desert sand and rock. Spiky wet bushes scraped my arms and left streaks of red mud on my face as they whipped across bare skin. We continued to follow the botanist with the long grey beard, trusting his navigation skills as we stepped slowly into the heart of the forest, our feet squelching on decaying wood and leaves. The air in the forest was about ninety percent water, so laden with moisture that you could almost drink it.

Thunder rumbled overhead. An afternoon storm was brewing, typical of the monsoon in this part of the world. I knelt by a creek, which flowed gently with clear, clean water that was as lukewarm as the humid air.

'You've got a leech, Tammie,' Jarrad said.

'Really? Where?'

Then I saw it.

'That's not a leech. That's a bloody anaconda!' I exclaimed.

Its slimy black form was already several centimetres long and engorging with my blood, fastened tight as it sucked on my ankle.

'We've got some salt in the car,' Dave said. 'Anyway, that storm's coming in. We should head back.'

I left the Tiwis streaked in red mud, drenched with sweat and rain, with a large bleeding sore on my ankle where the leech had fallen off. Flying back to Darwin, I had mixed feelings. I was sad and disappointed and happy and hopeful all at the same time. Sad because of the terrible state the Tiwi community was in, disappointed that we hadn't found a way to create local jobs and income that didn't rely on destroying forests, happy because they still had most of their forests left and hopeful because it wasn't too late to find a better way.

But it wasn't until after this trip, in the wild Kimberley region, that I really began to feel hope for the future of Australia's amazing wildlife. North-west Australia is the last part of this continent that hasn't yet seen mammal extinctions. Its ecosystems are relatively intact and teem with life. The reef-blue Indian Ocean off Broome bristles with migratory humpback whales, enormous whale sharks and a flat-nosed species of dolphin, the snubfin, which is only found in this part of the world. Several turtle species use this as a safe haven on their migration path throughout the South Pacific, laying their eggs on the beaches on which they were born in deep holes dug in the soft sand under the full moon.

It's not too late to keep the Kimberley intact, but new threats are already emerging in the form of oil and gas development, uncontrolled tourism and overfishing. Not to mention that the cane toad is on its way. These ugly brown South American toads are just about to cross the West Australian border in their inexorable takeover of the continent from east to west, leaving a graveyard of Australian native species in their wake. Indigenous people have lived in harmony with this place for thousands of years and in just a few decades we have started the process of degradation for which we westerners are infamous globally.

An Aboriginal elder called Micklo, whose people have relied on the sea to provide food for generations, told me, 'If my brother die or my aunty sick, I feel a twitch.'

He shook his finger, pointed at me and twitched it.

'This finger, see? He twitches like dat, eh. This finger it tell me when something happening to my family.'

A WWF colleague, Tanya Vernes, told me that Aboriginal people in the Kimberley were now restricted to the same fishing take as recreational fishers – two fish per day.

'When we don't be getting fish from the sea, this finger . . . my instinct . . . it going.'

Indigenous people there are so closely tied to the natural environment that this old man truly believed that if he didn't eat fish, he would lose his innate knowledge of harm to his family and an ability to read the health of the land. To him, fish was literally food for the soul.

As I scratched the surface of Indigenous Australia, I couldn't help thinking about the Bushmen. They suffered from similar problems of alcoholism and social decay as many of the Aborigines did, and likewise their culture was hanging on by a rope that was thinning by the day. I wondered, as a member of the human species, how much of cultures like these we were prepared to lose. I wondered how much of our own true selves would go with them, how much of the connection to the earth that nurtured our own bodies and souls was being bulldozed along with those trees on the Tiwis. It seemed to me that with so many seekers in the western world today, the answers could be right in front of us in the worlds we were losing without even noticing, if only we took the time to look.

In the west we are so removed from the natural world, it is no wonder this is happening. These days, most people don't associate the meat and vegetables they buy in the supermarket with anything from the natural world. Steaks come from plastic packets, not from clear-felled forests in South America. Tables and chairs and floorboards come from discount furniture stores, not from the vanishing homes of orang-utans in Indonesia. Until now, I hadn't realised that the fish and chips I was buying from the local store was often shark, labelled as flake, some of the most severely depleted species left in the ocean.

Everything we consume relates back to nature in some way. The least we should be doing is treating it with a little respect. Even if you look at it purely selfishly, without those natural resources *we* couldn't survive, so it makes sense to use them sustainably. Indigenous people realised this a long time ago, so why is it taking us, so-called advanced, westerners so long to grasp the idea?

In Australia, what with habitat destruction, feral animals and destructive bushfires resulting from a lack of traditional Aboriginal burning practices (largely the result of Indigenous people moving off country to towns), the last thing we needed was yet another threat, one that made all of the current threats much worse. But that was what we had, staring us square in the face on the nightly news, in one natural disaster after another – droughts, floods, cyclones and bushfires. Climate change.

In the face of staggering predictions that had even the most sceptical scientists shaking in their lab coats, turning around the global problem that was climate change would require everyone to get involved. That was where Earth Hour came in.

On 31 March 2007, after months of manic preparations,

everyone in the city of Sydney was being called upon to turn off their lights for just one hour, in a statement about climate change and the difference we can make when we all work together. Led by Andy Ridley, the funny Englishman, no one really knew if Earth Hour was going to work. Would the city skyline go dark as businesses and high-rises turned off the power? Would children encourage their parents to get on board? Would the Sydney Opera House and the famous Harbour Bridge switch off their lights too? Or would it all be a total flop?

Many of the staff of WWF gathered at a bar on the harbour to watch what we could only hope would be the opposite of the New Year's Eve fireworks – a darkening of the night sky. The cocktails flowed as seven-thirty approached and the tension mounted. A curly-haired *Australian Idol* star called Bobby and the fabulous Deni Hines entertained us with groovy tunes. Elsewhere, Andy and Greg were at an exclusive event where Cate Blanchett and Kevin Rudd, then federal opposition leader, were the prime attractions. I had taken my flatmate, Gabby, along as my date for the night and we were both dressed to kill, sisters in bling. I wore a bright red cocktail dress that floated around my knees and sparkled when I walked in red strappy high heels.

At seven twenty-nine, everyone went silent. I held my breath. Gradually over the next couple of minutes, light after light in all of the office buildings were switched off. High-rises darkened, big banks and investment companies illuminated signs were switched off and even the Opera House faded into the night. A cheer rose from the crowd as the darkness closed in through the city. Not all the lights had gone off, but it was still a great success.

I wondered how Andy was feeling right now. Since the leadership course we had spent many hours after work at the local pub, drinking wine and talking about conservation, changing the world, life, love and the universe. I enjoyed our discussions and he constantly made me laugh. He told me that he had recently come out of a long relationship that had ended badly and I sensed I barely knew the half of it. I'd heard Ray once say, 'Andy's lost his mojo,' and I thought that was odd, because he was always surrounded by women. He was fun-loving and a natural storyteller, someone who could regale a crowd with humour. In truth, I was pretty sure I had never met anyone like him. I found myself thinking about him, wondering what he thought of me.

'There's this guy at work,' I told Gabby one night after work.

'Oh, really?' Gabby smiled.

'Yeah, but it's weird. I honestly can't tell if he likes me. I mean, he's got this English aloof way about him that makes him very hard to read. I thought he was married, but he's not.'

Gabby nodded, encouraging me to go on.

'We're often the last ones left at the pub. That could mean he's interested or it could mean he's a drunk . . . and I am too.'

'Maybe he's on the rebound,' Gabby suggested.

'Well, yeah. Probably.'

'Is he flirting with you?'

'Well, yeah . . . I think so, but that doesn't mean anything. He flirts with everyone.'

I wanted to rule Andy out of the picture. The last thing I needed in a new job was a relationship with someone I worked with, let alone something that bound me in any way to living permanently in Sydney. Besides, he didn't wear khaki or have stubble. He was a suit who lived in a big city, the kind of guy I *never* went for. He really wasn't my type.

But when I saw him walk into the cocktail lounge late on the night of Earth Hour, dashing in a dark suit, eyes piercing behind square glasses, I grew so shy and nervous I almost dropped my champagne flute. I didn't know what had come over me. Standing beside the dance floor in my red dress, I tried to compose myself. He walked straight up to me, started to say a few words that I could barely hear over the music, then, mid-sentence, walked away to mingle with people outside.

Feeling slightly bereft, I told myself to forget him. *He's not interested. He barely spoke to you.* Then another voice said, *Don't give up on this one. He's just led the largest climate change campaign this country has ever seen. He's exhausted and probably slightly delirious. Swallow your pride. Give him another chance.*

Later that night, driving home to Bronte in a taxi, I was listening through a drunken haze to the news on the radio, thinking how ridiculous I had been to even contemplate a crush on the Englishman. He was always surrounded by women and clearly I had taken the subtle flirtations too personally. He was a Libran, after all, the sun sign of ultimate charm. Besides, having just come out of a break-up, he was hardly ready to launch into a new relationship. He really wasn't worth the mind space I was giving him. So, instead I thought of a half-a-dozen different and very sound reasons why I should forget about him as anything other than a colleague.

'Tonight in Sydney the lights went off for an hour in a statement about climate change,' the newsreader said. 'Even the famous Harbour Bridge dimmed its lights. The World Wildlife Fund says Earth Hour has been a resounding success. WWF spokesperson Andy Ridley.'

Oh, for God's sake!

Andy's voice blasted over the airwaves. 'It's amazing. Everywhere in Sydney, people got together and made something incredible happen tonight. Collectively, we can make a huge difference to the problem of climate change.'

I smiled, listening to his English accent and his words, vibrating with passion and belief. *This isn't over yet. Man, he's got a sexy voice.*

I flew up to my parents' farm for a week at Easter and didn't expect to hear anything from Andy during that time. So I was surprised when I got a text message from him on my way back to Sydney, saying, *How was your Easter? Did the Easter bunny come?*

I replied, *Yep. Me and five-year-old niece heavily inebriated with chocolate. Mission accomplished.*

Five minutes later my phone beeped with a response, *Well done. Me also inebriated. No chocolate involved. When u back in Syd?*

On way now. Bright lights calling.

Great. Dinner? Your side of town? Friday?

I almost fainted. Dinner? Was he asking me on a date? Maybe he had noticed me after all.

My heart racing, I texted back a highly composed *Sounds good*, then deleted 'good' and changed it to *Sounds great*.

Five days later, on a deserted Bronte beach, we were walking barefoot along the sand back to my flat under a globular full moon. The dinner had been wonderful and the conversation had flowed. Andy had all sorts of ideas about fixing the problems of the world and his passion invigorated me. We talked about the places we had travelled and when I spoke he seemed to really listen. He didn't fill silences with random chatter, but paused often to consider what I was saying. Andy's sense of humour was contagious and I found myself smiling and laughing all the time when I was with him. His charisma was magnetic and I knew I was melting under the weight of what had definitely become a crush.

Unfortunately there's a reason why they call it a 'crush'. That's what will happen to you if you let it run away with you too fast. I was in trouble and all the little voices in my head were screaming at me.

Watch out, girl! He's on the rebound. You work with him. He's obsessed with saving the planet – he won't have time for you. He's a Libran – an astrological disaster for a Cancerian. He's a city boy who wears a suit and he's never even been to Africa – he doesn't even like khaki! How on earth would he stand up to a lion? He's charming and flirtatious and dangerously charismatic and you better watch your step, Matson, because he's probably got a girl in every city. You're gonna get your heart broke . . .

The pearly moon reflected in a silver ocean. Waves rushed to the shore in frothy white bursts, whispering *Husssssshhhhhh* . . . I forced the voices of doubt to obey their command. The sand was cold and wet between my toes and the wine had fully permeated my senses. I was pretty sure I was slurring my words as I rambled about insignificant things, trying to banish the pestering voices from my head.

But for the first time in the evening I don't think Andy was listening to me at all. As we walked along the beach, he reached for my hand and held it firmly. Then he stopped me in the sand and I felt his arms curl around my shoulders. And that was the moment, under an autumn moon, that he decided to kiss me.

THIRTEEN

Contrary to everyone's expectations (including mine) Andy and I were still an item six months later. We had managed to keep it quiet until June, our own little secret, which both of us enjoyed while it lasted. Once people at work found out, we became a feature item on the rumour mill and it wasn't pretty. As anyone who's ever had a workplace romance knows, there's no way to deal with the tidal wave of gossip when it hits than to roll with it, letting it chuck you around for as long as it likes until it spits you out onto the shore covered in oceanic saliva. Don't expect to have good hair at the end of it.

My mother was delighted, of course, convinced that Andy would be the answer to my wayward wandering ways and that this meant I would stay in Australia and produce babies imminently.

'I'm just so pleased you've found someone to take care of you,' she said. 'I never liked the idea of you out there on your own.'

'Mum, I don't need someone to take care of me. I've been looking after myself perfectly well for the last decade. Besides, this isn't serious. I'm still going back to Africa.'

'Of course you are. Just remember, you're not getting any younger and it's not so easy to get pregnant after thirty-five.'

As usual, my father's response was the opposite of my mother's. My parents epitomise the cliché that opposites attract. Even after over thirty years of marriage, they still come from different planets. Like the poles of two magnets, it works for them, and it certainly makes for interesting dinner conversations.

'He's English?' my dad enquired, not hiding the disbelief in his voice.

'Yes, Dad.'

'English?'

'Yes, you know, the people that live in England.'

'A bloody pom? Send him up here for a week and we'll see what he's made of. We've got a whole load of calves that need castrating . . .'

When I took Andy up to the farm to meet the family during a particularly cold, dry Darling Downs winter, my brother Davo brought out an enormous bullet and placed it upright on the table in front of him. As it hit the glass table it made a loud clang.

'This is what my dad uses in his elephant gun,' Davo declared, grinning widely.

Before Andy could rise to the bait my father came in and announced that he was going out to send a bull off to be slaughtered.

'Why is that?' Andy asked innocently.

'His sheath's too long,' Dad replied flatly.

Later that night in bed Andy glanced down to his nether region and said, 'Remind me not to get on your dad's bad side. With a sheath this size I could be in trouble.'

On weekends away in the Hunter Valley wine region, swimming with dolphins in the glittering waters of Jervis Bay and hiking in the majestic Blue Mountains, Andy had filled my life with romance and fun and a healthy supply of sauvignon blanc. This unassuming Englishman was showing me the beauty of my own country and I began to see it with fresh eyes. He loved the energy of Sydney, and the fact that it was warm and sunny for more than half the year. And it's fair to say I grew to like it more than I had ever expected to.

But while there were still elephants out there, a part of me would always be torn. I had been a gypsy since I had left home at seventeen. Living out of a suitcase was second nature to me. Wild animals and wild places were where I drew my strength from, and after eight months in Sydney I could feel my energy waning. I had love in my life, something I had never expected to find here in the city, but it couldn't replace that basic need. While there was no way I was going to give up Africa for a man, I was pretty sure I didn't want to give up Andy just yet either.

So when I saw an opportunity to combine two of my favourite things – elephants and Andy – I jumped at it. But the elephants weren't in Africa this time. They were in India. Invited by my counterpart at WWF India, Sujoy Banerjee, to help them with some elephant problems during October, the peak of the human-elephant conflict season in India, I wasted no time saying yes. Andy was planning a holiday there around then too, so we decided to go together. This would be a good test. People told us that if we could survive a month together in India we could get through anything.

The elephant's skin felt hot and prickly beneath my thighs. Southern India's close, humid air stuck to me like a blanket, creating sweaty patches under my arms and in the small of my back. The muezzin was chanting the call to prayer at a nearby mosque, his deep, lilting voice blaring from the loudspeaker. The ethereal sound lifted me higher.

I'd dreamed of this moment for a long time.

'Okay. I think that's enough now,' Andy's voice cut into my thoughts.

I twisted round to look at him. His legs were even more distended than mine. He looked awkward and uncomfortable.

'Enough?' I was surprised.

'Yeah. That was fun, but I've had enough.'

Men, I thought.

'Andy, we've only been on the elephant three minutes.'

'I know, I know,' he replied. 'It's fine for you but I'm on the fat bit.'

'What do you mean, fat bit?'

'He's had way too many pies. You're sitting comfy on his neck, but I'm on the love handles.'

I laughed and both of us wobbled as we fought to keep our balance. Every movement threatened to pull us off the ambling giant. Soon we were in hysterics – unwise when you're four metres up on an Asian bull elephant without a seatbelt.

Earlier we'd watched the small, stern-faced mahout unchain the bull from the ankle, commanding him to reverse up to a concrete platform so we could climb on. It was fascinating to watch the little man shout commands to a colossus, which readily understood him. The elephant was called Anendan. The cab driver had told us that this is one of the names of the Hindu god Vishnu – the protector. The elephant's face and the ends of his ears were a pigmented pale pink and covered in black spots. He'd been blessed with a daub of red ash between the eyes.

Compared with the immense African savannah elephants I

knew so well, Anendan and the other elephants of this species were – there's no other word for it – almost pretty, and they're often used decoratively at Indian holy festivals. Not as large as African elephants, the heads are more conical, the ears smaller and lower. The features are altogether more delicate than their African cousins.

Most elephants in zoos and circuses are Asian (*Elephas maximus*) not African (*Loxodonta africana*), and there's a historical reason for this. In Asia elephants have been captured and used in agriculture and war for at least four thousand years, maybe more. The Egyptians and other North African races routinely used African forest elephants (*L. africana cyclotis*) and the now extinct North African elephant (*L. africana pharaohensis*) but were unable to domesticate the larger African savannah species (*L. africana africana*) that dominates the African continent today.

Hoisting myself onto Anendan's back, I'd been surprised by the sheer size of his girth, which forced my legs into their ungainly, yoga-like posture. A flimsy rope hung around the elephant's neck in a poor imitation of reins, providing a psychological rather than practical form of safety. Nonetheless, I clung on to them tightly while Andy grasped the leather belt round my waist. Led by the mahout, precariously balanced, we plodded slowly away down the narrow, palm-lined village street so typical of small beach towns in southern Kerala.

A thin, scratchy blanket was all that separated us from the bull's back and I could feel the warmth of his body, the hardness of the spine. I reached down to touch the rough skin of his neck, hard as concrete and covered in thick bristly hairs. With each slow flap of the giant ears a gust of warm wind blew into my face. Pachyderm airconditioning.

After a while I began to get into the rhythm, letting the moment take me to just being there, entirely in it. Even the sound of our rubbing against the elephant's back became syncopated to the rhythm of Anendan's massive strides. A gentle breeze rustled the palm trees and began to take the edge off the heat.

'This is awesome,' I said as Andy gripped my belt harder. Every time he moved, it threatened to plunge us over the edge. I tried not to think about the news report. *Two conservationists from Australia were killed today when they fell headfirst off an elephant.* What a stupid, inconsequential exit that would be – hardly a stingray barb to the heart or a lion dragging you off for a meal.

Suddenly the peaceful street was transformed by a bus heaving with noisy schoolchildren, which actually speeded up as the driver took in the two tourists on a bull elephant. Only an arm's length away children hung from the windows, laughing and calling and waving. Unlike horses – which would have been freaked out by this – Anendan regarded them evenly and continued plodding along. A motorbike clattered round us at high speed and was ignored. With chaos all around, on top of him there was a profound sense of peace, a kind of untouchability. We were riding the king of the jungle.

So this is how the world looks to an elephant, I thought. This was why I'd come to this place in southern Kerala – to ride an elephant. Even though I was in India to work as a zoologist I knew that sometimes it was really important to see things without scientific goggles. I wanted to see and feel what an elephant sees and feels. I wanted to go outside my human perceptions – really get a sense of the Asian elephant's side of the story – and this was the first step on that journey.

'It's *madness*,' declared Andy, 'madness.' Without turning around I knew he was grinning. From an elephant's point of view I couldn't disagree. To an elephant in India, the world must seem completely mad.

We'd known we were entering the mad zone well before we made it to India's far north-eastern state of Assam. The tone of the newspaper and internet articles we were reading in the south had been pretty explicit.

The state of Assam has been badly affected by armed insurgency over the last one and a half decades with various insurgent groups like the ULFA, NDFB, DHD, UPDS, NSCN waging a low intensity war against the lawfully established Government. Ever since they were formed, the major insurgent groups ULFA and NDFB have committed scores of incidents of mindless violence like murders, bomb explosions, kidnapping for ransom etc which have had a serious bearing on the law and order situation of the state.

A man called Sanjay Ghosh had been captured and killed by the ULFA in 1997 and it just so happened that he was an environmental activist, exactly what Andy and I were. As a result of this and other rebel activities, the state of Assam was on the no-go list for Australian travellers. Tezpur (the town in Assam where we were going to be based) translates literally to 'City of Blood'.

There was one big thing drawing me to Assam and I wasn't about to let any rebel activities hold me back. The human-elephant conflict situation there was extreme, far worse than anywhere I'd worked before. Headlines like ELEPHANTS TRAMPLE TWO PEOPLE TO DEATH and DRUNKEN ELEPHANTS RAMPAGE IN INDIA had become commonplace. Assam contains about 5000 of India's 25 000 or so elephants, a subspecies of the Asian elephant. Several BBC reports claimed that elephants in Assam were getting drunk on villagers' rice beer and charging through villages killing people. There were allegations of hundreds of people being killed by elephants and even greater numbers of retaliatory elephant killings. Then, the week before we were due to leave Kerala for Assam, we'd read in the *Times of India* that human-elephant conflict had broken out around the island of Majuli in Assam, taking several more lives.

Between the insurgency and elephant conflicts, Assam sounded like a war zone, but I had a feeling we weren't being told the whole story. Hundreds of killings? Drunken elephants? If these figures were correct, this was a big step up from my Bushmanland experiences in terms of the intensity of human-elephant conflict.

It takes eight hours to fly from one end of the Indian continent to the other, but our journey wasn't over when we arrived at Guwahati, the capital of Assam. Sujoy had invited me to advise the Minister of Forests in Assam on some techniques that were working in Africa to reduce human-elephant conflict, in the hope some of them might be applied in Assam. By email he informed me that he'd arranged for a cab to drive us to Tezpur, about five hours' drive east of Guwahati.

It had sounded simple enough but in India nothing ever is. Arriving at Guwahati airport, our cab wasn't there. My mobile phone didn't work (due to military security, we learned later) so I handed over a few rupees to a telephone shop at the airport and called Sujoy in Delhi.

'Hi, Sujoy. It's Tammie Matson from WWF Australia.'

'Tammie! How is your holiday?'

'Fantastic. We've just arrived in Guwahati.'

'Guwahati?' He sounded surprised. 'You are there now?'

'Yeah, we just flew in. But there's no taxi so I thought I'd give you a call and check that everything was arranged.'

'Oh. Please accept my apologies! I am getting the dates confused. I thought you were arriving in two days. I am very sorry. Please wait there. I will arrange one right away.'

'No problem, Sujoy. We'll wait till it comes.'

'Yes, and do not stray from airport. It can be dangerous in Guwahati.'

About half an hour later, a large older man with a paunch and a younger skinnier man barely out of his teens emerged and led us to a small hatchback in the car park. Looking skittishly aggressive, the young man leapt into the driver's seat like a rodeo rider jumping on a bull. Bellowing instructions the larger one clambered in beside him. Andy and I sat in the back, exchanging looks of excitement laced with fear.

Driving in India is challenging at the best of times but in Assam it's death-defying. Rickshaws darted in and out like mongooses. Ambassador cabs pushed and shoved and hooted. Pulled by blasé Brahmin bullocks with painted blue and red horns with gold tips, ancient wooden carts competed for space. Packed with sweaty, chattering passengers, windowless buses belched and farted their way down the road. Rickety bicycles and motorbikes whizzed in and out. Elephants with men on their backs carried palm leaves and logs at their own lackadaisical pace. Cows chewed the cud standing in the middle of the highway – bovine roadblocks with attitude. Everyone and no one owns the road.

Yet there's a surreal, counterintuitive sense of calm about the drivers who brave India's highways. Everyone ignores lines on the road and the beeping is incessant. I later learned that this isn't rude – people beep as a matter of courtesy to let other motorists know they're coming through. It's not uncommon to see an entire family on one motorbike – the husband driving, wife behind him, small child behind her and in the mother's lap, under her sari, a tiny foot with a gold anklet the only sign of the baby she's holding. The look of serenity on the woman's face as her colourful sari glides behind her, wisps of long dark hair escaping from a long plait threaded with white flowers is in stark contrast to the mayhem surrounding her. These women of the family motorbikes ride side-saddle without holding on to anything but their babies, balancing with so little effort that you'd think they were superglued to the seat.

There was another complicating factor in Assam – the army. As we drove out of Guwahati, the little hatchback had a face-off with a beast ten times its size. Our driver didn't slow down, but pulled off the bitumen as first one army truck then a convoy passed us, taking up the entire road. The military drivers glared down disdainfully.

Known worldwide for its tea – which grows in large plantations called tea gardens – Assam is a largely agricultural state. The lush, green rice fields that dominate the landscape are the result of extremely high rainfall, which reaches a peak in June during the monsoon. The magnificent Brahmaputra River snakes through the centre of the state like a huge artery, up to sixteen kilometres across in some places during the wet season. What the rural nature of Assam means for the roads is that there are probably more goats and cows than in many other parts of India, posing a direct threat to small cars tearing up the bitumen at breakneck speeds. As a result of the monsoon and the odd landmine laid by insurgents, the bitumen was heavily dented with potholes. In many stretches there were more holes than road, so we were often forced to drive on the dirt edging. The speedometer didn't work so we had no idea how fast we were going, but it didn't really matter because there weren't any speed signs and, as in Africa, the cops had more important things to do than issue speeding fines. We spent most of the five hours to Tezpur clinging to each other as our driver swerved round herds of cattle, potholes and army trucks, sometimes simultaneously.

There were signs of military activity everywhere. In each

town there were men in army uniform with automatics standing around or manning army bases under camouflage netting.

'Tezpur is military base,' announced the man in the passenger seat. 'Insurgents very bad.'

Seeking independence from the government, the rebel ULFA were still active in Assam, conducting regular kidnappings and killings to prove their point. The huge military presence suggested that the Assamese government was doing its damnedest to put the lid on them.

We stopped once for a train to pass. Beside us an army truck had also come to a halt. I looked up to see a dozen soldiers staring at me. After two weeks in Kerala I was used to this, but it was quite a different experience to see men with machine-guns doing the same thing. I pulled my sarong around my shoulders and leaned in to Andy. How strange, I thought, to feel this way here when just a few weeks ago I'd been strolling along Bronte beach in a bikini.

Our two guides were oblivious to this. The man in the passenger seat bought a handful of small green bananas from a hawker and presented them to us.

'You are my guests.' He waggled his head from side to side. 'Please take.'

After three hours of this alarming journey and the gawking soldiers, my appetite was suppressed but I gladly accepted the compensatory banana. The train passed and we were off, doing the sheep-swerving taxi dance again.

'We missed that one by a millimetre,' Andy observed.

I dragged my eyes away from the road ahead and raised an eyebrow. A minute later, another herd emerged. This was like being in some sick computer game. Sooner or later, we were going to get blown up and a sign would pop up, saying *Game Over*.

As yet another herd loomed, the driver neither slowed down nor prepared to weave between them. I watched the man's shoulders stiffen and rise. The tension in the car was palpable.

The hatchback hit a sheep and it rolled under the car, making an awful clunking sound as we bounced over it. All four heads turned to discover what had happened to it, only to see the sheep roll to a stop on the road. The driver never took his foot off the accelerator.

'Shouldn't we check if it's alive?' I shouted over the wind rushing through the car.

'Forget the sheep.' Andy shrugged his shoulders. 'Let's focus on us getting there alive.'

We arrived in Tezpur just after dark. The driver took us to the WWF office to meet the local manager of Assam's north bank landscape, Dr Anupam Sarmah, who extended a formal greeting and insisted he escort us to our hotel. We would begin work tomorrow, once we had rested.

After the hideous journey, rest was the last thing on our minds. We needed a stiff drink and invited Dr Sarmah to join us for a Kingfisher beer.

'No. I don't drink,' he replied. 'See you tomorrow.'

Feeling vaguely chastised we stood at the entrance to the hotel, but the guilt didn't last.

'So . . . Kingfisher?'

'Hell, yeah.'

We'd stayed in a wide range of accommodation in Kerala, but nothing compared to the Hotel Luit, Tezpur's top establishment. On entry I had to sign a form stating that I would be chaperoned by a male at all times. Incense smoked from a shrine in the entrance. We soon realised it wasn't just smoking – the shrine was actually on fire. Soon the whole foyer was thick with smoke and it crossed my mind that we might have to leap from our fourth-floor room if someone didn't put it out soon. But the front desk manager seemed blithely unconcerned.

We made our way through the smoke to the restaurant. The windowless room was dark and smelled of old curry. A Bollywood film was blasting from the television in the corner and two waiters leaned nonchalantly against the bar watching it. There were no customers.

'I don't think I'll be having the chicken,' I said.

Andy pointed towards moth-eaten drapes. 'I just saw a rat. It went under that curtain.'

We sank two Kingfishers, ate dhal and a 'vegetable' curry of unspecified origin (it might have been pork) and chapattis. The waiters stared at the Bollywood babes wiggling their way across the screen.

'Well, it's not the most atmospheric restaurant we've been to, but the dhal's good,' I volunteered.

'Dhalicious,' he replied. After a couple of Kingfishers, it was the funniest thing I had heard all day.

The next day in the WWF office, over many cups of fabulously strong, sweet Assam tea, Anupam described the human-elephant conflict in his region north of the Brahmaputra River.

'Population growth's the big problem here. Very big. It is not just the Assamese people. We have the issue of illegal immigration. That's a massive social issue. These people are pouring in from Bangladesh and other places and it's not controlled.'

Anupam paused, sighed, then went on, 'The government's been monitoring changes in forest cover in the north since 1991 and the loss is very bad. Almost a third of the forest went between 1991 and 2001.'

'What's the population growth been during that time?' asked Andy.

Dr Sarmah solemnly consulted his book.

'Eighteen percent,' he said, proud of his exactness and smiling for the first time.

I learned later that in fact about two-thirds of the lowland forest in Assam's Brahmaputra Valley had been destroyed since 1972, less than half an Asian elephant's life span. The human population had grown by twenty percent in the last decade. Anupam's smile faded as he showed us maps illustrating the extreme loss of elephant habitat.

With nowhere else to go, living in only a third of their former habitat, elephants were coming out of the forest and into people's small plots of farmland in search of food. That was where the conflict occurred, when people were defending their crops, homes and families. Every year, Anupam explained sombrely, dozens of people were being killed by elephants as they defended their meagre fields. In just one week in 1993 elephants killed fifty people. And at the desperate interface of human and elephant hunger, many elephants were being killed by humans too. In 2001 more than fifteen elephants were poisoned in one massacre by unknown perpetrators – retaliation for the deaths of humans caused by elephants.

He shrugged his shoulders. 'We're fighting a losing battle here. Just today in the paper six elephants were electrocuted in low-hanging powerlines. You can see the pictures for yourself.'

The newspaper headline read, ELEPHANTS ELECTROCUTED IN DRUNKEN RAMPAGE.

Allegedly the elephants had come to drink one of their favourite things, rice beer, which local people fermented in plastic drums in their huts. Some of the drunk and rowdy elephants 'went berserk', uprooting a power pole and causing several of them to get electrocuted in the live lines. It was a scene too awful to contemplate.

The following day we joined two of the WWF team, Hiten Baishya and Deba Dutter, on a journey through the northern part of Assam up to the border with the state of Aranuchal Pradesh. As we drove north the Himalayas loomed tantalisingly close in the distance but, being in Arunachal Pradesh we couldn't access them on foot. A wide river fed by water from the mountains formed the border between the two states.

On the Assam side of the border, little forest remained. We drove along narrow, potholed roads through a region that, in the last few years, had been converted to subsistence agriculture – largely rice paddies. The stumps of large trees in very recently cleared areas stood out like ugly scars. Piles of firewood for sale beside the road testified not only to the loss of forest but to the plight of desperate people trying to live here. The villagers were doing all they could to make a humble living off this land. Unfortunately, it was the same land that the last of Assam's elephants needed to survive. Until recently this had been their home.

Without the forest to feed and shelter in, the elephants were finding rice paddies in the place where trees had been, an enticing opportunity for hungry herbivores. The flimsy bamboo huts of the villagers would be little deterrent to an elephant with a rumbling stomach. None of the crops were fenced and these people had no materials to make fences, or money to buy materials.

'Many of them are illegals,' Hiten observed. 'They're coming in from Bangladesh. Others are tribals who have moved in recently.'

'Why doesn't the government kick them out?' I yelled above the roar of the diesel engine of the suspensionless Mahindra.

'The government won't do anything! You see, then they

will vote for them. No one has control over what these people do. They can do what they like. The legislation actually *supports* them to stay here.'

'A voter bank,' Andy commented. 'Smart politics.'

'So there's no rule of law here?' I said, incensed. 'Illegal immigrants can stay, chopping further and further into the forest every day, and elephants have to go. Then more and more people come and keep encroaching on the forest, making even less habitat for elephants.' I shook my head. 'No wonder this place has a human-elephant conflict problem.'

Later that day we obtained permission from the district forest officer to enter Nameri National Park, which sits on the border of Assam and Arunachal Pradesh. He informed us that his biggest problem was 'the buffer zone' – the region lying just outside Nameri.

'For some of the year we patrol. We are having twelve domestic elephants that we are patrolling with and there are two hundred wild elephants in Nameri. But for most of the year the park is impenetrable. When the floods come we can do nothing.'

The sun was setting as a young forestry ranger brandishing an antique shotgun rowed us across the Jia Bhorali river. The cold, grey water turned to silver as the hues of sunset washed over it. Water lapped at our wooden canoe. Before us lay Nameri, the full moon rising over the thick, old growth forest like something out of Kipling's *The Jungle Book*.

This was what we'd been waiting for. Andy and I had been in India for weeks, but we hadn't seen anything vaguely resembling a wilderness. Unfortunately there wasn't a heck a lot of it left in India. We stepped onto the bank and pulled the canoe out of the water. The ranger led the way across the sand as we scrambled up the bank and into the jungle along a wide path that had obviously been made by elephants.

The air felt fresh and healthy, rich with organic smells. I took it all in as if it were the first real oxygen I'd breathed for weeks. India is a festival of aromas, many of them very nice, like the sweet smell of incense, the wafting aromas of the spice markets or the enticing fragrances of hot curry. At the other extreme, the sheer mess of humanity in India means that other smells, like the stench of rubbish heaps along the roads and uncleaned, communal squatting toilets with excrement splattered on the walls, can be equally overwhelming.

The trees around us were at least twenty metres tall, their trunks thick with wide-leafed vines. The jungle was so dense and moist it looked almost impenetrable. As we walked further in I recognised the pungent smell of stink beetles, an odour I knew well from Africa. A chattering monkey leapt from a tree, the small, grey face full of alarm. My boots sloshed through the mud as I leapt over puddles and avoided piles of elephant dung.

When we entered a clearing a deer barked in the distance, holding the promise of far more animal life than we had time to see before nightfall.

I asked Deba, 'What kind of deer is that?'

'A barking deer,' he replied.

Andy rolled his eyes and said, 'Duh, Dr Matson.'

In Africa I'd always avoided walking in the bush at this time of day, even with an armed guard. At twilight it was just dark enough to obscure proper vision. Human faces fuzzed, shapes morphed and blurred, and elephants became ghosts of the night. In the African bush, this is when sight bows to hearing, when your eyes become your worst enemy, unworthy of your usual explicit trust. Predators love this time of day, when the senses of prey animals like us are confused, when you're not sure if it's a francolin in the bush behind you – that subtle shuffling of leaves, the crack of a stick – or a lion. Then you have only your ears to rely on and the big cats have the advantage.

As my sight became poorer I felt other senses kicking in – hearing, smell, peripheral vision, gut instinct – senses I hardly ever used now that I lived in Sydney, unlike in Africa, where they'd been finetuned by regular use. It felt good to be using them again.

'There are tigers in Nameri, right?' I whispered to Deba.

He smiled but there was concern in his eyes.

The ranger suddenly stopped in his tracks and studied something in the distance.

'We go back,' he announced.

I felt bereft to be leaving this beautiful place so soon but knew it was unwise to go further. The green grass that ran alongside the elephant track was taller than a man and perfect cover for the big cats that lived here – leopards and panthers, as well as tigers.

Back at the camp – a small wooden house overlooking the river – Hiten told us we had to wait for a couple of rangers who wanted to catch a ride across the river. By now it was quite dark, the only light in the camp coming from a pearly full moon and the candles illuminating the miniature shrine to Ganesh. The tiny, bright sparks of fireflies danced in the long grass. Save for the low murmur of the men's voices, it was quiet.

I squatted by the small shrine and watched the flames flicker over Ganesh, this Hindu god with an elephant's head and a mouse at his feet. Elephants are such an important part of India's culture, history and religion. Everywhere we travelled we'd seen signs of this – in museums, life-size sculptures carved out of rock and sandstone, ancient detailed paintings of armoured elephants going to war, holy elephants decked out in jewels and gold tassels carved into ancient temples and palaces, relics and monuments to both captive elephants and Ganesh. Half of the cabs we'd driven in had either a psychedelic flashing elephant on the dash or one hanging from the rear-view mirror.

For Hindus, Ganesh is the remover of obstacles and the lord of success. He is also, I was told, the protector of writers, signified by the broken tusk in his hand that represents a writing quill. This important deity, lovingly revered by many, has the head of an elephant, symbolising strength, and the body of a man, representing wisdom and intellect. He has a mouse at his feet, which represents presence of mind. Ganesh is the son of Shiva and Parvati, and holds enormous significance in the hearts and minds of many Indians. Before getting married, buying a house or doing anything new in India, one always starts with a prayer to the elephant god.

As I stared into the flames murmuring my own prayer to Ganesh, two gunshots broke the peace of the night and a man's voice shouted from somewhere in the jungle. No one seemed bothered.

I walked hurriedly back to where Andy was sitting with Hiten and Deba.

'What was that?'

'Warning shots,' explained Hiten. 'Keeps illegal fishing at bay.'

Then we saw the most amazing sight. Backlit by the gushing water of the river, the silhouettes of four men riding on two elephants appeared out of the jungle. The goliath profiles were like something out of a dream. They seemed to be moving in slow motion but covered the fifty metres between us in seconds. I watched as they knelt down to let the men off and pondered how a culture so steeped in elephants could have a human-elephant conflict problem. How could a people whose chief religion involved a prime god with the head of an elephant have a population threatened with extinction? It was such a bizarre contradiction.

As we strolled barefoot back across the moonlit sand to our canoe, the ranger told me that he and his men had been patrolling the park for twelve hours on elephant-back. The men spent their days with these domestic elephants, seeing elephants in the wild, protecting elephants and all the other creatures in Nameri from poachers. Beyond that, their lives were enmeshed in religion and worship of Ganesh. They lived and breathed elephants as if they were part of the same family.

My feet sank into the sand and I felt the spongy coolness between my toes. Turning my back on the park I prepared to return to the madness of civilisation, wondering how long the enchanting place behind us would remain.

FOURTEEN

The next day, our fourth in Assam, we were on the hunt for a wild elephant in a tea garden. You would think that finding a five-tonne bull in a relatively ordered plantation, where hundreds of people worked and claimed to have seen it just a short while earlier, would be easy. Not so. This made looking for a needle in a haystack seem easy.

The rows of lush green cropped tea bushes interspersed with tall shady trees were an oasis of order and precision in the chaotic madness of India that raged beyond its straight-edged borders. Ladies in colourful saris dotted the rows, picking tea leaves with nimble fingers and placing them in baskets. Some carried babies on their backs as they worked. Others sat on the ground eating meagre bowls of plain white rice. Most of them looked like they hadn't had a decent meal in quite some time.

As we lurched along bumpy dirt roads, past the manicured lawns surrounding the manager's sprawling home, we stopped regularly to ask workers where the elephants were, using the Assamese word for elephant, '*hathi*'. One man told us that six elephants had been there the night before. Another said there was only one and he had seen it with his own eyes just half an hour ago. Go that way, one said, pointing right. Go left, the next one said, just up the road. *Hathi* this, *hathi* that. Where the hell was the huge hiding *hathi*?

Despite Hiten the *hathi* hunter's best efforts, we couldn't find any elephants in the tea gardens, either real or imagined. Instead we found a small town with a curry restaurant, which wasn't a bad substitute. There we feasted on the hottest curry I have ever tasted. We were the only Europeans in sight and I the only female in the bustling eatery, so we found ourselves very much the centre of everyone's attention.

'This is where all the trouble is happening,' Hiten explained over lunch. 'The elephants are coming into the tea gardens at night. The workers are brewing their rice beer and the elephants love this. They drink it and then they cause trouble. That's when people get killed.'

Andy and I nodded vigorously. Tears were running down my face. Hiten paused to dip a handful of white rice into a chicken curry and chew it without even a grimace, before going on. I swigged lukewarm water from my bottle, trying to cool down.

'These workers in the tea gardens, some of the men, they go out at night and they are drunk too. Then when a drunk elephant is meeting a drunk man, well . . . you can imagine what is happening there.'

He paused again, waiting for some response from us.

'I'm listening,' I said, my voice husky with the heat of the dhal I had just swallowed. 'It's just that my eyeballs are about to explode.'

Shy Deba interjected, smiling, 'You are liking the Indian food?'

I nodded and smiled, wiping the tears from my eyes. 'I love it.'

Our Assamese friends laughed warmly and waggled their heads from side to side, the Indian equivalent of a nod.

Hiten went on, 'You must remember that so much of the forest has been cleared that the elephants will do almost anything to get food now.'

'But what can they eat in the tea plantations?'

'Nothing. They do not eat the tea bushes. In the day sometimes they stay in the gardens for the shade. The gardens are in the migration path to the rice paddies. You have seen yourself today how close people's crops are to the tea gardens. At night they come into the paddies and eat the crop, or in the villages near the paddies and tea gardens they go into the huts to drink the rice beer. When the rice harvest is coming, like is happening now, then we are getting a lot of elephants here.'

Hiten and Deba claimed that there were plenty of elephants around, but although we had seen a few captive elephants, we still hadn't seen a wild one. Determined to find some for us, they took us to a village that was a WWF-designated hot spot for human-elephant conflicts, a little way west of the Jia Bhorali River that we had crossed by dugout the night before. Hiten told us that elephants tried to raid there every night. It must have been part of an important migration corridor through the Himalayan foothills.

As the sun dropped through clear blue alpine skies, the distant peaks of mountains formed an imposing backdrop that was more like a painting than a real landscape. A slow stream of villagers carrying heavy loads on their shoulders waded through knee-deep water across a shallow river. One man, lean and muscled, led his small son across by the hand, using his free hand to balance a rickety old bicycle that hung over one shoulder. The river swallowed the boy up to the chest, but with his free hand the man nimbly yanked him up again, pulling him out of the deep water and dropping him in a shallow part. On the hunched back of an old white-haired man two large bundles of green grass hung off a wooden pole. His sinewy legs carried him across the gentle flow of the river and he squinted as sunlight streamed across the nutty-brown skin of his face. His faded military shirt was wet with sweat.

Just north of here was Arunachal Pradesh, 'land of the dawn-lit mountains'. We were told that it was off-limits without a special permit, so we would be able to explore the forests and rivers at the base of the Himalayan foothills in Assam, but, unfortunately, not the famous mountains. They were just over the border – we could look but not touch. Just to the north-west was the Buddhist country of Bhutan, and a little north of Arunachal Pradesh was the vast land mass of Tibet.

'The elephants will be here at five-thirty,' announced Hiten with absolute certainty.

'Five-thirty? On the dot?' I responded, thinking that Asian elephants must be a lot more predictable than their African cousins.

'They have watches?' Andy joked.

'What?'

'Watches,' Andy gestured to his wrist. 'You know, to tell the time.'

Hiten laughed, and his tightly cropped moustache wobbled. 'Oh no, no, no! Mr Andy, you are a very funny man!'

As we waited, troupes of small children in ragged, dirty clothes gathered around us, giggling and watching us with the intensity of people who hadn't seen too many Europeans before. One by one, the group of barefoot children edged closer to us, led by the smallest and the bravest, a boy in a ripped singlet top. My smile drew them closer and incited a lot more giggling and whispering. Suddenly Andy took a few large, rapid steps towards them and made a loud roar, sending the group into a panicked run filled with hysterical, high-pitched laughter. A few seconds later, they snuck back with tentative smiles for more, daring Andy with their cheeky eyes to try that again. Some games are guaranteed to win over kids no matter where in the world you are.

Like many people in this part of India the families of these children were poor rice farmers. Their small grass-roofed houses with walls of bamboo and clay were laid out in an organised row alongside a field. In it the long green leaves of rice ripening formed a luxuriant carpet.

In contrast to the otherwise traditional setting, an electric fence several metres high had been put up by the Department of Forestry rangers between the river and the villagers' crops and homes. It wasn't turned on all the time, Hiten explained, because the elephants only came at night. Sometimes, when it hadn't been turned on in time, elephants came and tried to push it over. Snapped wires and severely bent metal posts were the result. Hiten told us that some repairs had to be done on the fence every day. The elephants were *that* keen to get through at this time of year. It was October and almost peak season for human-elephant conflict in Assam because of the ripening rice crops.

A few minutes after five-thirty, just after the sun had set, a wild herd of elephants appeared.

'Right on time,' Andy declared, a wide grin spreading across his face. 'Let's go and have a look.'

In the faltering light of dusk, the ethereal, dark silhouettes of a small breeding herd emerged from the steep bank of the river. There were some very small ones amongst them, which the elders held between their legs protectively, keeping them in the centre of the herd. Milling around on the bank, the elephants seemed undecided about what they were going to do next.

I tried to imagine what had brought the elephants to this moment of indecision. The herd had probably walked for many miles through the foothills of the Himalayas, looking for food in disturbed forests that now were a fraction of what they had once known. Many of the adult elephants could probably remember the time thirty years ago when their range had been much bigger, when they didn't need to come down from the forest and face confrontations with noisy, aggressive primates.

Now, after a long, tiring walk through the foothills, they had coaxed their small babies across the river, choosing a place to cross where the water was not too deep or rushing so fast that a baby would be swept away. After the long walk, perhaps the herd had enjoyed the luxuriant touch of the cool alpine water on warm wrinkly skin. Or maybe, so close to a village, they could think only of the impending danger they faced by being there.

These wise old mothers must have known they were trading off safety for food. Drawn in by the luscious smell of ripening rice plants, intensifying the closer they got to the crop, their enormous tummies must have been rumbling with anticipation. It was so great a desire that even the mingling of the smell of rice crops with that of danger – the pungent aromas of human sweat and toil, the smoke of wood fires and the acrid stench of buses packed with people – couldn't keep them away. Theirs was a hunger that subsumed fear. And now that they were there, at the source of that delicious smell, a barrier stood in their way. The old ladies knew this barrier. They had been here before and been stung by its vicious steel threads of pain. It had burned their skin like fire. The first time they had recoiled instinctively in terror, shuffling small babies away from its electric charges and out of harm's way. But now they were just angry that it was there at all. It must have been infuriating and frustrating, having come so far, being so hungry and able to smell the delectable rice grass right there, just metres away, only to be prevented from reaching it by the electric fence.

A couple of dozen villagers had gathered around us and were creating a ridiculously noisy din. They were all watching the elephants and talking animatedly about them as though commenting on their favourite television comedy. Their voices were loud and intrusive, interspersed by even louder laughing. They didn't seem at all worried about the elephants a hundred metres away. A mobile phone blared through the cacophony and a man yelled 'Hello! Hello!' at the top of his lungs. Everyone seemed to be enjoying themselves, except for the elephants.

They continued to mill around on the bank, rumbling in what seemed to me to be anxious tones, still unsure after ten minutes about what their next move would be. Hiten told me that to the right of this village was a large tea garden, and then another even larger one. There were many large tea estates in this part of India. The tea gardens were where elephants often went during the day, seeking respite from the sun under tall trees that were planted in order to shade the rows of tea bushes. To the left was a town, and then another town, and then another, all merging into each other in a steaming urban sprawl of human civilisation.

To the right, tea gardens. To the left, towns. Straight ahead, an electric fence. Behind them, heavily cleared forest. What were these elephants going to do? What choice did they have but to seek out whatever food they could for their families? They had nowhere else to go.

I felt tears welling in my eyes. I wanted to yell at all the noisy people around me, 'Shut the hell up! Just shut up! And turn off your damned phone!'

But I didn't. Instead, I watched the elephants move into the disturbed forest on our side of the riverbed. Moving closer to the rice paddies, it seemed they weren't giving up on their dinner. When the elephants left, with the sunset show over, all the people went home.

'Come, Tammie, Andy,' Hiten said. 'They will try and get through the fence now. Let us go and see.'

We crawled under the fence back to the side where the village was. By now it was dark. A full moon began to rise over the river. Soon its generous illumination shone so brightly that I could see my own fingers quite clearly. We could hear the elephants nearby but we couldn't see them. Their regular rumbles and the occasional frustrated shriek were the only signs that they were there.

As we waited to see what the elephants would do, I listened to the night sounds of the village. A dog barked. Busy insects whirred and chirped. The low hum of people's voices could be heard as families enjoyed comfortable conversation and ate their evening meals. In the distance, I could hear what sounded like gunshots. We'd already seen that the military had a large presence in Assam and the newspapers reported regular confrontations with insurgents. More than once, I had heard gunshots from our hotel in Tezpur.

'Are people shooting?' I asked Hiten.

'Perhaps,' he replied, his eyes distant, 'but mostly it is the villagers using firecrackers. The loud noise, it is keeping the elephants away.'

A trail of candles flickered in the darkness along the small track that separated the rice crop from the villagers' homes. One flame burned for each house. Outside one hut was a shrine to Ganesh, decorated by more small candles. Hiten explained that the candles had been lit tonight because there was a festival on.

Of course, a festival. In our short time in India they seemed to happen every second day. This one was in honour of the goddess of wealth and wellbeing. I could only imagine she was something like an Indian version of Oprah.

Tiny glowing insects fluttered all around us like iridescent fairies swirling through the darkness. When they landed and stayed still, they flashed on and off like Christmas lights. There was no electricity in the area, but it wasn't dark. Between the glow cast by the bulbous moon, the flickering of festival candles and the dancing fireflies, the night was a spectacle of lights.

After about an hour of waiting to see if the elephants would try to break through the fence to get to the paddy, they still remained there patiently. Perhaps they were waiting for us to leave so they could make an attempt. They had all night. Where else were they going to go for food? At some stage during the night they would find a way to get through the fence. They had to. Just like these villagers, they had families to feed.

I heard a new sound then. It was the clang of metal on metal, a rhythmic jingle. *Clangy-clang. Clangy-clang*. I heard men's voices, deep and solemn, coming from behind us in the sky. I turned around to see the awesome sight of three elephants emerging from the darkness, walking ponderously down the track towards us. Giant padded feet delicately avoided the tiny festival candles with each lumbering step. They were *kunkies*, working elephants that had been trained by the forestry department to maintain the peace in the war zone between elephants and people. Their main job, Hiten told us, was to keep wild elephants away from villagers' crops. On each elephant's back were two men. They wore official military-style caps and carried single-shot rifles slung over their shoulders.

It was a scene so striking that I will never forget it. I heard one elephant rumble gently, nonconfrontational, almost a greeting. A sense of calm descended over us all in the presence of these trained giants. But I was under no illusions. Gentle as these elephants seemed with their mahout riders, I knew they could crush me in a single rapid movement. I gave them several metres of space. A couple of the men spoke to Hiten in low, deep voices, discussing in Assamese the location of the wild herd.

One of the elephants was much bigger than the other two and I guessed it had to be a bull. I'd read that the largest of Asian elephant bulls are twice the size of the females, weighing up to six tonnes and standing up to three metres in height (which is still a couple of tonnes lighter than the biggest African bulls). A chain around one of his legs was what was making the clanging sound. The other two were considerably smaller than he was and didn't have tusks, so I guessed they were females.

After a few moments of conversation between Hiten and the riders, the elephants left in the same surreal, regal manner in which they had arrived. Their boulder-like shapes seemed to drift into the darkness. I watched the giants perambulate purposefully along the electric fence and out to the other side where the wild herd hovered under the cover of forest, not wanting them to slip out of my sight. But within moments, darkness closed in around them and all that was left was the sound of the clanging chain as the bull led the way into the forest.

I expected some kind of confrontation as the *kunkies* met the wild elephants and pushed them away from the village. Would the wild ones trumpet and charge the *kunkies*? Would they rise up and thump each other with the brunt of their foreheads the same way elephant bulls in Africa fought over oestrus cows? I waited for the clash, anticipating the worst. In India, I had seen that things could get crazy very fast.

A man spoke in encouraging but nonaggressive tones, perhaps urging the bull forward. And, as if they understood, without retaliation or anger, the wild herd moved away back towards the river with no choice but to look for food in the forest. Peacefully they were followed by the three persuasive *kunkies* who would trail them across the river until they were well out of the way.

In contrast to what I had expected, there had been no tempestuous clash of domestic and wild elephants, no mad trumpeting or obstreperous screeching, just a subdued acquiescence in response to some gentle encouragement. Perhaps all of the conversation between the *kunkies* and the wild elephants had been in ultrasound, in tones that are too low in frequency to be heard by humans.

'What do you think those *kunkies* are saying to the wild ones?' I asked Andy.

'Let's hope they're saying, "Don't come here. These humans are crazy," he responded sombrely, putting his arm around my shoulder.

The *kunkies* had an important job, protecting people's livelihoods by keeping wild elephants away. But I wondered how the wild elephants perceived them. I imagined them saying, 'Traitors! You have food in your stomach because you are slaves to the humans who are destroying our home. How can you push us away, your own species?'

And I imagined the *kunkies* responding, 'You are right. We are sell-outs. But you have something we will never have. Freedom.'

The Asian elephant is in terrible trouble. India has most of Asia's wild population of around 35 000 elephants. Compared with Africa's hundreds of thousands of elephants (easily more than half a million), Asia is struggling to maintain a piddly wild population of just tens of thousands. There are about 15 000 captive elephants used in things like construction, festivals and tourism, but wild Asian elephants are on the brink of extinction in every country in which they exist (Indonesia, Myanmar, Sri Lanka, Thailand, India, Laos, Cambodia, Malaysia, Borneo and Vietnam).

In Assam, WWF had found donors to pay the cost of the *kunkies*' upkeep by the forestry department. Most of the conflicts were happening in tea plantations, and during the peak conflict season, the *kunkies* were used in what they called 'flying squads' to drive wild herds out of the plantations. Ironically, several of the tea companies proudly used elephants in their logos.

Earlier in the day, after seeing one such logo, Andy had said, 'So WWF is paying for the *kunkies* to stop conflicts in tea gardens. Workers and elephants are being killed, but even though the tea companies use elephants in their logos, they still pay nothing to help fix the problem. Sensible.'

We learned that several of the Assamese tea companies sold tea to the developed world, including England. Would people in the western world still buy tea if they knew that it came from plantations where elephants and poverty-stricken workers were dying in the dozens every year? Perhaps. But would they be *more* likely to buy tea if it came from plantations that looked after both elephants and people, even if they had to pay a little more for it? Given a choice, would you buy 'elephant-friendly' tea from plantations that were turning the problem into the solution?

Andy said, 'These tea companies are missing a brilliant marketing opportunity. Just like dolphin-friendly tuna, you could have elephant-friendly tea.'

As we walked back to the vehicle in the dark with our WWF colleagues, I wished I could say that my first sighting of wild Asian elephants had been inspiring, but it wasn't. It was sad. I wondered what the future held for India's wild elephants. It seemed unlikely that elephants would become extinct, because so many were kept in captivity. But what kind of fate was that?

I tried to imagine a world in which there were no wild elephants left in India. Disturbingly, it wasn't that hard. We were already well and truly on that downhill bus journey.

FIFTEEN

One place that was apparently full of wild elephants, and that we were determined to see, was Kaziranga National Park on the south bank of the Brahmaputra River. This four hundred square kilometre world heritage site was also where we would find the last of India's rhinos, the largest remaining population of the greater one-horned rhinoceros. The park was known for its impressive population of tigers, water buffalo and a high diversity of deer and birds. We booked a room at the Wild Grass Lodge at the edge of the park and Anupam kindly arranged for us to be transported there, a couple of hours' drive from Tezpur.

But before we left Tezpur, Anupam asked me to spend a couple of hours with his team talking through some of the options that were working in southern Africa. An economy based more on wildlife, coupled with some long-term land-use planning, was an obvious long-term solution, but while the political unrest continued in Assam, neither was likely to happen. I kept coming back to the idea of elephant-friendly products. What if WWF got the tea companies in Assam interested in marketing themselves as elephant-friendly, as Andy had suggested? And what about growing chillies and using them to deter elephants, as was working in Africa?

I knew that all over Africa the Elephant Pepper Development Trust was training local people in chilli-growing and in how to use the hot peppers as an elephant deterrent. Two years earlier, after John Hanks had told me about their chilli program, I had read as much as I could about chillies – how to grow them, how to use them as a mitigation measure in human-elephant conflict, what countries were using them. I was no expert, but I knew enough to be certain that they had to be worth a try in India.

Unfortunately, no one at WWF in Tezpur shared my enthusiasm. The year before, they had done a trial by walking a domestic elephant up to a chilli fence. The elephant had baulked, stopped in its tracks by the acrid smell, suggesting that Asian elephants, just like African ones, were indeed turned off by chilli. However, the trial had cost them an arm and a leg, so they had ruled chilli-based deterrents out as too expensive for the average villager.

I tried to convince them that growing their own chillies, not buying them, was the answer. That was why chillies had been successful in Africa; not only were they unpalatable to elephants, they provided a crop that was worth more than traditional crops like maize and sorghum. People there grew the chillies themselves. But Anupam, in particular, was quite sceptical, and no one else in his team seemed willing to support the idea.

'It won't work,' he said bluntly. 'Just because it is working in Africa does not mean it will work here.'

There were murmurs of agreement from the others. It was incredibly frustrating that they had ruled the idea out so early when their trial had actually suggested it might work. Although I wanted to scream, I couldn't blame them for their attitudes. This little team of dedicated conservationists was so entrenched in the overwhelming problems of human overpopulation, poverty, illegal immigration, civil war and human-elephant conflict, that they couldn't see out any longer. They were doing the best they could, but negativity is contagious and it seemed like they were now almost at the point where they didn't think *anything* would work to save Assam's elephants.

Andy and I left Tezpur feeling drained and wondering if we had made any kind of difference at all. There was nothing else we could say to convince them, so we headed off to Kaziranga National Park in the hope of seeing some rhinos.

An hour or so later, we met a WWF representative on the side of the road near the park, a vet and conservationist, Dr Garga Mohan. Garga's enthusiasm was a breath of fresh air after the morning's discussion.

'I am so happy that you have come to Kaziranga, Mr Andy and Dr Tammie. I am only very sorry that I must leave you tomorrow for Guwahati. And there is a problem, you see. It is a problem, but not a very big problem. The park is not yet open. It is only opening in November.'

I glanced at the date on my watch. It was 27 October. We only had three days there before we had to return to Guwahati to begin the long trip back to Australia.

'Oh, no! You mean, we can't go in?'

We both so desperately wanted to see the famous rhinos of India. Had we come all this way for nothing?

'Strictly speaking, no. You cannot enter. But we will meet with the director of Kaziranga. In fact, I will phone him this very moment and if he is available, then we will go there and talk to him.'

Garga walked to one side and spoke on his mobile phone for a few minutes before returning to us with a large smile. 'We go now to see the director. He is expecting us.'

The director's house was much larger than any others we had seen in Assam. He was clearly a man of status. Our new friend Garga, boisterous and confident a few moments before, shrank before him, despite being a head taller than the gruff little spectacled man in front of us. He introduced us in humble tones. The director nodded impatiently, putting Garga firmly in his place, grunted, shook Andy's hand and then, as an afterthought, shook mine, avoiding my eyes. Then, in a commanding tone, he invited us into his home for tea and biscuits.

The director strutted ahead of us with the authority of an army commander, and in some ways, I suppose, he was. Here, there was a war on poachers and he was in charge of the army of men tasked with fighting it. And the truth was that in Assam there weren't only the poachers to contend with. On patrol deep in the forest, you never knew when you might come across ULFA rebels and find yourself fighting for your life.

Inside the director's house it was fastidiously clean and had a stiff air of regimented colonialism. Dusty pink curtains. Buttercup yellow walls. Either he had a wife hidden away here somewhere or he was batting for the other side. The former, I was pretty sure. A small fluffy white dog that looked like it had just been to the salon for a blow-dry stayed close by the director at all times, staring at us disdainfully from the far side of the couch.

We sat on firm lounge chairs while the director ordered a manservant to bring us tea. The man returned shortly after with a silver tray balancing a plate with four plain biscuits and teacups of strong, sweet Assamese tea in which slithers of lemon floated. He placed the cups and plate on the table delicately, avoiding eye contact with everyone in the room.

Dr Garga explained that Andy and I worked for WWF in Australia. He told him that I had worked in Africa on human-elephant conflict and was here to advise the minister on how to reduce the elephant problems in Assam. The director nodded, but continued to avoid looking at me directly. I told him about a few of the things that were working in Africa, from band-aid treatments, like chilli-based deterrents, to longer-term solutions like transfrontier conservation areas. He barely glanced at me as I spoke, but he must have been listening, because after I stopped talking he directed a couple of relevant questions to Garga and Andy. Naturally, I replied, since neither of the two men had been to Africa. Garga looked decidedly uncomfortable. He reminded the director that it was I who had the expertise and that Andy was here on holiday. But it didn't make any difference to the awkwardness in the room. The man simply wasn't used to dealing with women. I had dealt with sexism before in large measure in Africa, but this was something else.

We had seen on the front page of the paper that day that a good quantity of rhino horn had been apprehended by the police near Kaziranga. Unfortunately the poachers had got away over the border before they could be caught. I asked the director about what they were doing to protect the rhinos. He explained to Andy and Garga that eighteen rhinos had already been poached this year.

'Eighteen rhinos – this has no impact on the population,' the director said, waving his hand in the air, 'but it is an ongoing problem. Our men are not well equipped to deal with these poachers. We have to be smarter than them, because they have automatic rifles and our men do not.'

I was surprised to hear him say that eighteen rhinos *wasn't* a significant loss to a global population of just a couple of thousand. In Namibia, black rhinos were the highest-priority species for the government. There, the loss of a single rhino's life was considered devastating.

'Our men patrol every day and night. You will find them in a jeep, on an elephant or in a raft. They are always patrolling, looking for poachers.'

Just then, a man in uniform arrived at the door and spoke humbly to the director. The men exchanged words in Assamese before the director waved him away with a dismissive flick of the hand.

He turned to Andy and said, 'If you want to see the conflict, you can go out with the patrol tonight. They are leaving in an hour.'

'That would be great!' I exclaimed, assuming it would be fine for me to go too.

I felt scorn from the lap-dog and the manservant for daring to speak in the presence of their king, but the director himself continued to pretend that I wasn't there. His behaviour was so odd that it was almost funny.

As we left the house, Andy reminded the director that I would be meeting the forestry minister in a few days in Guwahati. For the first time the man looked me in the eye.

'Look after Kaziranga,' he commanded, and thereby granted us permission to enter the park before the official opening.

I fought the urge to salute.

An hour or so later we were trailing a team of rangers on patrol in their open jeep, led by a bearded man who, I think, was called Sherman. I had been hoping that we would get to see a little of the human-elephant conflict in and around the paddies my WWF colleagues had been telling us about, but what we saw that night was beyond anything I could have imagined, much worse than I had seen in Africa. It was a war zone. Within minutes of setting out to the tea gardens and paddy fields on the edge of the park we saw the first elephant bull. He was standing under a tree, the undulating sea of tea bushes obscuring his feet and lower legs. He was in transit, Sherman said, on his way to the rice crops on the other side of the highway.

I learned that the mad highway we had driven on that afternoon followed the park all along its southern border and in a couple of places divided it from new additions to the park, essentially splitting wildlife habitat in two. We had noticed the warning signs on the road, urging drivers to slow down due to the high chance of hitting crossing animals. The signs hadn't made any difference to the buses and trucks that had catapulted past us at breakneck speed. We noticed fresh road kill, a deer that had been dragged to one side of the road, evidence that the signs weren't really working.

Elephants regularly crossed the road, Garga told us, looking for food outside the park. It was completely possible that they would be hit (though it was hard to imagine who would come off worse – the elephant or the car). I had heard that recently in another part of Assam several elephants had been killed by a train as they crossed from a forest into a neighbouring district. Such incidents were more common than you might think. Where elephants and people were travelling fast in the same small space, devastating collisions were inevitable.

Perhaps responding to the men's voices, the bull ambled off into the night.

'He will come back,' Sherman said knowingly.

We followed the forestry jeep into the heart of rice paddy country and parked the cars at the edge of a verdant field that gleamed faintly silver in the starlight. It was about eight o'clock and the waning moon had not yet risen. The only light to guide our way was the generous incandescence of a sparkling Milky Way and the dim beams of a couple of torches.

Led by rangers dressed like soldiers, lugging old rifles over their shoulders, we set off on foot into the night. I breathed in the rural air of Assam deeply, its crisp freshness such a stark contrast to the humid, heavy, polluted air we had breathed in other parts of this continent. Firecrackers blasted like gunshots close by, frequently filling the night with piercing reports. We walked along risen contours paved with elephant footprints that had hardened into the mud, being careful not to twist an ankle in the deep hollows.

In convoy with the rangers, we weaved in between the lush rice paddies, the green leafy plants providing the life source for entire families. With every breath of that cool night air I felt more and more alive. I could sense myself falling into a familiar rhythm as my feet trod upon the earth in the footsteps of giant mammals. No longer just an observer of the world around me, I was fully immersed in it, vulnerable to whatever the elephants, gods and demons of this night held in store. It was scary out there, with firecrackers blasting off at regular intervals, knowing that we were on foot in elephant country at night. The adrenaline focused my senses. I felt tapped into something bigger than my own little universe and it felt good.

I had felt this way a few times now in Assam, first while crossing the river by moonlight from Nameri and again in the presence of regal *kunkies* on the night of the goddess of wealth and wellbeing. Andy told me he had felt it in Nameri too, that same sense of satisfaction and awe that he had once felt as a twenty-one year old sitting on the bow of a felucca on the River Nile. This feeling of wellbeing was one I associated with being in the wild parts of Africa, so I was surprised that I had felt it several times in India.

In general, India was rushed and confusing and loud, dominated by people and their ever-advancing civilisation, leaving little room for nature to survive. In contrast, I associated Africa with a slow pace, large tracts of nature without people and the peace of the bush. Yet, both continents held a fascination, each mystical and inspiring in their own ways. India had a frenetic energy about it that was contagious, and its people had a generosity and warmth that made you not want to leave. Its rich colours and smells and sounds were entrancing. And now, out here in the rice paddies at night, I felt my spirit come alive just as it did in Africa.

What was it about these places that invoked such feelings? Was it nature? Human nature? Or the combination? Was it the change of perspective that made everything seem clear? People here were living on the edge. Just like in Africa, life was too tenuous to think far beyond today. Perhaps that was what it was: a simple appreciation of the preciousness of the present. Maybe it had something to do with the elephants. Whatever it was, my spirit felt alight, ready to face anything. I was glad that Andy felt it too.

I looked at Andy's broad frame walking ahead of me behind the stocky silhouette of one of the rangers. I could see that he was enjoying this as much as I was. I couldn't help remembering what a man who claimed to be an astrologer had said of him a couple of weeks before in Tamil Nadu.

The astrologer's generous Buddha belly wobbled as he shuffled forward on his plastic chair to examine Andy's palm. He leaned over, sweating profusely as he held my sceptical boyfriend's hand. Scrutinising its lines and creases with a large magnifying glass, his brow was furrowed in studied concentration as he muttered to himself. The man looked up suddenly, gave Andy and me practised looks of deep concern, interspersed by moments of crazy-eyed madness. He wiggled his handlebar moustache vigorously, the dark hair breakdancing above his upper lip with every discovery he made about Andy's future. Finally he looked up, with the toothy smile of a professional conman.

'King of a thousand men,' he announced with certainty. 'Many, many men you will command . . . And I see you like the drink . . . and gambling, yes . . .'

The astrologer turned to me and nodded encouragingly. 'You lucky! He good man, yes. You very lucky!'

'This guy is a genius,' Andy grinned, clearly enjoying himself.

He would milk the 'lucky' line forever after at the most annoying moments.

A few minutes before, the man had examined my palm. To my alarm he immediately began to shake his head, his features twisted into a look of grave concern as he tut-tutted grimly. He tapped the side of his head with his knuckles, trying to explain what he was seeing. Judging by the look in his eyes the destiny he could see in my palm wasn't pretty.

'What is it?'

He shook his head again, sighed, tapped his head harder and drew out the agony.

I waited anxiously.

Finally, apparently hesitant to tell me the bad news, he announced sadly, 'Man mind. You have man mind.'

Given that the women in India seemed to have all the lowly jobs and little status (allegedly, in the Hindu tradition women can't reach the ultimate spiritual state of nirvana, liberation from the cycle of rebirth through reincarnation), I could only imagine that having the 'superior' mind of a man must be a disadvantage for a woman in India. Clearly it would be kinder not to be smart enough to be aware of one's own stupidity, hence the pitying look the astrologer was giving me now.

He pulled Andy in close, put his arm around us paternally, still holding my hand tightly with the magnifying glass pressed onto it.

'You! He! Lifelong . . . lifelong!' he exclaimed, using his free hand to draw a circle of loving destiny in the air around the two of us.

Bang! A firecracker shot like lightning through the night, jolting me back to reality. I didn't know what Andy and I had or whether it would last, and I was highly suspicious of the supposed astrologer, but in my heart I hoped he was right. Andy shared my passion for adventure and hanging out with him was always fun. *Maybe, just maybe, this can work . . .*

'This is unreal,' Andy said, unaware of my train of thought. 'There are so many people out and about. I'm so glad we got to see this.'

Every few hundred metres at the edge of every field was a stand made of bamboo and grass where men huddled next to campfires or nearby up in watchtowers of bamboo, guarding their crops from marauding elephants. If one came too close, they would run towards it, holding flaming wooden spears up high and yelling at the top of their lungs.

High above a rice paddy, with a bird's-eye view, two men had nestled into a watchtower in a tree for the night, looking out for the enemy. On our path through the fields, we met two young men carrying barbaric weapons, long, sharp spears with evil hooks that could be used to gore elephants. Another man carried a primitive bow and arrow with steel barbs at the tips of the arrows. We were told that people also used home-made guns created from plastic and poly pipe.

'This is what they use to attack the elephants,' Garga explained. 'They cause terrible wounds to the elephants, but usually don't kill them.'

I wouldn't have liked to be up close to a grumpy elephant and have only those weapons for self-defence.

As if reading my mind, Garga said, 'You can see this is why many people get killed. A wounded elephant is more likely to attack.'

We walked over a bamboo bridge to a small island in the middle of a dam where a man had built a house of reeds. He told us that he had been a farmer, but had now become a fisherman. Elephants don't eat fish, he said. This had to be a better living for him and his family.

Up the bamboo stairs to the upper level of his simple house there were two rooms. A demure lady, his wife perhaps, greeted us shyly, '*Namaste*'. From up there, without any windows, just large rectangular openings in the bamboo wall, I looked out over a moonscape that was far from serene. It was a battle zone of burning fires, men with all manner of weapons, and encroaching elephant enemies, punctuated by aggressive yelling and random shots of firecrackers.

No one was winning this war. I had begun to see that in the world of human-elephant conflict, everyone loses. The only question was who lost more? Was it the elephants, whose numbers were dwindling due to habitat destruction and conflict with people? Or was it the local people who had lost brothers and fathers, livelihoods and homes to the elephants?

That night we met a woman who had lost more than most. Her husband, the father of her two children, had been killed by an elephant bull the year before. Sadly, her story wasn't unusual. If there were ever a tale that contradicted the image of elephants as gentle giants, this was it.

When the elephant came on that fateful night, the woman huddled in the house of clay and bamboo with her two children, both under the age of ten. An elephant bull had been drawn by the rice beer brewing in a room by the house. Her husband stood out the front of the house to defend his small family, yelling vehemently at the bull. Sometimes this was enough to drive an elephant away, but not this bull. Perhaps he was in musth, high on testosterone, or perhaps he carried wounds from previous attacks by humans and sought some kind of revenge. For reasons unknown to those we spoke to, this elephant was angry. It grabbed the man with its trunk and dragged him screaming around the side of the house. The huge creature knocked down a large part of the house as its body slammed into the clay walls, its trunk locked around the man's body with an anaconda-like grip. No one knows for sure what happened next, but typically elephants will throw their victim to the ground with a mighty force, then crush them with a tusk or a knee.

Terrified, inside a home that was caving in, no longer hearing her husband's voice, the woman cowered with her children. She prayed to her gods that the bull would not come for them inside the broken-down house. She stuffed cloths into the mouths of her children to stop them making any noise. There was nothing between them and the elephant but flimsy walls of clay that were crumbling down around them. She didn't know what had happened to her husband, she said. She didn't know that he was dead. She could still hear the elephant outside the house, looking for food, rice beer or rice from the granary, rumbling and crashing around like a rampaging monster. Her survival and that of her children depended on them all being deathly quiet. She hugged her children tightly, praying for the nightmare to end.

Amazingly, they survived that night. In the weeks that followed, the government compensated them with enough money to build a new house. But the house, like the old one, was built of clay and bamboo. The woman was scared it would happen again. She told us that her two children were too afraid to sleep in the house. She pointed to a tall tree close by where a bamboo ladder led up to a horizontal reed and bamboo frame. There, beneath a grass roof, two small children slept on mattresses, hemmed in by mosquito nets. To them, their treehouse was a safer place to sleep than the house.

Sadly, I would learn that this woman's story was common in this part of the world. There are hundreds of widows, and even more fatherless children, as a direct result of elephant attacks. A few days before, watching wild elephants with nowhere to go, I had taken the side of the elephants. Now, listening to this woman's story, I was definitely on hers. In truth, there was no wrong or right side in this war. There was only bloodshed driven by the need to survive. While hunger on both sides continued, elephants and people would keep dancing around each other in an awkward flamenco, standing on each other's toes. There were too many dancers in this ballroom and simply not enough space.

SIXTEEN

Andy and I were still recoiling from the impact of the battle when we woke up the next day in the comfortable beds (as always in India, it was two single beds that we had pushed together) of Wild Grass Resort. It was a relief to open my eyes after disturbing dreams of raging elephants bearing infected wounds from makeshift spears and guns. Images of the conflict were still fresh in our minds.

Our room was high up in the treetops and large windows with mosquito netting let the dawn light filter in. A wooden fan spiralled on the high ceiling, circulating air that smelled crisp and clean, fresh from the jungle. Without question this was the loveliest place we stayed in our entire time in India. At the other end of the accommodation spectrum had been the hotel in the town of Mammalapuram, where, on our arrival, a fresh human turd lay in wait for us on the couch. I had retched, and then called for help from a ratty little man in a turban. He retched too, but perversely seemed unable to remove his gaze from it, perhaps trying to think of someone – *anyone* – in the hierarchy of the hotel lower than himself whom he could designate to clean it up.

'Maybe a monkey did it,' Andy suggested, not nearly as nauseated as I was and enjoying my response.

'No way, man,' I said, trying to stop myself throwing up. 'Trust me. I'm a doctor. I know my shit and that's no monkey turd.'

So, to say the least, I really appreciated the cleanliness of Wild Grass, with its crisp sheets, rustic feel and close proximity to nature. Today we were going to Kaziranga in search of the greater one-horned rhino, a species that had almost become extinct in the early 1900s. Back then, only a hundred or so remained. Now there are about two thousand five hundred, most of which are in Kaziranga, and a few hundred in Nepal's Royal Chitwan National Park. The population had bounced back well after the slaughter of the late 1800s, following a ban on rhino hunting in 1910. Unfortunately, illegal hunting remains a problem, driven by the demand for horn, a prized ingredient in Chinese medicine.

There was no fence around the park, only a gradual transition from farmland to jungle. Villagers and goats milled around the fringes, tending to crops, goats or children. Our jeep drove over rough muddy tracks that hadn't been used much since last year's tourist season six months earlier. In the vehicle with us were four Indian men – a guide from the lodge, a driver who came with the car, Dr Garga and an armed forestry ranger.

Thick, verdant jungle rose up around us, blocking out the sun with a dense ceiling of arching boughs and broad leaves. It felt dark and damp in there, like being cocooned in a clean wet cloth. The smell of earthy, living forest was overwhelming and compost-like in its pungency. As I inhaled its rich scent, I spotted something in the middle of the road that sent a frisson of excitement up my spine.

'Shit!' I exclaimed.

'What is it?' Andy replied, startled by my unladylike language.

'Shit!' I said, louder, 'Hold on, we're going to hit it!'

Our jolting jeep bounced and jerked over a large mound of fresh rhino dung, almost the width of the car.

'Is that a dung midden?' I asked Garga breathlessly, preparing to leap from the moving vehicle before he could answer. 'Can we take a look?'

'Yes, it is a communal dung pile for the rhinos,' he answered, then, more quizzically, 'You want to look?'

I nodded enthusiastically. It is the affliction of a zoologist, I'm afraid, to be obsessed with dung. Inside a turd's soft warm coils are all sorts of biological secrets about animals' diets that warrant a thorough investigation and can invoke fleeting, but euphoric, moments of discovery. This opportunity was too good to miss. I leapt out of the car and charged back along the road.

Andy stood back, shaking his head, and said to Garga, 'I don't know what to do with her. She's obsessed with . . . shit. I can't take her anywhere any more.'

Quite formally, Garga replied, 'Mr Andy, she is a scientist. She must do what she must do.'

I chuckled. But I noticed that he, too, stood well back from the dung pile, disinclined to get his hands dirty with fresh pachyderm crap. Poking through the dung with a stick I could tell that these rhinos were largely grazers. Undigested grass was clearly visible in the large brown boluses.

'Are you done yet?' Andy asked, rolling his eyes.

Within minutes of driving into the jungle, we spotted our first Indian rhino. A distinct dark grey shape stood to one side of the road on a shaggy carpet of lime green ferns. Behind her was a much smaller rhino, peeking out from behind her mother's ample thigh. Camouflaged by the thick greenery under a heavy canopy of trees, their concrete-grey skin was dappled by shadows and gentle sunlight. It wasn't until they stepped out onto the dirt road that we were able to take a close look at them.

The mother was well aware of our jeep parked about thirty metres away, but she looked straight ahead as she crossed the exposed road in front of us, focused on reaching the thick forest on the other side. Her small round ears were pricked up and zoning like sonar dishes as she walked through the open, watching and listening for any threat. Her baby trailed close behind, its hornless nose almost touching the female's blistery buttocks as it bumbled along. As they surged into the thicket the rhinos were a vision of something ancient and primitive. They didn't seem to belong in the present, but in the age of the dinosaurs. With armour-like plates over short, stocky legs and bubbly skin, they are creatures designed to fight battles. And, indeed, these half-blind, blundering creatures have been embroiled in a war, first with legal hunters and now with poachers, for decades.

Greater one-horned rhinos are of a similar size to Africa's white rhinos and share the habit of grazing on grass, which is why they also have a wide, flat mouth, not pointed and beak-like ones as black rhinos do, which is designed for browsing on leaves. But that's about where the similarities end. Indian rhinos have one horn, instead of two like the African black and white rhinos, and all of the rhinos I saw over the next few days had horns that were decidedly smaller than their African cousins'. Compared with the long horns of black rhinos I'd seen in Namibia, these stumpy unicorns barely seemed worth a poacher's effort.

Over the next few days we had several rhino sightings, including a few females with young and a male with a large bloody gash across his hind leg. We watched one female at sunset teaching her small baby how to use a dung midden. Even those in the jeep less dung obsessed than I couldn't help but be intrigued. The female plodded heavily out of the high grass before stopping abruptly over the midden. She wiggled her butt to aim, lifted her tail like a lever, and then left a healthy deposit on the pile, a hormonal calling card to any other rhinos in the area. She waited for her calf to copy her, which he did with a wiggle and a plop. Then together they bounded off into the grass, considerably lighter and with a spring in their steps. Even Andy couldn't help but comment, 'That's pretty cute.'

Kaziranga was a treat. Interspersed with the jungle, large wetlands teemed with birds. Our guide told us that almost five hundred different bird species had been spotted in the park. Herds of swamp deer lay on the grassy fringes, contemplating their breezy existences. As we drove through the park a solitary hog deer darted out of the long grass and bolted across the road. Asiatic buffalos soaked waist deep in swamps, lazily chomping on a feast of water plants.

Tigers prowled in Kaziranga too. There were perhaps a hundred of them in the park, but in the high grass they weren't easy to see. We were fortunate to see a tiger pug mark in the mud and also a scratching tree where one big cat had left his territorial markings with razor-sharp claws. The scratchings were twice the height of a man.

'Tigers? I have seen many, many tigers!'

These were the words of the ebullient Mr Boro, a ranger with over twenty years' experience in Kaziranga, with whom we were fortunate enough to spend an afternoon. Relaxed in his khakis, the symbol of the game warden, he had the look of a man who had faced his fears and lived to tell the stories. There was a gentle wisdom in his eyes that I had seen before in people who had spent a lot of time in nature.

Anyone who has ever seen the famous YouTube clip of the tiger attacking the men on the back of an elephant will know Mr Boro. He was one of the guys on the elephant.

Mr Boro explained that they had been tracking the disgruntled tiger for some time. She had been attacking (and been attacked by) people and was pretty riled up. Now she had become a problem animal and it was Mr Boro's job to immobilise her.

On elephant-back, three men to every elephant, the team of rangers glided slowly through the long grass. They had glimpsed the burned orange blur of the tigress as she skulked away from them a second earlier. She was clearly not enjoying the invasion of her privacy by the species she disliked more than any other. Everyone was nervous, including the elephants.

On one elephant's back, Mr Boro was sandwiched between two men, one in front, the other behind. He was concentrating hard. The dart gun was cocked and ready to fire as he aimed into the sea of grass, looking for a telltale glimpse of striped fur. Hold . . . Hold . . .

He couldn't see the tiger, but she could see him. Up until then the rangers had been hunting her, but the tables were about to turn. The hunters had become the hunted. Out of sight, stalking with the same stealth she used to kill deer, the tigress took slow, deliberate steps, her back hunched low to the ground as she slunk closer. Softly, softly . . .

Mr Boro held his dart gun poised for the shot. But the tiger was as invisible as a ghost in the long grass. When she charged towards the elephant no one was ready for her fury. Quite definitely, she was aiming for the men on the elephant's back, not the elephant itself. The men yelled at the top of their lungs, one hitting the saddle with wooden sticks, trying to stop the charge. But she was beyond fear. A split second later she had leapt up onto the elephant's back and grabbed a man.

As the tiger's dagger-like claws struck human flesh, the arm of the man in front of Mr Boro was shredded. Somehow he held on. But Mr Boro was thrown off the elephant onto the ground next to the tiger. Amazingly, as he lay there dazed and confused, instead of taking the opportunity to maul him, the tiger fled.

No one was killed that day – and all of it was captured on film. Mr Boro told this story as if it were the sort of thing that happened every day. He had seen men gored by rhinos and others who had lost limbs to tigers. A tiger attack was all in a day's work for him. Wildlife conservation wasn't just his job. It was his passion.

'My wife, she say to me,' Mr Boro chuckled, 'You spend so much time with the rhinos! You are bald. Soon you will grow horn through your head just like rhino!'

He leaned over to show us his bald head. 'See! No horn yet! But three children, yes. My one daughter, she is becoming doctor.'

As we drove with Mr Boro around the park it was clear that he commanded the respect of all the Department of Forestry staff that we met.

'Do you think there is a future for elephants in Assam?' I asked him from the back seat of his four-by-four.

He turned away to conceal a look of deep concern and sadness, and shook his head.

'I cannot say yes for sure,' he shrugged. 'There are many, many people in India.'

Doubt and despair hung in the car for a few seconds as we all contemplated the growing problem of human overpopulation. India now had the fastest growing population in the world.

But then I watched Mr Boro's features grow determined. 'All the doctors, teachers, nurses – everyone has a role to play in conservation. We must all help. It is not just a job for forestry.'

'That's exactly right!' Andy exclaimed. 'We can't just rely on conservationists to solve the problems any more.'

The whole ethos of Earth Hour was based around this idea of empowering everyone to get involved. Andy and I had talked about it at length before. The more I was learning about conservation problems around the world, the more I was beginning to see the sense in this idea. We can no longer depend on the environmental movement to save species. It has gone too far. Now we need everyone to help.

The conservation movement has had some big achievements since its inception in the 1960s, and there are many committed, passionate individuals who dedicate their lives to conservation. Some species, like giant pandas in China, greater one-horned rhinos in India and savannah elephants in southern Africa, have increased in numbers as a direct result of human intervention. But, by and large, we are not winning the conservation battle.

Some say that the situation would be a lot worse if it weren't for the environmental movement and I'm sure that's true. Sadly, it simply isn't enough. Until everyone takes ownership of the species extinction crisis that the planet now faces and accepts that we are a part of the natural world and dependent on it for our own wellbeing, we will continue to see species decline. Like Mr Boro said, doctors, teachers, nurses! Let me go further and say children, firemen, check-out chicks! In the face of global climate change, which, at current rates of warming, is predicted to put thousands more species on the threatened species list in a matter of decades, there is no more time to waste.

The thing is, we *are* responsible for this mess in a much more personal way than you might think. Andy had immediately made the link between the tea that was being grown in Assam and sold to consumers in London. Although the tea growers were using elephants in their business logos, they weren't doing anything to reduce the problem of human-elephant conflict in their plantations. People in England and elsewhere were buying the tea of Assam, so they were connected to the problem. With every tea bag they dunked in their porcelain cup, they were unknowingly helping Asian elephants on the path to extinction. Conversely, tea drinkers could be part of the solution if they demanded that tea growers help conserve elephants and sell elephant-friendly tea.

In other parts of the world, consumers were linked to other wildlife problems. Palm oil plantations are the cause of massive, large-scale clearing of forests in Indonesia, Malaysia and Papua New Guinea. Most people buy vegetable oil for cooking, not knowing that if the oil has saturated fat in it, then it is probably palm oil. Palm oil is also used by many manufacturers of products like biscuits, chips and cosmetics. Usually the labelling isn't clear. Many fast foods are fried in palm oil. When you buy palm oil in any form, knowingly or not, you are contributing to the extinction of Asia's only great ape, the orang-utan. In the last decade, the population of orang-utans in Indonesia and Malaysia has declined by between thirty and fifty percent.

'It's not about blame,' Andy explained. 'It's not that the tea companies are doing the wrong thing necessarily. They're just doing it by default. I'm sure they're not happy that so many people and elephants get killed in their tea gardens. Imagine if we convinced them that elephant-friendly tea was a superb marketing opportunity? Imagine if they were the chief sponsors of the elephant-conservation program in Assam? If the world knew they were helping save elephants and reducing conflict, they'd be bound to increase their sales.'

I thought of all the things that hadn't been done yet in Assam to conserve elephants – population estimates were tentative at best, data on conflicts were equally tenuous, and no one had any idea what the home ranges of these elephants were, how many state and country borders they crossed. With sponsorship they could revegetate the forest, reconnect elephant habitat and explore alternative fuel sources to wood to stop the logging. There were all sorts of potentially useful techniques being used in Africa, like fences with cloths doused in chilli grease, trip alarms and even African bees. With the right amount of funding, a full program of elephant conservation, research and community education could be implemented in Assam. I imagined a scenario in which the business world was funding elephant conservation, so becoming the solution rather than part of the problem.

Assam, with its populations of rhinos, elephants and tigers, had all the right attributes for a flourishing tourism industry based on its wildlife. Unfortunately, due to the military and rebel activity, it was still on the no-go list for most foreign tourists. I had never heard of the state before this trip and nor had most people I knew, even the better travelled ones. What it needed was a really good publicity campaign letting the outside world know how utterly fantastic it was. Above all, it needed an end to the *human* conflict so that tourists would return and bolster the economy.

Perhaps what it also needed was a dose of African perspective. In southern Africa, elephant populations were escalating, to the point that in South Africa's most famous game park, Kruger, the government was considering culling again (as a last resort). What was Africa getting right that India wasn't? Could transfrontier conservation areas work in India too, allowing elephants to move naturally back into their historic range and giving local people benefits from wildlife? I couldn't see why not, except for one big fat problem. In Assam the government hadn't blocked deforestation. There was no point allowing elephants to roam free if there was no habitat for them to move to.

The first step had to be to recognise the economic value of Assam's forests as a refuge for its elephants, tigers and rhinos. These natural assets were worth more as tourist attractions than they were as short-term homes and firewood for illegal immigrants and villagers. The loss of the forests was at the source of human-elephant conflict. We needed to speak to someone with influence, someone who might share this vision, someone prepared to take risks to sort out the growing problem of human-elephant conflict. I hoped that man was Minister Rockibul Hussein, Minister for Forests, Tourism, Environment and, last but not least, Public Relations.

'Don't expect him to come soon,' Sujoy Banerjee, who had just flown in from WWF India's head office in Delhi, said with a resigned smile. 'Last time we waited four hours.'

But, luckily for us, the minister only kept us waiting for about ten minutes, impressive for a politician. Earlier Sujoy had waltzed us past the long line of hundreds of people in saris and business suits hoping to get a meeting with their government representative at Parliament House. Stuck to a pillar beside the throng of people were dozens of A4 pages with lists of names scrawled on them. Apparently, if your name wasn't on that list you couldn't get in. If you were on that list, you could line up and wait in the hope of a meeting, but apparently this could take days.

Time with the minister was not easy to get, but we were here to offer him solutions to a problem that was now in the news every day. As we waited in the airconditioned boardroom, our WWF team took up both sides of the rectangular wooden table.

Andy and I sat on one side, with Anupam, Sujoy and Pranab Bora, in charge of WWF's program at Kaziranga, on the other. The room was less palatial than you might expect for a politician with four ministries to his name. An old photocopier sat in the corner collecting dust.

The guys were nervous, as evidenced by their silence. One thing I had learned about India is that it's almost never quiet. Talking over others is not considered rude. It's normal. We had discovered that it's quite okay to answer your mobile phone and talk to someone else when you're in the middle of a meeting. None of the rules of conversation that exist in the west count for anything in India. Sujoy, bless his soul, tried to break the silence by telling an awkward joke. That was when the minister walked in.

As Rockibul entered the room, the men rose like startled meerkats to greet him in submissive tones. Andy and I followed suit. The ample spread of middle age formed a rotund hillock beneath the minister's black pin-striped shirt and matching trousers. Around his waist the environment minister wore what appeared to be a crocodile or snakeskin belt. He was a large, imposing figure with a commanding presence. He truly lived up to his name – Rockibul, a cross between Sylvester Stallone and a Spanish bull. The minister reached over to shake Andy's hand and then made to sit down, the assumption probably being that I was there as his secretary. Before he could sit I reached over and forced a handshake. It felt uncomfortable on both sides, but I knew I needed to assert some power from the beginning. Otherwise he wouldn't listen to anything I had to say.

Sujoy jumped in, leading the conversation in gushing, flowery tones, and generously introduced me in Hindi. The minister looked a little surprised that the WWF team had brought a woman to him, but he was polite. He offered me an awkward smile as Sujoy indicated that I should tell the minister a little about Africa.

Nervously I began, 'I want to thank you for having us here. Assam is beautiful. I have been to many amazing wildlife parks in Africa and I can say that Kaziranga is one of the best wildlife areas I have seen.'

He acknowledged the compliment with a nod.

I went on, 'The best thing about India is that the people worship Ganesh, the elephant god. In Africa this is not the case. There, people need economic incentives to conserve elephants. In Namibia elephant populations are now increasing because they have an economic value. So, in some ways, here in India you have the advantage.'

The minister nodded and grunted. I wasn't sure that he was really listening, but I continued and tried to keep my nerve. I told him about some of the approaches that were working in southern Africa. When I mentioned chillies, his ears pricked up. Assam, after all, produced *Bhut jolokia*, the hottest chillies in the world according to the Guinness Book of Records. He leaned forward and I saw a glimmer of genuine interest in his eyes.

'This . . . chilli? How does it work?' the minister asked.

'You can use it in lots of different ways. You can put cloths in a mixture of chilli and oil and hang them up on a fence around a crop. Or you can make a brick of chilli mixed with elephant dung and put a hot coal on top, then the chilli smoke will keep the elephants away.'

The minister leaned back in his chair and smiled. He liked this idea.

'In Africa, this is working?'

'In some places, yes.'

Anupam interjected then, speaking in Assamese. Andy and I sat in silence, waiting to be called upon. Twenty minutes passed.

I wondered for how much longer we would have the minister's attention.

Finally, Sujoy, ever the consummate professional, cut in and asked Andy to give his opinion.

Andy spoke a little about the possibility of improving the branding of the state to the outside world, through things like 'elephant friendly' tea and chilli.

'Here in Assam you have chilli that is so hot, it even scares the elephants!' Andy said.

The minister chuckled to himself and nodded.

'In Namibia,' I said, 'up until 1990 the country was at war. Just ten years later their wildlife populations were increasing and now the country is making a lot of money out of its tourism industry. Tourism there is all based on wildlife – elephants, rhinos, lions. It is the fastest-growing economic industry in Namibia. You can do that here too. Assam has all the right ingredients. You have Kaziranga. You have tigers, elephants and rhinos.'

The minister was listening intently. 'Do you think Assam can be like Africa? Like the big national parks? The Serengeti?'

Before I could reply, Anupam answered for me in Assamese. Although he may only have been trying to help, it made me want to scream. Andy looked at me. We both knew what was going on. There was no malice. This was just India.

He leaned over and whispered, 'Interrupt, babe.'

But I couldn't. India had its culture and I had mine.

The next time the minister asked a question about Africa, Andy raised his hand to stop Anupam from answering.

In a firm but not impolite voice, he said, 'Let her speak.'

'Please,' the minister encouraged, gesturing for me to answer.

'If you want to make Assam the elephant and rhino state, you can do this, but the elephants need a place to live. If all the forests are gone, there will be no elephants left to show tourists.'

I could sense the minister's attention was waning. We had kept it for about forty minutes. As Anupam continued to speak, Sujoy translated in my ear. Apparently Anupam was saying that WWF was testing chillies as a mitigation measure against elephants and would continue these efforts. It was hard to believe what I was hearing. Hadn't Anupam been the one most opposed to a chilli program when I had first mentioned its success in Africa? *Just because it is working in Africa doesn't mean it will work here* . . . Still, I couldn't help being delighted. With the minister clearly in favour of a chilli program, everyone in the WWF team was behind it too. Where a day before there had been negativity, now there was local ownership. It was the best possible outcome for the elephants. Without that, the ideas would go nowhere after Andy and I flew back to Sydney.

'Minister,' Sujoy cut in eloquently to close, 'we need the kind of leadership that you are showing not only in Assam but also in all of India, the kind that stands up for wildlife and sees the value that it has for India.'

The minister enjoyed Sujoy's masterful flattery. It had been a good meeting. He called on his press officer to take our names and we all huddled together for a group photograph for the next day's papers.

Sujoy kept us busy with more meetings with until almost midnight. As we collapsed on our beds, Andy said, 'You know, I saw a glimmer in the minister's eye today when you spoke about chillies. Even if he takes nothing else away, he will remember that. You had him with the chillies.'

I realised then that I had found someone who wasn't in the least threatened by who I was or what I did for a living. He didn't need to prove himself by outdoing me in any way. We brought different skills to the table, so there was no competition. Andy actually encouraged me to be stronger and admired the part of me that usually sent men running, that never-say-die zeal that I had needed to survive in Africa for so long.

In previous relationships I had found myself pretending to be weaker in order not to threaten my partner's ego. Perhaps it's because I work in a traditionally male domain, but many of the guys I had dated before exhibited a weird need to outdo me. Once, a boyfriend claimed my project as his own when meeting some local people in a village, even though I was standing right beside him. The small amount of power I had in this traditional environment was taken from me before I could even shake the chief's hand. As a result, I often found it easier to be alone. Back then it had seemed the impossible quandary of my life that I couldn't do the work I loved without wishing I had someone to share it with.

'You're stronger without a man,' my dear friend Shelby had said to me after the last break-up.

Then, she was right. But that was before *this* man. With Andy I knew I would never have to be 'the little woman'. He simply wouldn't stand for it. It dawned on me that I may have finally found what I had been looking for all these years, someone who completely supported me. After such a long bout of khaki fever, I was in love and there wasn't a trace of khaki to be seen.

Some girls want to hear three particular words in order to know they have the right guy. I wasn't looking for them at all. Andy had said the three words I needed to hear. Let Her Speak.

The next week, newspapers in India and Australia reported the story. Assam's forest minister was committed to sorting out the human-elephant conflict problem in north-east India. We read his words to state parliament in the *Australian*, quoting our meeting almost directly: 'We have begun working on the chilli-smeared rope fencing. These chillies are too hot even for the elephants and we are banking on this experiment to check man-animal conflicts.' Recognising that the destruction of forest habitat in northern Assam was the principal cause of the problem, he said, 'Man-elephant conflict has taken a serious turn because of large-scale encroachment on elephant corridors'.

And it wasn't only Rockibul who was taking a stand in the media. Paris Hilton had jumped in on the action, allegedly sympathising with the elephants' problems with rice-beer binge drinking. 'It's just so sad,' she was quoted as saying. 'The elephants get drunk all the time. It is becoming really dangerous. We need to stop making alcohol available to them.'

Andy and I wanted to leap for joy. The minister's public statements and WWF India's commitment had added momentum to what I could now see was an opportunity to adopt some of Africa's successful elephant conservation measures in India. The continents were vastly different in some ways, but quite similar in others. The question was, could India act fast enough to turn around the perilous state of its elephant population? Bureaucracy, politics, territoriality and egos would need to be overcome if the last of India's elephants had any chance of survival in the wild. If two-thirds of the forest in Assam had been destroyed in the last three decades, the rest would be gone very soon. There was no time to waste.

My heart sped up as I realised what I needed to do. I needed to learn more about how Africa was fixing the problem, to see how the chillies worked with my own eyes. I had to go back to the place with the largest population of elephants in the world. The coincidence of it all made me smile. Having missed out on the opportunity to work with John Hanks on a chilli project in Africa, an alternative adventure with a different species of elephant had opened up for me. Through WWF, although it wasn't a core part of my job, I had found a way to use my human-elephant conflict experience in a place I had never imagined I would visit, let alone work. In a land of tea, incense and curry, I was doing a chilli project with elephants after all.

SEVENTEEN

Seven months later, in May 2007, I was back in Africa, this time in Livingstone, Zambia. A series of strange but wonderful coincidences had led me to do some work for the group that pioneered the use of chillies as an elephant deterrent, the Elephant Pepper Development Trust (EPDT).

The ball had already started rolling while I was in India. One of the two founders of the trust, Australian entrepreneur Mike Gravina, gave a presentation to WWF staff in Sydney about the work they were doing in Africa. I tracked him down as soon as I heard about his talk, only to discover that he just moved back to Sydney after five years in Zambia and was living in the suburb next to mine. Once again I marvelled at the smallness of the world. Always, when I have been on the right path, things seem to happen to help me along. Even though I was living in a city as far from the elephants as I ever had, it was beginning to feel like they were now chasing me, not the other way around. Perhaps

Ganesh was standing beside me, removing the obstacles in my path.

Mike and I met at a dark little pub in Surry Hills, Sydney.

'We know that chillies work,' Mike told me. 'I mean, you just have to look at the branding on our sauces to know we're pretty confident about that. You've seen our sauces, right?'

He pulled out a pamphlet. The hot chilli sauces that the trust's sister company, African Spices, sold brandished the slogan *Elephants hate chilli!*

'People living in Africa just don't see elephants as the gentle giants of Attenborough documentaries,' Mike went on. 'They need options that allow them to feed their families. That's what chillies do. They're a high-value crop that elephants don't eat. It really is that simple.'

I told Mike about the situation I had seen in India, and asked if he thought chillies could work there too.

'I don't see why not,' he replied. 'It's about adapting the techniques to the local situation. If it rains a lot there, they might have to replace the chilli cloths on the fences more often.'

Talking to Mike I realised just how little I knew about the practical side of chilli-growing. He and EPDT co-founder, Dr Loki Osborne, had been doing this for years with their local team in Africa.

'I'd kill to see how chillies actually work,' I said. 'It's one thing to see pictures, but it's not the same as seeing it yourself.'

'Well why don't you go and have a look at what we're doing in Livingstone?'

'I'd love to . . .' I trailed off, wishing that were possible. The truth was, my boss, Ray, had been pretty lenient letting me spend the time in India, away from my primary focus on Australian threatened species. I was pretty certain he wouldn't let me go to Africa so soon, especially when the problems at home were so pressing.

'The fact is, we really don't have enough capacity,' Mike went on. 'We could really use your help. Leave it with me.'

A week later Mike phoned with a proposition. He wanted me to help the main guy who ran Elephant Pepper on the ground, Zimbabwean Malvern Karidozo, design a monitoring program for their activities. It sounded like a great excuse to see the way chillies worked, but I was doubtful that my boss would let me go. Even though WWF is a global network, most country offices are focused on their own priorities and, understandably, elephants weren't high on WWF Australia's agenda.

So, when an email came through signifying Ray's approval of the trip I was astonished. He had given me a month off in May, and wanted a full report on my return. I could have hugged him I was so ecstatic. I might have been living in a world of suits and stilettos, but that didn't mean I couldn't still have adventures with elephants.

With a few months to go before I flew over there, I set out to learn more about the Elephant Pepper Development Trust in my spare time. I discovered that the organisation was registered as a trust in Zimbabwe in 2002 by American scientist Dr Loki Osborne after many years of research and community work in Zimbabwe looking at the effect of chillies on elephants and on people's livelihoods. Loki hailed from the McIlhenny family of Louisiana, the company that manufactures Tabasco sauce. He teamed up with Mike early this decade to build a commercial arm for Elephant Pepper – African Spices – that would buy the chillies harvested by local communities at fair trade prices and sell them overseas. One of their biggest buyers was Tabasco. The resulting chilli sauces were marketed as 'elephant friendly' because they returned ten percent of their profits to the trust. Also, the company provided an instant and guaranteed buyer to rural people who established a chilli crop. Now the trust was primarily a training organisation, providing practical courses in chilli-based deterrents and chilli-growing for people all over Africa.

By late March my flight was booked and I was raring to go. The next question was, would my Indian partner in crime join me? It was just after the second Earth Hour and Andy was desperately in need of a holiday. This time Earth Hour hadn't just been held in Sydney. It had reached three hundred and seventy other cities and towns in more than thirty-five countries, an amazing feat for a tiny team of people with almost no resources. With over fifty million people turning their lights out, Earth Hour had demonstrated again that more and more people everywhere cared about the issue and wanted world leaders to take action on climate change. Earth Hour 2009 was set to be even bigger, aiming to reach more than a billion people in a thousand cities, but before that journey could start I knew just the place for Andy to gather his strength again. It didn't take much to convince him to join me in Africa.

We arrived in Livingstone on a scorching day in early May, exhausted after the two-day journey from Sydney to Zambia. The next day we met Malvern Karidozo, a softly spoken, humble young Zimbabwean man whom Andy and I both liked instantly.

'Would you like to see a chilli farm?' he asked. 'There is one close by.'

We piled into Elephant Pepper's old Isuzu and Malvern drove us through the busy streets of Livingstone. He told us it had become a much more bustling town for tourists visiting Victoria Falls since 2000, when Zimbabwe took a turn for the worse.

We wound through a maze of dirt roads to a village on the outskirts of town. When Malvern pulled up, several barefoot children ran out to greet us. Judging by the size of the trees in the bush nearby, I guessed we were pretty close to the Zambezi River, where elephants crossed over between Zimbabwe and Zambia. We were just a few kilometres from the famous Victoria Falls and microlight aircraft and helicopters full of tourists whirred above us just out of range of the cloud of spray that billowed up from the churning water. Lively African township music blared from outside one of the brick huts. Scrawny chickens pecked at scant pickings in loamy red soil. The children led us past several grass-roofed brick huts, typical of so much of Africa, to a very large garden. Giggling, they practised their English on us.

'How are youuuu?'

'What is your naaaame?'

A bushy bearded man in the garden smiled warmly and waved.

'This is Mr Kanga,' Malvern introduced us.

Our new friend wiped hands covered in soil on his shirt and self-consciously proffered one of them to shake.

'You have come to see the chillies?' he asked. 'Come, I will show you.'

We followed him into the field where he tended all sorts of vegetables in random rows, including maize and capsicum. A couple of young boys followed Mr Kanga's every move, watching and learning. The rich fiery hues of chillies on robust, dark green bushes were striking in between the other plants, standing out like Christmas trees with bright yellow, orange and red decorations.

'You see this? This is the chilli fence for keeping the elephants out.'

The entire perimeter of the garden was surrounded by a fence consisting of tall wooden poles placed about five metres apart, connected by two strands of thin rope. Attached to the ropes were one of Elephant Pepper's chief weapons against elephants, cloths doused in a strong combination of oil and chilli.

Under a tree nearby lay dozens of rectangular bricks made of dried elephant dung mixed with chillies. Each brick was roughly the size of an ice cream-container. In the centre of each one was a small indentation.

'These are the chilli briquettes,' Malvern explained. 'The people put them around the perimeter of the crop with a hot coal on top. The smoke smells like chilli.'

'Is the chilli working?' I asked Mr Kanga. 'I mean, do the elephants come now?'

'Oh no! The elephants are not coming any more. My field is protected. Before the elephants were eating everything! Now, I have time for my beautiful family.'

We laughed as he smiled proudly.

Mr Kanga paused for a few seconds and scratched his thick beard. 'You know, now I am too busy with growing the crop. I am not even having time for shaving!'

Over the next week Malvern took us to several chilli farms: some subsistence farms, like Mr Kanga's, that provided an income for a family or two; others that funded entire communities. At one village, the home of an influential Zambian elder, Chief Makuni, a lady told us that she had been allocated three rows out of a crop of about thirty rows. It wasn't enough, she said. She wanted more. Each family had an allocation and was responsible for their designated rows. The entire communal cropland shared a loose perimeter fence made of wood and wire, which would have been easy for an elephant to push over. But there was no sign of elephant damage whatsoever, despite the evidence of elephants we had seen not far away.

At another village, I joined Malvern as he handed over wads of Zambian kwatcha in payment for the chillies. About twenty men and women gathered in a circle on plastic chairs under a shady tree, while Malvern and some other men leaned over a low wooden desk. The women, wearing bright sarongs around their waists and on their heads, all sat together in a parade of colour.

An old man with a few missing teeth gave me a gappy grin and encouraged me to sit on a chair beside him. He proudly showed me his record book. I glanced down the tattered page where numbers had been roughly scrawled in jagged columns. The scruffy notebook was this man's bible. Every day during the harvest he had weighed his pickings then handed them over to the village representative for delivery to African Spices, making a note in his precious book. He told me that today he was happy because he was being paid for several weeks' worth of crop. Chillies were worth more per hectare than any other crop being grown in the area – about US$1 per kilogram.

Like the other chilli-growing villages I had seen, people seemed less worried about elephants than they did elsewhere, even though they lived among a dense population of them. And they were all very happy to be reaping the benefits of their chilli crops. The system wasn't perfect. As in any communal system in a poor country, there were things to iron out to ensure fairness and transparency. But, hey, it wasn't a bad start. I was impressed.

The Elephant Pepper Development Trust had established chilli programs in seven African countries so far, and the only thing stopping them establishing more was a lack of funding and human capacity. Now that I had seen how simple it was to establish a chilli crop, I felt certain that if chillies could work in Africa, they could work in India too.

EIGHTEEN

In Zimbabwe, Elephant Pepper's program had been working really well, Malvern told us, until the trouble started in 2000. After years of work in Zimbabwe, political strife and instability under Robert Mugabe's merciless regime had forced Elephant Pepper to move its headquarters to Livingstone in Zambia, on the border with Zimbabwe. It was a good thing they did, because things had been going downhill in Zimbabwe ever since.

I knew it was absurd, but I still longed to return to Zimbabwe. I had left in 2000, the year that Mugabe's war veterans had first invaded white-owned farms under the pretence of a free and fair land redistribution program. Then I was convinced that Zimbabwe's troubles would be over in a few years, at worst. But now it was 2008 and the country's problems were worse than ever. After three hoax elections that kept Mugabe in power, the once thriving agricultural economy had crashed, the Zimbabwean dollar was worthless, inflation was through the roof and there were dire fuel and food shortages. Every tragic news story I saw about Zimbabwe broke my heart.

Although I wasn't born in Zimbabwe some part of me came alive when I travelled there at the age of fifteen as an emerging adult. In the seven years that followed, as I went back again and again as a volunteer, worker and researcher, it became a strong part of my history. I felt I would always be indebted to the place and the people who had shown me my calling in wildlife conservation. I still loved the country, but I knew it must have changed a lot from the carefree days when I had been there. Was the Zimbabwe I knew and loved still there? Was I ready to confront it after eight years?

I wanted Andy to see the Africa that I knew, the wild creatures that roamed free in national parks and reserves. We had been in Zambia for almost a fortnight and had seen plenty of chilli farms but not a lot of animals. So, since we were only a few hours' drive from one of the most amazing wilderness areas in Africa, I knew exactly where to take him.

'Don't make any sudden movements,' I whispered in Andy's ear.

The lion padded with slow and purposeful grace towards our open Land Rover.

It was about eight o'clock at night in the southern part of Hwange National Park, Zimbabwe. Just weeks away from winter, the evening was freezing cold and pretty close to pitch-black. We had been on a game drive all afternoon and now, nearing camp, I was looking forward to a stiff drink and a hot meal. But Africa is always full of surprises and the show's never over till she says it is. As our safari vehicle turned a sharp corner on the dirt track, an earth-shattering roar filled the night. Its deep resonance reverberated in my chest. Our guide, Charles, hit the brakes as the feline form of a male lion loomed large in the headlights right in front of us.

He was young and strong, his full blond mane endowing him with a regal presence. His eyes were piercing as he looked out into the night at something we couldn't see. Charles thought that he was calling to his brother, who we had seen earlier that day. The lion continued to lie there for a few minutes, allowing all in the vehicle to admire him, cameras flashing and clicking furiously. Shortly after, perhaps annoyed by the headlights and the flashes, he pulled himself to his feet and began to walk towards the vehicle.

There's nothing like being in an open vehicle in Africa at night with a lion walking towards you to send a jolt of wake-up juice into your veins. You know that if that lion wants to eat you, he can. He knows that too. And in a deep part of your soul a primordial memory is triggered and you remember that it wasn't so long ago that your species was his prey. To say the least, it's a little disconcerting.

I watched that ancient recollection brush over Andy's features as the lion walked beside the vehicle on his side, just a metre from where he sat. I was pretty sure he wasn't breathing.

The lion slunk past and disappeared into the night, probably more interested in the herd of zebras he could smell nearby than the enraptured humans holding their breath in the Land Rover.

'Wow,' Andy finally exhaled.

Wow, indeed. It was good to be back in the wilds of Africa.

Arriving in Zimbabwe the day before, Andy and I had been the only tourists lining up at immigration to pay the US$30 single entry fee. On foot we had traipsed across the Victoria Falls Bridge, dragging backpacks and small suitcases on wheels around slushy mud and brown pools of water where the inverted rain had fallen. Mist from the falls clung to our skin, cooling our faces in the midmorning heat. *Mosi-oa-tunya*, the locals called it – the smoke that thunders. We weaved between the long lines of large transport trucks laden with goods, a caterpillar of vehicles that stretched for kilometres. One driver told us he had been waiting for two days to get through the border post.

I felt the atmosphere change as soon as we set foot on the Zimbabwean side. This was a country on the verge of collapse. A desperate throng of taxi drivers flocked towards us and begged to be the chosen one to take us up the hill to the Victoria Falls Hotel.

'How much?'

'Ten dollars.'

'US?'

'*Ja*.'

'But it's only a five-minute drive.'

'Ten dollars.'

'No thanks, we'll walk.'

As we strode away, one man with pleading eyes ran after us. 'Please, madam, five dollars to help me eat.'

It worked. The man led us to his taxi, an early 1980s Mazda 323 that looked like it had been driven off the falls and reconstructed piece by piece. Every panel on the dilapidated sedan had been replaced or was broken. There were no functional door or window handles on the inside. In the back seat, I could feel sharp springs jabbing me in the butt through the tattered upholstery.

We chugged up the hill at twenty kilometres per hour, powered largely by our driver's ecstatic smile and the small amount of fuel that he had lined up for for days to put in his car. He told us that there were new rules in Zimbabwe. Due to the fuel shortages, vehicles were limited to five litres of petrol per car.

Some things in Zimbabwe hadn't changed. The famous

Victoria Falls Hotel still shone as a tall beacon of colonial charm overlooking the falls. The paint had not peeled, the service was still impeccable, the grass lawns were perfectly clipped and green, but it wasn't crawling with foreign tourists as it had been in 1993 when I had lunched there with my father while a vivacious local marimba band played. After so many years with a depressed tourism industry, I was surprised that it was open at all.

At the hotel we met a driver from Wilderness Safaris who would take us into Hwange National Park, two hours' drive away. My old friend Dave van Smeerdijk, now head of marketing for Wilderness Safaris in Johannesburg, had arranged this trip for us. Little Makalolo Camp, he said, had just been renovated.

'You'll love it, mate,' Dave said. 'It's really wild.'

'But, Dave, are you sure Zim's okay after the election and all?' I asked, for my mother's benefit more than my own.

'It's fine. We've still got guests booking in there. It's a lot quieter than it used to be.'

'Sounds perfect.'

As we drove through, the once bustling town of Victoria Falls was like a ghost town. Most of the shops were open, but their shelves were almost empty. I remembered the vibrant, crowded marketplaces where I had once bargained with local salesmen for wooden animal carvings and crocheted shirts in a throng of other tourists. Now those same thatched stands stood bare and desolate beside the road, not a carving in sight. No tourists meant no buyers, so many Zimbabwean craftspeople had moved their wares across the border to Zambia.

But perhaps the most striking difference was the complete absence of cars on the road. In the two-hour journey from Vic Falls to Main Camp at Hwange National Park we passed only two other vehicles, both of them semi-trailers carrying loads of what looked like construction materials bound for the Zambian border. The highways were in outstanding condition, just as I remembered them, but there wasn't a car in sight. It was eerie, as if everyone had just disappeared, abducted by aliens.

We were stopped twice at police roadblocks as we wound through undulating rocky outcrops dotted with baobabs. At each roadblock the uniformed men searched our vehicle. Given the paucity of traffic on the road I suspected they were happy to be doing anything. I listened to the conversation between our driver and one policeman, and was surprised that after all those years I could still understand some of the Shona they spoke. He wanted water – *mvura*. Our driver knew better than to argue. He gave him several bottles of water from our cool box. The policeman arrogantly waved us off.

It was almost winter and the sun set early shortly after five. After the boiling day, the temperature dropped sharply. It was night-time before we arrived at Little Makololo Camp and, despite the blankets covering us in the back of the open vehicle, my teeth were chattering with cold. I had forgotten how much the temperature dropped at night in this part of the world.

'I need a stiff drink,' Andy declared.

'Me too,' I slurred through frozen lips.

Charles's teeth shone like fluorescent lights as he smiled and led us to the campfire. I squatted close to the flames to warm my freezing fingers. There we met Colin Gillies from Bulawayo and his daughter, Brigit, with whom we would share the camp for the next few days. The camp, which was set on open plains near a large waterhole, was unfenced, so Charles reminded us that walking even the short distance from the dining area to the tent required an armed guard with a good torch.

It's the little things in Africa that are for me so soaked in familiarity that it only takes a small dose to remind me this is my second home. I had forgotten how good it felt. Africa is raw and immediate when it hits you, rushing in through the sweet scent of smoke from a mopane campfire, the sight of triangular grass-roofed huts hugging the bases of *kopjes*, the eerie cry of a jackal at sunset. As I lay in bed hugging a hot-water bottle, I heard elephants drinking at the waterhole and their tummy rumbles and splashing lulled me into a deep and contented sleep.

I woke before dawn to the familiar sounds of guinea fowls, francolins, babblers and wood doves. I kept my eyes shut and listened blissfully to their orchestra. A spotted hyaena laughed some distance away, a cackle of delight before bedding down for the day. I could have stayed there listening to the dawn chorus of the African bush forever.

The last time I had been in Africa I had been single, penniless and without a roof over my head I could call my own. That had been less than eighteen months earlier and a lot had changed since then. Now I had a paid job with a global conservation organisation and I was in a rare position to be able to influence mammal conservation in some small way in India, something I had never imagined I would do. At thirty, I had finally saved a little money for the first time in my life and had moved in with Andy to a peaceful flat overlooking the ocean at Clovelly, in Sydney's eastern suburbs. And now I was back in Africa in a canvas tent, in the land that I loved, with a new love snoring gently beside me. I had everything I wanted. So why did I feel so unsettled?

Long before the sun rose, my mind buzzed with questions that I didn't have answers for. Would I be able to return to work in Africa again? Would Andy like it here? What would he do for a living? And above all, where did Andy fit in this tight relationship I had had with Africa for so long? Could I really have them both?

In Africa I was independent and strong. It was, after all, the place where I had forged my identity, my character built and nurtured by nature's daily lessons in life, death and survival. But I knew too well that it was a relationship that was fickle and sometimes abusive. 'Africa can chew you up and spit you out,' my father once said. I knew he was right. Africa had slapped me around, knocked me down, then pulled me up for another beating time and time again. I had found love in Africa then lost it. I had almost been eaten and stood on numerous times. I had felt genuine fear here, and learned how to control it. I had reached the peaks of happiness in this place, and at other times fallen into depths of despair. I had felt euphoric and inspired by the simple, unadulterated beauty of Africa, but I had also seen its dark side. At times I had felt lonely and lost and loveless.

In the male-dominated environment of African conservation world, I had worked hard to build a career and a life for myself. While I loved the irresistible men in khaki, it was almost impossible to juggle being the type of feminine lady they sought with the strong woman I needed to be.

Decades after the feminist movement opened up all sorts of opportunities for women, I was one of a generation who wanted it all and knew I could have it if I worked hard enough. But that didn't mean I knew exactly *how* to do it and be happy. I knew I wasn't alone. Plenty of female friends my age were staking new ground as women in a world of high speed, deadlines and cut-throat competition. I knew I was a great *do*-er, capable of managing lots of things at the same time, but that didn't mean I was a great *be*-er. The opposite was more likely. While my mother was always the first to tell me that there was no greater source of happiness for her than being a wife and mother, the truth was that for me that simply wasn't enough. I wanted the cake *and* the low-fat cream too.

I still wanted Africa, but in the eighteen months I had been away I could feel it slipping from my grasp. I was changing and so was my relationship with the continent. So assuming that I could have anything I wanted now, what *did* I really want? Having all the options open to you is one thing. Narrowing them down to what your heart truly desires is entirely another. The single life of a roaming, twenty-something zoologist had had its perks but, by accident or intent, being back in Africa I realised I had moved into another era. Things were different now. I no longer wanted to lie alone in a tent while elephants jostled around me and wonder if I were going to die. At the very least, if I were going to do that, I wanted someone to cuddle up to while the elephants farted furiously around us.

At thirty, I still wanted the freedom to fight conservation battles in the developing world, but I had also begun to think about other things, things that had never really entered my consciousness until now. Like kids. A black-listed term in my vocabulary until then. Suddenly the 'K' word was featuring heavily in my thoughts and an arrow shot straight from it to another formerly taboo word – marriage. The question was, could I have them all? The answer had to be yes. So then it became, okay then . . . *How?* I heard a long hollow whoosh and then a plonk as the question fell down the deep well of my brain and hit the floor without catching any kind of response on its way. The question brushed itself off, stood up and repeated insistently, *How?* I had no idea. In the past when I was seeking answers I had often found them in the African bush. This was where I hoped I would find them now.

Over the next few days I explored the national park with Andy where, fifteen years earlier, I had first come with my father. We watched a majestic lion stride through grass the colour of his fur, scenting the dawn air for prey or mates. We shared a tree by a waterhole with a large breeding herd of elephants resting in the shade. Protective adult females stood watchfully over carefree young ones lying on their sides, gently fanning their ears in the midday heat, eyes half closed, aware but restful. They accepted our presence just metres away with generous tolerance. Common impalas pranced and barked, stocky Cape buffalos grunted and tussled, handsome sable antelopes strode elegantly across the savannah. The deep throaty sound of ground hornbills reverberated like drums through the bush. An elephant bull in musth left a pungent vegetative odour behind him as he mock-charged the vehicle, showing off his formidable strength. Raging eyes flared with testosterone in a square forehead caked in dried mud. This was Andy's first African safari and Hwange put on one hell of a show.

It was all too easy to forget that Zimbabwe was in a state of crisis, and that just outside the park this once flourishing country had ground to a halt. We heard rumours – whispered, always – of beatings in the rural areas, torture and rape. Local staff told us that it was almost impossible to get food. Prices for mealie meal, used to make Zimbabwe's staple diet, *sadza*, had gone through the roof, and, even if you could afford it, sacks of the precious powder were thin on the ground. How Wilderness Safaris kept Little Makololo Camp running at all was a miracle. The chefs prepared meals fit for kings out of whatever they could get a hold of, doing their best to uphold the standards of the camp even while Zimbabwe crashed down around them.

The Zimbabwean dollar, worth more than the US dollar when it was introduced in 1980, had eroded to over ZWD$7 million to US$1. Inflation at that time had reportedly jumped to 355 000 percent. Notes now started at ZWD$10 000 but were worthless.

'It affects your business in ways you can't imagine,' Colin told us. He owned a printing company. 'Simple things like accounting systems. You lose track of all the zeros when you add things up. I mean, you sign a cheque for millions of dollars just to pay for a small order.'

I asked him what he would do if things got worse, if the planned run-off election led to more years of oppression by Mugabe's government.

'We have to carry on,' he replied. 'We must. I'm too old to start over somewhere else. Zimbabwe is my home. We'll get through this.'

I sensed that his daughter, Brigit, who had lived in England for several years, was desperate to come home to Zimbabwe. But in the current climate, for her and her husband with a new baby it just wasn't an option. She had to listen to her head and not her heart.

As a long-time active member of the Zimbabwean Wildlife Society, Colin was depressed about the poaching that was decimating the country's once flourishing conservancies and game farms.

'It breaks your heart,' he said, his voice trailing off as he stared into the flames of the campfire. 'In the national parks there is no money to buy petrol to pump water. Tourism operators like these guys are the ones pumping the water. They're keeping the wildlife alive in places like this.'

At the waterhole nearby, an elephant trumpeted and we heard water splashing.

Among the local staff in the camp, however, there was a growing sense of hope. Things couldn't go on like this much longer, they felt. Few dared to say aloud what they hoped for, that Zimbabwe would soon have a new president and food in their bellies, but most felt that change was coming, that they just had to hold on a little longer.

Resilient as I knew Zimbabweans were, I wondered how much more they could take. I asked Charles what he thought.

'Change is coming,' he replied stoically. 'People would rather put up with the beatings and the hunger than face more of the same in the future.'

In Zimbabwe, although things had never been worse for people, they soldiered on. I had expected to find disaster in this country, to see it destroyed by one man's greed and his addiction to power. But in the midst of perhaps the darkest, longest night in Zimbabwe's history, a light was still shining. It shone brightly from the strong hearts of her people in their incredible tenacity. Through eyes wet with tears, they still saw a hopeful future. They had nothing else to hold on to. Hope was all they had left.

Even in the mess that was their present day, Zimbabwe still had a resilient, ravaged magnificence about it, as you would see when staring into the eyes of a brave soldier who has seen hell and lived to tell the story. It had changed, but the essence of the country and her people was still the same.

As we walked back across the Victoria Falls Bridge to Zambia I realised that although Zimbabwe and I had both changed, we would always be old friends. A little piece of Africa would always be with me wherever I went, no matter how much I changed or how long I stayed away. And both of us had to keep moving forward.

NINETEEN

At the confluence of two giant rivers, somewhere in the junction of four African countries, I was up a tree. Close by, a herd of hippos honked and yawned, their enormous gapes revealing pearly whites that could chomp a man in two. I clung to a precarious branch overhanging the rushing water of the mighty Zambezi and glanced at my hand. A small black ant crawled onto the top of it as if my skin were an extension of the tree limb on which I was perched like a pale, hairless baboon. A lime green chameleon swivelled an eye in my direction in a passing assessment of my potential as predator or prey. 'G'day, mate,' I said.

What was I was doing up a tree on a tiny island on the Zambezi talking to a chameleon? Beneath me, looking up with a strange mixture of trepidation and confusion on his face, that was exactly what Andy was thinking. He had just asked me a very important question, and I had scrambled up a tree.

It had all started a couple of days earlier when, after a couple of weeks of work with Malvern, Andy had, unbeknown to me, been on the phone to Dave and arranged another weekend in the bush for us. All I knew was that we were on a low-slung ferry with dozens of local people crossing into Botswana and I wasn't quite sure why.

A baby was crying. I watched the mother, young herself, her curvaceous hips wrapped in a brightly patterned sarong, pop out a plump breast and shove it in the child's mouth. She caught me watching her and looked away shyly, muttering something to the gathering of voluptuous African mamas around her.

I looked away, caught in the act of people-watching. Casting my eyes over the expanse of water we were crossing I tried to work out if this was the Zambezi River, linking Zambia and Zimbabwe. Then again, I pondered, it could have been the Chobe River in Botswana or Namibia. Andy leaned over the ferry's railing beside dozens of local people, trucks and cars crossing the border out of Zambia. At that moment we were in the no-man's-land at the junction of four countries: Botswana, Zimbabwe, Zambia and Namibia.

'Where are we going exactly, babe?' I asked Andy.

'It's a surprise.'

'At least tell me what country. Is it Botswana? Namibia?'

'Strictly speaking, I think we're going to Namibia.'

'But doesn't this ferry take us to Botswana?'

'I'm not exactly sure . . . Possibly. We'll find out on the other side. All I know is that we have to meet a transfer at midday at Kasane.'

'Is Kasane in Botswana?'

'I don't know . . . This is killing you, isn't it?' Andy chuckled.

'Not at all, I love surprises,' I lied.

I hate surprises. I love the *idea* of going with the flow, but every cell in my body resists relinquishing control. I was delighted with the surprise adventure, but now that we were on our way my natural control-freak urges were taking over. I had no idea where we were going or how we were getting there. I had no currency on me other than a few Zambian kwatcha and some US dollars. I sure hoped this mad Englishman knew what he was doing.

It turned out that the ferry we were on took us to Botswana.

I asked a man in a suit and tie in the immigration line-up, 'Is this Kasane?'

'No. You must get a taxi. It is eleven kilometres that way.' He pointed into the hot, dry bush where a tar road wound off into the distance. It was too far to walk with bags in the midday heat.

I spotted a local minibus taxi and the driver encouraged us to jump in. Squished inside with about ten other passengers, I sat between Andy and a rotund, well-dressed lady from Zambia. The taxi smelled strongly of hot, sweaty humans.

'Do you have any pula on you?' I asked Andy.

'What's pula?'

'The Botswanan currency.'

He looked at me blankly. I was waiting for him to give me his standard answer whenever I asked him something he didn't know the answer to – 'Detail, darling. Detail.'

'It's okay, I'll ask if they will take US dollars.'

I scavenged around in my bag, trying to find some small currency. As I was searching, the lady beside me leaned over and passed me a five-pula coin.

'Here,' she said, smiling. 'You can take this.'

Surprised, I thanked her and asked if she would like to exchange it for some US dollars.

'Oh no,' she protested kindly. 'You can just have it.'

It's one of the most inspiring things about the developing

world that it is the poorest of people who are the most generous. Tears pricked my eyes.

I was about to protest again when she raised her hand to stop me and exclaimed with a laugh, 'I am giving it to you.'

We struck up a conversation and I learned that she was a radiographer who lived in Lusaka, the capital of Zambia.

'What are you doing here in Botswana?' I asked.

'My husband is here. I am visiting him.'

'Oh? What does he do here?'

'He is in the prison,' she smiled, as if that sort of thing happened every day. 'He works for a mining company in Zambia and he bought a car in Botswana. Then when he gets to the border the officials say it was stolen.'

'Oh, that's awful. How long is he in for?'

She sighed. 'Already he has been there for two weeks. He has a hearing in ten days.'

We dropped the lady off at the barbed-wire fence of the prison gates and she wished us luck. I thanked her again for shouting us the cab fare. As we watched her lug her small suitcase up the hill I remembered yet again how generous the spirit of Africa is when you allow yourself to go with its flow.

I looked to my right over Andy's shoulder, where large fields of sugar cane and mealies stretched into the distance. The fields stretched long and luxuriant across the landscape, fed by the ample rainfall this part of Africa received seasonally. Suddenly two terrified creatures came into view. Elephants! And they were running. Awkward and ungainly legs pelted across the field, trampling clipped green crops; their ears were flapping and their eyes were wide. I couldn't see what they were running from, exposed in the open field in broad daylight, but they were going like the clappers.

I wondered where these elephants were from. Were they

Botswanan elephants or Namibian ones? So close to the border they could be Zimbabwean or Zambian too. The truth was, in this part of the world they were simply elephants of Africa, probably crossing a national border regularly. Elephants, after all, had no need for passports on their traditional migration routes. Their ranges encompassed vast areas that often included more than one country. That was why transfrontier conservation areas were so important; they allowed elephants to move freely across their natural range.

I was deep in thought about these cross-border elephants when the taxi dropped us off at the Kasane Immigration Office. Half an hour after our passports had been stamped into Botswana, they were stamped out again. A man from the place we were going to, a lodge that I now knew was called Ntwala, met us there. He helped us into a small speedboat and we sped off onto the wide sapphire Chobe River.

Ten minutes up the river our driver slowed down and skilfully manoeuvred the boat off the main stretch through a thin channel lined with reeds and lilies. We pulled up on the bank of a small island where local people sat chatting.

'Where are we?' I nudged Andy.

'I have no idea,' he grinned.

'Here, you take your passports,' our driver instructed. 'It is for entry to Namibia. Just walk up the hill. You will see it there, the customs office.'

And so it was. A small brick building with one room, the official border post between Botswana and Namibia materialised as we walked up a dusty path through the bush. There was no line-up. Behind a glass window a smiling official stamped us into Namibia.

'Do you think we have to go through any more countries today?' I asked Andy. 'I'm running out of pages in my passport.'

'That's it, I think. It takes about half an hour to get to the lodge from here.'

The journey had taken us the best part of the day. Three countries, six customs officers, four passport pages, two elephants and a prison visit. But it was worth it. Ntwala, an intimate five-chalet lodge on a tiny island in the Zambezi River, was the kind of place that dreams are made of.

Chobe National Park is elephant city. With somewhere in the realm of 120 000 elephants, Botswana's first national park managed to avoid the slaughter that decimated elephants in other parts of Africa. Andy and I arrived in the park by boat with our guide, Albert, and within half an hour we were watching dozens of elephants from an amazing floating vantage point on the Chobe River.

Several large herds drank at the river's edge, wading in up to their knees and spraying cooling water over their backs. There's nothing like the jubilant enthusiasm of elephants as they approach water. As the day heated up, the numbers of elephants continued to grow, thirsty new herds emerging from behind the bank, gaining speed in saggy, baggy pants as they approached the river. Little ones bumbled close to their mothers, ears flapping, heads shaking and trunks flailing, unable to contain themselves at the sight of the water. The atmosphere was charged with social tension. It was fun and exhilarating, a real pachyderm party, where old friends caught up and new ones joined the social circle.

A tiny baby stood near his mother trying to work out how to use his trunk, flinging it around like an unmanageable plaything. While his observant mother drank close by, he plunged headfirst into the dirt on the bank and vigorously rubbed his trunk and head in the dust while wiggling his butt in the air. Ecstatically, he tumbled over on his side and began to roll around in the dirt, scratching his back and covering himself in dust. He was really enjoying himself. Each time he rolled up he flung his tiny trunk in the air and swung it around crazily, having so much fun with his unruly appendage that we couldn't help but laugh at his antics.

His mother, watching him out of the corner of her eye as she drank, didn't seem to know how to react to her calf's rambunctious behaviour, preferring instead to pretend it wasn't happening. I imagined her embarrassedly chastising him, 'Oh, for goodness sake, Charlie, everyone's watching! Will you just settle down? Your father would be mortified if he saw you behaving like this in public!'

Several other elephants were watching him now and another calf, a female who was slightly larger than him, came over to investigate. Wanting to put him firmly in his place, there was only one thing she could do in a situation like this – she sat on him. Quite literally, in a big-sisterly fashion, she planted her podgy arse on his as though sitting on a comfortable lounge chair. She stayed there sitting upright for a few minutes, her body rocking as though she were on a washing machine as the calf tried to fling her off, his trunk still flailing around. When she finally stood up and ran off, the small calf chased her and trumpeted as loudly as he could, flinging his untamed trunk at her in retribution.

To hell with scientific rules about anthropomorphism, I thought. Who wouldn't love elephants? They played. They felt joy and excitement, truly revelling in the pleasure of water on a hot day. They formed loyal family bonds and, it seemed to me, deep friendships that lasted lifetimes. They could be courageous matriarchs in the face of lions and hyaenas. I'd seen elephants show compassion, like the herd that had waited for the female with the dying calf in Khaudum. I knew they grieved lost loved ones, but then got on with their lives. They had long memories and formidable tenacity in the harshest of conditions. And then it dawned on me. It wasn't actually that elephants were so much like *us* that made them so endearing. It was that they showed us the best side of ourselves.

Later on, in the deeper waters of the Chobe, we watched a large bull standing waist deep in the river surrounded by an aquatic field of lilies with white and purple flowers. He was feeding on river plants while having a good soak in the cool water, the perfect way to cope with the dizzying midday heat. Nearby, African jacanas, or 'Jesus birds', walked on water, treading lightly with splayed feet on round floating lily pads. Darters gathered in large flocks to dry themselves on crags of wood and fallen trees in the river, holding their wings out like clothes on a line to catch the gentle wind. At sundown they skimmed just above the water, almost touching it with wings stretched out flat in flight, flying as fast as our boat was travelling. Tiny malachite kingfishers, resplendent in a garb of bright blue feathers and fiery red beaks, perched on swaying reeds on the banks of the river, fluttering from stalk to stalk, chasing insects and small fish.

A fish eagle, the king of the avian world, pulled a large slippery catfish out of the river with sharp talons. The feathers of his stark white chest ruffled in the wind. The catfish must have been too heavy to be lifted up to the nearest tree because the eagle began to devour him on the riverbank, ripping at flesh with its piercing beak. Hippos lazed on islands in the river, sunning their huge bodies and oozing pink secretions that acted like suncream. But above all, by their sheer size and numbers, it was the elephants that dominated this kingdom.

On our way back to the lodge Albert suggested we cast our lines into the Zambezi at a couple of his favourite spots for tigerfish. Africa's tigers are fierce freshwater carnivores and game fishermen from all around the world come to catch them.

They're known for putting up a fight, although I was told they are bony and don't make good eating. I grew up fishing in North Queensland but I was no fisherman and nor was Andy. It had been a long time since I had cast a line in the water. What the heck, I thought. As Albert let the boat drift along on the fast current we cast our lines behind the boat near the long reeds, reeling in slowly as he instructed us.

'If you get a bite, reel in fast,' Albert said. 'Then he will fight you!'

The midday sun burned fiercely down on us, its rays reflecting off the water. The tigers weren't biting. We tried a couple of other spots on the way back, Albert insisting that these were good spots for catching tigerfish. Andy got a bite – or, at least, he thought he did – then got snagged.

'I've had enough,' I announced, impatient as always. 'I can feel my forehead burning.'

'Just a little longer,' Albert insisted. 'I've got one more spot to try.'

By now we were almost back at the island where the lodge was. I could hear the rapids that rushed past our chalet. With the engine off, Albert let us drift over them, steering the boat carefully in order to stay in the deep part of the river. We were drifting fast, the boat bobbing up and down over the rapids as the channel narrowed and the reeds closed in around us. Suddenly we bobbed past a family of hippos resting on a sandbank in a break in the reeds, just metres away. Too close. I held my breath, knowing that hippos could charge our small boat quickly and with little provocation. They glanced up with piggy eyes as our boat floated past them. Three slow seconds ticked by and we were out of their sight. 'Phew,' I breathed, 'that was close.' *Splash!* In a delayed response about five seconds later they all bombshelled into the river, led by a spooked baby.

Watching the river with expert eyes, Albert said, 'Just one more here'.

He took my rod and cast spectacularly out near the reeds where the rapids started. As the bait hit the water, the reel whirred into life.

'It's a tiger!' he exclaimed, then passed the rod to me. 'Here, take it!'

'Me? No, you!' I protested.

But he wouldn't take no for an answer. I held on to the rod, held it high and reeled in like a madwoman. The fish dragged on the line, pulling it up river. Every time the fish slowed, I reeled fast. When it was close to the boat it leapt out of the water, a flash of silver and red.

'It's big!' Andy said, reeling his line in so he would have free hands to help me.

The fish pulled away again, determined to put up a good fight. But by now, so was I. I reeled and reeled and reeled, arching my back to hold onto the rod, ignoring the sweat and suncream pouring into my eyes.

'There he is!' Andy exclaimed. The silvery form of the tiger was right beside the boat. Alfred leaned over the side with a hand net and scooped up the fighting fish. He deftly pulled the hook out of its mouth and held the fish up with both hands. It was beautiful. Black zebra stripes flanked glistening silver metallic skin along its length. The broad, strong tail flashed a magnificent burning red.

'You want photo?' Albert said. 'Quick. Get camera.'

He was about to hand the heavy, slippery five-kilogram fish to me, but I insisted that he hold it. Andy snapped a picture of our team effort, with me standing beside a grinning Albert holding a five-kilogram tigerfish, before Albert let it go back into the river.

By now it was after one and we had worked up a healthy appetite. Briefly we returned to our chalet to wash up before lunch. While I was in the bathroom, Albert arrived at the door. I heard the two men conversing from the other room, but I couldn't make out what they were saying.

'You're not going to believe this but there's a sitatunga on the island next to this one,' Andy relayed the message. 'Shall we go and have a look?'

A sitatunga is a rare swamp-dwelling antelope found in wet parts of Africa like the Congo and Botswana's Okavango Delta. I had never seen one and had mentioned to Albert that morning that I would love to. What a coincidence, I thought, that there was one on the island next door!

Andy and I got back into the boat and drifted down the rapids to the small island just a few hundred metres away. Immediately I checked for tracks. Albert pointed out the fresh tracks of an elephant that had been there a few days before, leaving deep imprints in the mud. We walked through the thick forest of the island along a game trail frequented by hippos, being as quiet as we could so that we didn't disturb the sitatunga. Albert repeatedly pointed at the ground, pointing to tracks that didn't look like a sitatunga's to me. But then again, what did I know? Although I had worked on antelope for many years, I was certainly no expert on sitatungas. I knew they had long splayed hooves for living in water but I had no idea what their tracks looked like.

Albert tracked slowly and meticulously, followed closely by Andy and then me at the rear. I scanned the bush carefully, looking for the telltale white stripes or the downy red fur of an antelope. My senses were on high alert. I could hear hippos in the river nearby and I knew that we could easily come upon one on foot. As always, I kept an eye on the tree situation, making sure there was a climbable one close by.

As we came around a bend the forest opened up into a sandy clearing surrounded by palm trees. On the far side of the clearing on a sandy river beach were two tables covered in white tablecloths. A bottle of champagne rested in a silver bucket of ice at the centre of a lavish lunch spread. A platter of vegetable samosas, marinated chicken legs, ham quiches and honey-glazed carrots graced one table. The other table was set for two, and was decorated with all sorts of jungle leaves, purple flower petals and native melons.

The two men watched my face as I registered the surprise that had been planned for my benefit under the guise of a hunt for the elusive sitatunga. In contrast to the wide smiles on theirs tears filled my eyes. I threw my arms around Andy, unable to find the right words. While this was happening, Albert made a discreet exit.

Overwhelmed, I said, 'You planned this?'

'Well, yes,' Andy grinned. 'With quite a lot of help from the lodge staff. Now, come and sit down while I pour us both a drink.'

While hippos gaped in the background, Andy popped the bottle of champagne.

'This is so beautiful, babe. I can't believe you did this,' I said, taking a large gulp of champagne.

'I'm glad you like it. Now I have to ask you a question . . .'

Andy knelt down in front of me and pulled something out of his pocket.

I think at that point all of the colour must have drained from my face because I felt as though I might faint. It was a good thing he had told me to sit down. He took my hand. It was shaking and although it wasn't hot in the shade I could see he was sweating. In his hand he held a white-gold ring with a dozen tiny diamonds on each side in the shape of a Zulu shield. In the middle was a deep violet tanzanite rock with flecks of pink light in the centre. It is a truly special African stone, because tanzanite is only found at the base of Mount Kilimanjaro and is apparently rarer than diamonds.

'Tammie Matson. I really love you. Will you marry me?'

An audience of hippos gawked at us from the mighty Zambezi. A large male honked brazenly, demanding my answer. A gentle breeze rustled leaves in the palm trees. Sweat beads glistened on Andy's forehead. There was no more time for the questions that had plagued my mind for months, about whether saying yes to marriage and children was the same as saying no to freedom and adventure, about whether I could have Andy and Africa too. Now was the time for answers.

Two hours later, Albert arrived to pick us up and take us back to our island. He found me up a tree, with Andy standing underneath pleading with me to come down. I was trying to get a better look at the hippos and had decided to demonstrate to Andy what one should do if charged by one of these cantankerous amphibious mammals. As a co-conspirator in the surprise marriage proposal, Albert took one look at Andy's confused expression and at me up the tree, and his face dropped.

'Don't worry, mate,' Andy exclaimed. 'She said yes!'

POSTSCRIPT

Andy and I tied the knot in early November 2008. A barefoot local priest in a traditional skirt led the small ceremony on the soft sand of a South Pacific island. The heady perfume of scarlet hibiscus and frangipani flowers mingled with air that was humid and salty. Waves lapped gently at our feet. And as the sun set over an ocean as tranquil as my heart, a new chapter began for both of us.

Two weeks later, fresh from the honeymoon, I was back in Assam, this time to work with Dr Stephen van Mil's production company Animal Media Australia on a film about human-elephant conflict. But crazy, unpredictable, contradictory India! A fortnight earlier, as Andy and I had been exchanging vows, insurgents killed eighty people in and around Guwahati in a devastating series of bombings targeting public places and civilians. Along with the bombings in Mumbai, which happened while I spent the night there, it felt like India had become a war zone.

What on earth was I doing going back to this mad place just a fortnight after getting married to the man of my dreams?

And yet, as soon as I landed in Assam I was surprised at how happy I was to be back. This place had crept under my skin in a different way to Africa but was no less addictive. Women in bright, colourful saris worked sun-ripened fields of golden rice, sprawled beneath the snow-capped peaks of the Himalayas. They stacked small bundles of harvested rice by hand in neat little rows before gathering them together in village granaries. Lean men in knee-length wraps and scuffed sandals bent over and strained to pull heavy loads of rice hay three times their height on wooden carts along the main potholed highway. A sheep strapped to the roof of a bus along with dozens of suitcases and bags occasionally looked up to take in the scenery. Women glided along the street in glittering saris, the soft fabric flowing behind them elegantly. Whenever we stopped, friendly, curious locals asked to take photos of us with their mobile phones. A road sign by the highway stated, *Don't gossip. Let him drive*, which the almost all-male crew found hilarious.

Nothing had changed since Andy and I had been there, which was both good and bad. Close to where we were based at the delightful Nameri Eco Camp, I felt a strong, sad sense of deja vu as I watched truck by truck, bicycle by bicycle, cart by cart, all loaded with wood from the forest blatantly whittling away what was left of Assam's remaining elephant habitat. I tried not to think about the fact that this had probably happened every single day since I had been there a year before.

There is nothing underhand or secret about what's going on here. Everyone knows what is happening and no one is stopping it. Assam has a long, cold winter and villagers need to keep warm and cook curry to fill empty bellies. Wood costs them nothing but a little physical exertion and people are so poor that they have no alternative. Little bit by little bit, the forest is being destroyed and soon it will all be gone.

It is no wonder that dozens and dozens of people and elephants are being killed by each other every year in Assam. This is the only place where I have heard elephants make a sound that is so raw and angry it is like a scream. At night in the villages I saw desperate elephants with nowhere left to go literally running scared across croplands as large, noisy crowds of villagers charged after them with burning spears. These images still haunt me. There is so much fear and rage in these elephants; it is not surprising that they are retaliating against the species that has stolen their home. Almost every week at this time of year, someone is killed by an elephant. The widows wear white saris in grief and often do not remarry. Although extended families usually adopt them, their lives are harder without husbands.

While we were there, an elephant killed a boy and the community was so incensed that they attacked the Forestry staff and broke one man's legs. At another village they burned down the Forestry office after elephants destroyed people's homes. It is not only the elephants who are subject to revenge by people; it is the underpaid staff of the Forestry Department, who are also now seen by some as the enemy.

People will do anything to protect themselves from rampaging elephants, but they do not want them killed unnecessarily. Some of the people I spoke to actually called elephants 'Ganesh' or 'baba' (god), not *hathi*, in regular conversation, which shows the almost indistinguishable link between the elephants they fight and the god they worship. A widow told me that although her husband was killed by an elephant, she does not hate elephants. She just wanted to get on with her life and sleep easily. Through a translator, she told me, 'What can I do? I will pray to Ganesh.'

But these people need more than Ganesh now. They need

support from their government to improve their standard of living so that they do not need to get wood from the forest. They need a government committed in the long term to protecting what is left of the forests and revegetating corridors so that elephants have somewhere to live and do not seek rice paddies. They need support to explore alternative crops like chillies, ones that elephants won't eat. They need it now, not tomorrow. Tomorrow will be too late.

On my return to Assam I was heartened to hear some villagers talking about 'hot chillies' and the possibility that this could be an alternative crop to rice and a barrier to elephants. WWF Assam's Soumen Dey was working closely with local people to see how well they would grow. He was seeking funding to establish a crop three kilometres long that could form a trial buffer between forest and paddy.

"First we must show people that chilli pays. It must come from the people, not from outside. Then it will have a life of its own," Soumen said. "After all, our chillies are the hottest in the world. It is saying so in the Guinness Book!"

With the help of WWF and the Forestry Department, strategically placed *kunkies* are helping to reduce the amount of conflict in parts of Assam. For now, these flying squads of elephants are stopping wild herds destroying people's livelihoods by driving them back to the fragmented forest. But there are only a dozen or so *kunkies* used for this purpose in the whole state. As the forests dwindle and the human population grows, how many more *kunkies* will be needed? And for how long will this approach work? When all the forest is gone, replaced by rice paddies and tea gardens, an agricultural landscape will become the new habitat of Assam's elephants. If human-elephant conflict takes hundreds of lives now, how many more will it take then?

There are other victims of the conflict, too, those that no one ever hears about. They are the calves of elephants that are killed, maimed or herded away. These tiny babies fall into trenches in tea plantations and their mothers cannot get them out. When people come and scare away the herd to get a trapped baby out, the young ones smell of humans – a scent laced with memories of fear and persecution. As a result, even when an attempt is made to reunite the baby with its mother it is usually rejected by the herd. Others get separated from their herd at night in the paddies when their mothers are frightened away or wounded by people wielding spears and other weapons. They become orphans. These are the refugees of the war between people and elephants.

Thankfully, there is a place for these motherless babies. They find sanctuary at Kaziranga's Centre for Wildlife Rehabilitation and Conservation (CWRC) where a husband and wife veterinary team from the Wildlife Trust of India, the Boros, care for half a dozen pachyderm victims of conflict, as well as many other rescued species. When the orphaned elephants are very young, some of them brought in at just a few weeks old, they are bottle-fed with formula milk and tended to day and night by their carers. If they make it to a few months old, they join a small family of orphans and spend their days foraging in the forest near the sanctuary. Their carers stay with them the whole time and the babies seem to need their company as well as that of their adoptive sisters and brothers.

"You see this one," Dr Boro told me, pointing out a small male with particularly fuzzy hair on his head. "When he came in, his herd was attacked in a village. He was having a slash across his trunk."

As if the small elephant had heard us talking about him, he stopped leaning against his adopted sister and wandered over to us. He held his little trunk high, wobbling it in the air as he smelled us. It looked like a drunken cobra. Curious and unabashed, he bumbled over until he was standing beside us. He wasn't any higher than my waist.

His trunk ventured up my body and around my leg, sniffing and exploring my scent. Perhaps judging me to be non-threatening, he ventured further, gently wrapping his trunk around my wrist. The calf held it there firmly for a second, surprising me with the strength in the serpentine appendage, even at his young age. It felt like a hairy python, muscular and warm, a living proboscis on a journey of discovery. I felt like a specimen being investigated; no longer the scientist, but a subject of inquiry.

Then, in a gesture I can only describe as one of the most endearing things I have ever experienced, this little elephant pulled my hand past his floppy lips and into his pink, moist mouth. He began to suck on it gently, still with his damaged trunk wrapped around my arm, holding it firmly in his mouth. Occasionally he glanced up at me in the unaffected way of toddlers, as if the whole world were there for him and no one else. He seemed quite content suckling there for several minutes with my now slimy hand ensconced inside his soft mouth, dripping with elephant saliva.

The elephant did not judge or condemn me for what my species did to his. Perhaps he was too young to understand how he had personally been a victim at the hands of people. Right then, what separated our species didn't matter one bit, either to him or to me. I smiled, smitten by the affection of this precious, fuzzy-headed pachyderm. It was just me and the elephant, in a perfect moment, connected by a tiny trunk.

AUTHOR'S NOTE

Despite the Kenya-led global ivory ban in 1989, poaching of elephants and the illegal trade in ivory continues today, although to a lesser extent. There is still a demand for ivory to make things like carvings and jewellery, especially in Japan and China, and to provide for domestic markets in parts of Africa and Asia.

However, in much of southern and east Africa, elephant populations are growing, especially in Botswana, Namibia, Zimbabwe and South Africa. By the end of last century, these countries had accumulated large stockpiles of legal ivory and they wanted to be able to sell it. This ivory was not from poached elephants, but from natural mortalities and legal culling. Any profits from its sale, the governments declared, would go towards elephant conservation and management. When CITES; the Convention on International Trade in Endangered Species, approved the sale of stockpiled ivory from Namibia, Botswana and Zimbabwe in a one-off sale to Japan in 1999, these countries welcomed the decision. Elephants were doing so well in places like South Africa's Kruger National Park that the government started talking about culling again.

Then, in late 2008, CITES made one of the most momentous decisions since the ivory ban, to allow China to trade in ivory taken from official stockpiles in Namibia, Zimbabwe, Botswana and now also South Africa. Dr Sue Lieberman, then head of WWF's global Species Program, told me that this reflects how successful southern Africa has been in its conservation efforts.

'They've earned it,' she said. 'And so has China. China has made enormous progress with the number of ivory seizures. They really have come a long way and they deserve some recognition of that.'

Not everyone in the conservation community agreed with WWF's stance on China. Some felt that allowing China and Japan to buy legal ivory would only increase the demand and result in more illegal hunting. Opponents of the decision called it a 'poaching smokescreen'. Only time will tell whether allowing China to trade in legal ivory will elevate levels of poaching and illegal trade. CITES is confident that they have adequate controls and monitoring in place to track the ivory and ensure that there are no loopholes for poachers to step through. But the point is, the fact that this conversation has happened at all reflects just how far African elephants have come since the late 1980s, when the situation was so dire that the Kenyan government torched ten tonnes of ivory in a symbolic gesture to stop the killing of elephants for their tusks.

While the overall picture for African elephants is getting better, it's not rosy for the species all over the African continent. Poaching, habitat loss and human-elephant conflict remain serious threats to African elephants to varying extents in different countries. The population in West Africa is small and highly fragmented due to extensive loss of habitat, and time is running out to protect the remaining forests. The future for the remaining four to ten elephants in Guinea Bissau looks bleak and it's even worse in Senegal, where they cannot confirm the existence of more than one elephant. Côte d'Ivoire, which was named for its abundance of elephants, has a declining elephant population due to severe poaching. In central Africa, forest elephants in the Democratic Republic of Congo share their habitat with armed militia, and extractive industries like logging and mining are further reducing their habitat. In the last thirty years the amount of elephant range across Africa has more than halved and the majority of habitat left is outside protected areas. The future of African elephants will require international cooperation to protect, connect and manage their habitats across their range through transfrontier conservation areas.

Conservationists are just now starting to take into account the impact of climate change as well, which some scientists predict may reduce the persistence of many species, including elephants, in Africa. National parks like Kruger may have a lot of elephants now, but some climate change projections suggest that by 2080, many of their current protected habitats may be unsuitable for them. The International Panel on Climate Change predicts that Africa will be the continent hardest hit by global warming, in part because of its high dependence on rain-fed agriculture. Climate change is predicted to increase the aridity of much of Africa and, coupled with more extreme droughts, this will put further pressure on the natural resources people and elephants share. Human-elephant conflict is increasing as human and elephant populations grow, but climate change could exacerbate this even further by increasing competition for land and water.

Although poaching and illegal trade in ivory are still rampant in some parts of Africa, the success of conservation measures in southern Africa demonstrates that we can turn the page for a species and build a brighter future. By providing economic incentives to local people to conserve elephants, countries like Namibia, which now have thriving wildlife populations, have become role models for the rest of the world. The Bushmen of Nyae Nyae Conservancy, Namibia's first communal conservancy, have shown what can be achieved for elephants when local people are empowered to move forward sustainably. There, proactive measures like concrete enclosures are helping to protect people's water resources, and socio-economic benefits from elephants are flowing in from trophy hunting, reducing the cost of living with elephants.

Although the South African government approved culling as a last resort to manage elephant populations in places like Kruger, these days there are much better options that allow elephants and people to thrive without a need for mass slaughter. Transfrontier conservation areas like the KAZA are some of the most exciting and challenging developments in elephant management because they allow elephants to move across their natural range, incorporating long-term integrated land-use planning with community-based incentives so people can cohabitate with elephants. Good progress has been made with some of these initiatives already and more are emerging across the continent.

When people ask me if I am optimistic about the future of the Asian elephant, I hesitate – and then I say yes. If we can turn things around for the African elephant in parts of its range in only a few decades, we can do it for Asian elephants too. The difference in Asia is the surging human population and extreme loss of habitat. It means that we have to act fast and furiously to save what is left.

Elephants are powerful flagships for all the ecosystems they inhabit. If we allow the planet to lose a species as impressive as the elephant, what hope is there for other species? I can't let that happen and, with your help, it won't. Preliminary programs are starting in Assam to grow chillies and deter elephants, but there is much more to be done. If you would like to learn more about what you can do to help, log onto www.tammiematson.com

Let's work together to make sure these extraordinary animals not only survive but thrive on the amazing planet we share with them.

ACKNOWLEDGEMENTS

I have been incredibly fortunate to work with some amazing people in Africa, India and Australia. It is because of them – and the incredible animals with which we share the planet – that the inspiration for this book came about. With thanks:

In Namibia, to Dries Alberts of the Ministry of Environment & Tourism and Stacey Main for great support and friendship, Leon #Tsamkao for his impeccable translation and patience, Chief Bobo #Tsamkao and the management of Nyae Nyae Conservancy for the opportunity to work in their magnificent part of Africa, and the people of Bushmanland for sharing their lives with me. The gentle encouragement and can-do attitude of my treasured friend, Dr Jennifer Lalley, helped me get this project off the ground, the fine company of Dr Kisa Baldwin, Ron Swilling and Warren Tapp in Bushmanland ensured I maintained my sanity when the going got rough, and the awesome job at Wilderness Safaris thanks to Dave van Smeerdijk made it possible for me to complete it. Jen and Dave were also kind enough to give me a place to live in Windhoek (and co-conspirators with Andy in setting up the location for the best damn engagement ever). To Moremi and Chobe, the dalmations, Mosi and Malelo, the cats, and Zepa, the pug for keeping me company on lonely Sundays in Windhoek. The project was financed by the Rufford Foundation, the Wilderness Trust and the Namibia Nature Foundation. Also, to the Ozquest and local volunteers who slogged away in the crippling summer heat to build cribs for elephants in Nyae Nyae in 2006.

In India, Sujoy Banerjee, formerly of WWF India, a real gentleman, devoted conservationist and closet rock star, who made it possible for me to continue my journey with elephants in another pachyderm kingdom. To the tireless team at WWF in Assam for making me so welcome and for their bravery in the face of many conservation challenges, especially Dr Anupam Sarmah, Pranab Boro, Hiten Baishya, Deba Dutter and Dr Garga Mohan. To the Wildlife Trust of India's Virek Menon and the wonderful team at Kaziranga's Centre for Wildlife Research and Rehabilitation who keep on saving orphans. To the Department of Forestry rangers in Assam who simply never give up.

In Zambia, to the gang at the Elephant Pepper Development Trust, especially Mike Gravina and Dr Loki Osborne, the men behind the chilli idea, and Malvern Karidozo, who is the quiet achiever behind the scenes. To Dr John Hanks for the ongoing mentoring and encouragement.

In Australia, to WWF's Greg Bourne and Dr Ray Nias – for enabling me to continue my journey in conservation through a global organisation with clout. Many friends at The Panda in Sydney made my time there so memorable, including those who dragged me to the pub regularly (you know who you are – well, okay, not that much encouragement was required).

To Alex Craig, my publisher at Pan Macmillan, a like mind who really 'gets' Africa and its pull, and Charlie Viney, my wonderful agent, who saw the value in what I had to say. Editors Ali Lavau, Julia Stiles and Joel Naoum greatly improved the manuscript with their insightful and gentle critiques. To my great friends, artist Nafisa Naomi for the beautiful elephant art in this book and film producer Dr Stephen van Mil for the chance to return to the elephant kingdoms. To Nafisa Naomi, Adam Harper, Kisa Baldwin and Andy Ridley for letting me use their photographs.

My family and friends are the solid ground beneath my mad existence and without them I couldn't do what I do. My wonderful mum, Rhonda doggedly supports my lifestyle even though she doesn't like it, and my dad, Allan, who I have to thank for getting me started on my African journey, just wishes he could afford to go back every year. My amazing sister Kek (Kiri Rheinberger), a country vet, provides constant inspiration to me and everyone around her, and my brother Davo, a kindred spirit, is always up for a chat about the meaning of life. My six-year-old niece Ella keeps me real and does a wicked impersonation of a zebra. Michelle McKemmy (Shelby) is that rare and cherished loyal friend who keeps me grounded but won't let me lose sight of my dreams. Fellow Africa addicts and dear friends Sally and Jeremy Henderson's optimistic view of life is an essential tonic in mine. And to the fabulous Kellie Marshall, Gabby Shaw and Nicola Keays, thanks for the ever-essential girlie chats!

Finally, my husband Andy, who came up with the title, is truly my hero, not only because he respects my 'man mind' and always finds the humour in my too often too serious existence, but also because he is so determined to make the world a better place. To the many I have inevitably neglected to mention who have helped me on my journey, thanks a million.

Sally Henderson
Ivory Moon

Sally Henderson's long love affair with Africa and its elephants was brought to life in the bestselling *Silent Footsteps. Ivory Moon* continues that affair in one of the most inhospitable landscapes on the planet . . .

When Sally and her husband, Jer, volunteer to run a remote safari camp in the parched Namib Desert where existence depends on the life-giving fog from the Skeleton Coast, she has no idea if it is heaven or hell that awaits her. Her longing for a wilderness experience where elephants roam the dunes is tried by the extremes of climate and by dangerous encounters with wild animals, but Sally does not expect it will be camp politics that take her to the edge.

A woman running a camp in a man's world, Sally is tested by the staff, who come from many different tribes, and challenged by the intractable men's men who make Africa their hunting ground. Her quest for equilibrium is intensified by the haunting presence of intangible things and the echoes of an ancient mystery.

Vivid and immediate, Sally's depiction of the wildlife that rules Africa is unparalleled. *Ivory Moon* takes us into the heart of a strange desert world where nothing is as it seems.

Jane Stork
Breaking the Spell

Growing up in post-war Western Australia, and embarking on the familiar path of marriage and raising children, Jane Stork's semblance of a normal life began to unravel as she entered her thirties.

She sought answers at a meditation centre, and quickly became devoted to the Indian guru Bhagwan Shree Rajneesh, changing her name, adopting the orange robes of a 'sannyasin', and uprooting her family to live first in an ashram in India and then in the Bhagwan-created city of Rajneeshpuram in Oregon, USA.

It was here that Bhagwan's behaviour became increasingly bizarre. He began promoting a siege mentality among his followers, ordering them to amass firearms. He encouraged his secretary Sheela to use drastic methods to take over local governments and punish the local communities who objected to their 'utopian' city.

For Jane, what started out as a journey seeking spiritual enlightenment descended into darkness as she sacrificed her marriage and children, and eventually – through a monstrous act of attempted murder – her freedom.

After serving time in the US, Jane started a new life in Germany, but soon realised she could never truly be free until she faced up to the past . . .

With an international arrest warrant hanging over her head, and a son who is gravely ill, Jane finally does so with devastating clarity.

Utterly compelling and deeply moving, Jane's incredible true story is a profound meditation on the nature of self-determination and the human spirit's capacity for redemption.

Fiona Higgins
Love in the Age of Drought

When Fiona meets Stuart at a conference in Melbourne she isn't looking for a relationship, let alone the upheaval of falling for a cotton farmer from South-East Queensland. But then life never quite goes according to plan . . .

When Stuart sends Fiona a pair of crusty old boots and a declaration of his feelings sixteen days into their relationship, it's the start of a love story that endures – in spite of distance, the strain of Stuart's farm entering its fourth year of drought, and Fiona's issues with commitment.

Something's got to give, and eventually Fiona puts everything on the line – her career, her Sydney life, her future – and moves to Stuart's farm. Nearest township? Jandowae, population 750.

Here, Fiona encounters an Australia she's never really known, replete with snakes on the doorstep, frogs in the toilet and the perils of the bush telegraph. Gradually, she begins to fall in love with rural life, but as Stuart struggles to balance environmental and commercial realities, she realises that farming isn't quite as simple as she'd imagined. Ultimately, Fiona has to learn how to cope with the devastating impact of the drought that grips the countryside, and what it means for Stuart, the farm and their future together.

Love in the Age of Drought is a delightful fish-out-of-water story about the city–country culture clash overcome by the course of true love. Written with heart and humour, it's also a moving portrait of country Australia's capacity for survival and renewal amid a drought that won't be broken.

ADAM HARPER